MARGARET - A WOMAN OF CONFLICT

Other books by Paul James include:

Diana: One of the Family?
Anne: The Working Princess
At Her Majesty's Service
At Home with the Royal Family
Prince Philip's 101 Great Games
The Royal Almanac
Excuses, Excuses . . .
It's a Weird World

MARGARET
A Woman of Conflict

Paul James

SIDGWICK & JACKSON
LONDON

First Published in Great Britain in 1990 by Sidgwick & Jackson Limited

ISBN 0-283-99904-7

Typeset by Matrix, 21 Russell Street, London WC2

Printed by Billings and Sons Limited, Worcester.

for Sidgwick & Jackson Limited
1 Tavistock Chambers, Bloomsbury Way
London WC1A 2SG

CONTENTS

ACKNOWLEDGEMENTS

Anyone who writes about the Royal Family automatically lays their head on the proverbial block. Discussing a biography of mine on television, presenter Fern Britton asked dismissively, 'How does he *really* know?'

It is a justifiable question. First and foremost, I come from a long line of royal-watchers. My great-great grandfather saw the then Prince and Princess of Wales (later King Edward VII and Queen Alexandra) at every available opportunity, as his diaries reveal, and began a continuing tradition.

Born a stone's throw from Sandringham House, I grew up with family and friends who worked in the various palaces, and was frequently taken to see the Royal Family. Maybe it was patriotism on my family's part or mere curiosity to see how the other half lived, but in this climate I developed a vast and intimate knowledge of royalty long before it became a full-time career. Occasionally now I meet authors who have been on one overseas tour as part of a press contingent covering a State Visit and they return as 'royal experts'. My knowledge is on a much more basic level. Over the years I have known those who take princes and princesses their morning tea in bed, run the royal bathwater to the correct temperature and squeeze the right amount of toothpaste on to the regal brush; those who experience, on a day-to-day basis, the fascinating foibles and eccentricities of their employers that have helped me build up a realistic picture of each royal character. I now have the advantage of being able to attend engagements myself, and piece more of the jigsaw together from first-hand experience. Learning about the royal way of life is continually exciting, and not without its surprises. When Princess Alice, Duchess of Gloucester, visited friends of mine at their flat in York House to see their new-born baby, she pointed to the cooker in the kitchen and asked, 'What is that?' She had not seen a stove before.

During the time that I was writing this book the Princess Royal had four letters stolen. An unidentified man subsequently offered the letters to a journalist of *The Sun* newspaper, who eventually passed them on to the police at Scotland Yard. A few weeks later, two journalists arrived unsolicited on my doorstep and openly accused me of being the mystery man. They stated that I had been positively identified by the *Sun* journalist, that Scotland Yard had a photofit picture of me and that it was only a matter of time before I would be arrested. All this was, of course, a blatant lie. Fortunately I knew exactly where I was at the time the letters were handed over, which was beyond dispute, and when I later saw the photofit picture it naturally looked nothing like me. Needless to say, Scotland Yard did not come and arrest me.

Although the tabloid press's heavy-handed attempt to get a story caused me, and those who overheard their wild accusations, a great deal of laughter, and I thoroughly enjoyed recounting the episode on radio, on a much more serious level it brought home to me the dangers of bad journalism. They could so easily have written a story in such a way that would have implicated me in the royal letters scandal to millions of readers.

So it is for the Royal Family, who have no effective means of redress.

One afternoon I watched the Princess of Wales on an official engagement. She was in a particularly buoyant mood, laughing and joking continually. At one point she looked down, her expression momentarily serious. Click. A photographer took a picture that appeared in a tabloid newspaper the following day, accompanying an article that claimed Diana had argued with Prince Charles and was desperately unhappy. Every picture tells a story, but not always an accurate one. Princess Margaret understands more than most the character assassinations of the press, and any writer hoping to give an accurate portrait of her must steer clear of media myth and prurient gossip. Although I have consulted various books to check dates, places, and accuracy of basic facts, the major instruments of my research have been my eyes, my ears and my own judgment. Any opinions expressed are my own, as are any unwitting errors or omissions. Over the years so many people have given freely of their time to provide me with greater insights into the Royal Family and to all those concerned I offer my heartfelt thanks.

Many people who have helped with information for this book have, for various reasons, requested anonymity which I respect. I would like to express particular gratitude, however, to: The Lord Napier and Ettrick, Muriel Murray-Brown, the Press Office at Clarence House, Dr June Paterson-Brown, Joan Disley, Elizabeth Jorden, Giles Pegram, Patrick Murtagh, Susan Conrad, Paul Hodgkins, Carey Smith, David Horne, my agent Andrew Lownie and the invaluable 'Trish' – Patricia Reynolds, Julian Clegg and the staff of BBC Radio Sussex for the many 'royal scoops' we've had on the programme, and last but by no means least, my editor Annie Jackson, for her hard work and astute judgment, as always.

In any book of this nature there are invariably anecdotes and stories which are apocryphal or open to conjecture. In her biography of Queen Elizabeth the Queen Mother, author Penelope Mortimer wrote that it is far more difficult to find out the truth above a live person than a dead one and that to discover the truth about a living royal is 'virtually impossible'. This is true, and I have, therefore, tried only to include facts that I have personally been able to verify. I hope that ultimately Princess Margaret will be better understood as a result.

PAUL JAMES
Brighton, 1990.

INTRODUCTION

Her Royal Highness the Princess Margaret has been parodied to such an extent by the popular press that the line between gross caricature and stark reality has become indistinct. Until overtaken by Princess Michael of Kent and then the Duchess of York, she was the media's Aunt Sally, always there to be knocked down from her pedestal and fair game for the snipers who portrayed her as an overweight moll, sunning herself on the Caribbean island of Mustique, surrounded by toy-boys and squandering her Civil List allowance. From time to time the angle changed and she became the 'tragic' Princess, divorced, depressed, diseased and alone, with the rumour rife among royal watchers: don't write anything bad about Margaret – she's only got a year left to live.

Like her niece, the Princess Royal, she is a no-nonsense lady who does not suffer fools gladly. A little too grand, publicly aloof, she can quickly pull rank on anyone who dares to become overfamiliar. When an aged American celebrity approached the Princess at a private party in the Dorchester Hotel ballroom, curt-seyed and then to maintain her balance and her dignity grasped a royal arm as she rose unsteadily, she received nothing more than a piercing look of cold, naked steel. Through such actions Princess Margaret perpetuated the media myths. Her public performance needed better direction.

As a youth I waited in a prime position for three hours to witness the arrival of the Queen's only sister on an official visit to my home town. At the appointed moment, Princess Margaret swept out of the station entrance, not pausing even to wave but merely raised her gloved hand in acknowledgment. Before I could place the camera to my eye, Her Royal Highness was under the railway arch and out of sight. It is an image of the Princess that was to colour my view of her for many years. Arriving at a school as part of that day's itinerary, Princess Margaret was equally brusque. Unimpressed by the reception committee, she looked at my mother (who was there officially) and snapped, '*Where's* the headmaster?' The Princess had no time for hangers on.

Having reached the milestone of her sixtieth birthday in August 1990 Princess Margaret has mellowed. It is not just the media image that has turned in her favour; she has weathered the storms of a colourful and restless life, and a stronger, wiser woman has emerged. As a child she was continually cast in the shadow of her elder sister, Elizabeth, who was being groomed for queenship. When her father ascended the throne in 1936 the young Margaret Rose is reported as saying, 'Now that Papa is King, I am nothing,' and to make herself noticed she developed a defiant streak that incited conflict. Her life has been one of mixed emotions and full of pressure. The onus was on her as a Princess of the royal blood to find an appropriate marriage partner, a burden which pushed her into the arms of the wrong man. With no real role in life, other than being born sister to the Queen, she lacked the sense of purpose that was instilled into Elizabeth from an early age, and as she was not blessed with such a robust constitution as the rest of the family, it became more noticeable when Princess Margaret was forced to cancel public engagements through ill health.

Often called 'the theatrical Princess', Margaret's greatest conflict has perhaps been within herself, the true character of Princess Margaret at odds with the public idea of how a member of the Royal Family should behave. Too often in the past she has overplayed the part of Princess and, instead of allowing the woman to shine through, she has acted the prima donna, with unfortunate results. At the age of sixty, the Queen's only sister has a reputation that precedes her. Yet, she insists that since she was seventeen she has been 'misrepresented and misreported'. The greatest challenge to any writer, therefore, is to delve through the myth and seek the fact amongst the fiction.

Princess Margaret is an enigma. She has the resilience and rebelliousness of the Princess Royal, and many people forget that she was the Diana of her time. Women everywhere followed the fashions of Margaret Rose and when she lit a cigarette in public for the first time it meant liberation for thousands. I first saw the Princess in the early 1960s at Sandringham, near my childhood home, and heard how she would remain in bed while the rest of the Royal Family would brave the icy Norfolk winds to undertake fire practice. 'Let Margo burn then,' the Queen is reputed to have said gleefully. It was the first of thousands of stories I was to hear about the Princess over the next three decades, and one that has been repeated to me from different sources ever since. Queen Mary called her grand-daughter *espiègle* – roguish – and to me Princess Margaret became one of the most fascinating royals because of her apparent inability to conform.

This is not a biography in the traditional sense that begins with Princess Margaret's birth and follows her life chronologically through to the present day. This has been done before. Instead I have attempted to give a closer impression of the real woman that the public does not have an opportunity to see. I have looked at the key areas in her life which have fashioned Princess Margaret's character, and will, I hope, give a greater understanding of her as a person and explain, perhaps, her sometimes unexpected behaviour. This is not an official biography; these are commissioned only after a royal personage's death, but the Princess has known of my work from the outset and noted that my approach would be 'entirely sympathetic'. I hope that I have followed the Princess's wishes and looked at her benevolently, but it would be misguided to be too sycophantic or uncritical. I have gone instead in search of truth. Occasionally the truth hurts.

Neither is this book intended for those in search of trivia. Yes, I could tell you that Princess Margaret is frightened of the dark, adores Tchaikovsky's *Swan Lake*, dislikes champagne, can sing madrigals and once had a Sealyham dog called Pippin, but where such facts do creep in they are intended to illustrate a point. My goal has been to find the person behind the princess. The life of Princess Margaret has been an obstacle course, a conflict between private desire and public duty, a struggle for privacy in the glare of national scrutiny, a fight for independence in a family dominated by tradition. That she has ultimately survived more than her fair share of attacks says much about Princess Margaret's resilience and strength of character. Whether she has achieved lasting peace or a temporary truce, only time will tell.

CHAPTER ONE

In Lilibet's Shadow

First-time guests invited to a small private lunch party at Windsor Castle were surprised by what they saw. The two women on opposite sides of the table often spoke in unison as if they were telepathic. Their conversation was so sharp that it could have been rehearsed. Even if their faces had not been so familiar, and their background unknown, the physical resemblance was so obvious that it became difficult not to stare in comtemplative comparison, yet from such close quarters the contrasts between the sisters became unexpectedly striking. As the Queen sipped a sweet Sauternes, Princess Margaret opted for lemon barley water in preference to her once-favourite tipple of Famous Grouse whisky. The high-pitched tones of one volleyed with the deep mellow voice of the other.

Margaret and Elizabeth are like chalk and cheese. Whether of her own volition or through media invention, the former has always seemed to court controversy while the other has conscientiously avoided any trace of scandal. Princess Margaret has changed her style and appearance to such an extent that any photograph of her can be clearly dated, whilst the Queen has remained reassuringly the same. One's hair has been long, short, curly, straight, bouffant, back-combed, permed, bobbed and back to long to suit her mood rather than the mode; the other adopted the familiar, now classic style in the early 1950s and it has remained unchanged for forty years, with the introduction of two prominent grey streaks as the only concession to age. Princess Margaret's weight, like Elizabeth Taylor's, has fluctuated with her state of mind – plump in times of trouble, slender during periods of contentment – yet her sister's

1

figure has remained consistent. Never will you find a photograph of Her Majesty looking embarrassingly overweight, neither do you ever become conscious that she has dieted; the only obvious change is the inheritance of Queen Mary's matronly bosom. On a superficial level, the close observer cannot fail to notice that the functional attire of the monarch appears dowdy beside the panache of Princess Margaret who has the confidence for deep décolletage and the Caribbean suntan to carry it off. Her five-strand pearl necklace is just a touch more elegant than the conventional three rows worn by the Queen.

The most significant difference between the Queen and Princess Margaret over six decades has been hostility, not necessarily between the two sisters themselves, although they have not always seen eye-to-eye, but for as often as Elizabeth has received praise, Margaret has been attacked. When, in September 1989, the eminent author A.N. Wilson, in a television documentary, criticised Queen Elizabeth II as a modern constitutional monarch, claiming that her only requirement was 'sufficiently powerful reading spectacles to be able to drone through the speeches written for her by the Prime Minister', he found few supporters. It has become sacrilegious to say anything scathing about the present incumbent of the throne. Yet for almost a lifetime, it seems, it has been both fashionable and permissible to condemn Princess Margaret.

'When my sister and I were growing up, she was made out to be the goody goody one,' revealed the Princess on the eve of her fortieth birthday. 'That was boring, so the Press tried to make out that I was wicked as hell.' It is an image that she has been unable to live down. She has suffered not simply through being the second-born and therefore constantly upstaged by her sister, but more fundamentally because she was the *only* other child to counteract Princess Elizabeth's character and thus the odds were against her. Had there been a brother, he would have taken precedence in the order of succession and the two girls would have been allies. Had there been more 'little Princesses', young Margaret Rose would not have been the sole target for media combat. Just as the current Duchess of York, the much maligned 'Fergie', bears the brunt of public criticism today, resulting in a more dignified and glamorous image for Diana, the Princess of Wales, so Princess Margaret suffered in the wake of her sister's majesty. Sadly, for her, the injustices began in the nursery.

By the time Princess Margaret was born, Elizabeth – nicknamed 'Lilibet' after her first childish attempts to pronounce her own name – had made an enormous impact on the public, not only in Britain but especially in America. Ranking third in line to succession, the prospects of her acceding to the throne appeared remote. It seemed likely that her parents the young Duke and Duchess of York (later King George VI and Queen Elizabeth) might have a son who would become heir-apparent. Her uncle David, the Prince of Wales, and first in line to the throne, was free to marry and produce offspring of his own; no one could possibly foresee the path that lay ahead. Although not obviously born to be Queen, the fascination for Princess Lilibet stemmed from the fact that she was born less than eight years after the Armistice of the First World War, and the echoes of the guns still sounded in the hearts and minds of many who had lived through what they hoped had been the war to end all wars. Great Britain was experiencing the Depression, and just two weeks after her birth the General Strike began. Starting with a major dispute in the coal industry, exacerbated by the ever-increasing power of the trade unions, soon all major industries ground to a halt in sympathy with the miners' cause. Printers, builders, electricity, gas and engineering workers all downed tools in a direct challenge to the Government. Within a few years the Depression spread across the Atlantic, as confidence in American companies began to wane and European countries were asked to return capital that had been loaned to them. Fear of the probity of a number of businesses caused panic on the New York Stock Exchange in Wall Street leading to the 'Crash,' when more than 13 million shares changed hands in one day. Share prices fell, businesses collapsed and thousands of families were financially ruined.

In this harsh international climate, the Royal Family became a focus for attention, and Princess Elizabeth a symbol of hope. Crowds gathered daily outside her parents' home at 145 Piccadilly in London and it is reported that open-topped buses were seen to lean sideways as they passed the house with passengers rushing across to peer into the nursery window. It was deemed unsafe for her nurse, Clara Knight (known as Allah), to wheel her through Hyde Park, and so the baby was taken for walks around the private gardens of Buckingham Palace. Known as 'the Empire's Darling', at the age of three Lilibet appeared on the cover of the American magazine *Time*. It instantly created a new fashion, for the article mentioned that the Princess's nursery clothes were yellow. Out went pinks and blues and soon every fashionable toddler was wearing yellow. For the Christmas before Princess Margaret was born Princess Elizabeth was given her first pony and long queues formed outside the recently opened Madame Tussaud's exhibition when a waxwork of the Princess astride a Shetland pony was put on display. Interest in her was insatiable and her young face and blonde curls appeared on chocolate boxes, china mugs and plates, and in Newfoundland her head appeared on a 6-cent stamp.

However much the Duke and Duchess of York tried to protect their daughter from the attention, inevitably, as an intelligent child, she must have been very much aware that she was different. Harold Nicolson, King George V's biographer, revealed that when the four-year-old Elizabeth became fidgety at a concert, her grandmother, Queen Mary, suggested that they leave. The little Princess asked to stay so as not to disappoint the crowds outside who were waiting to see her. She was swiftly removed through a back entrance and home to Piccadilly in a taxi with a Lady-in-Waiting. The crowds missed her departure. It was an object lesson from Queen Mary that has never been forgotten. Even today the Queen and Princess Margaret do not pander to the crowds, and as children were frequently terrified of visiting their grandmother for fear that she was going to admonish them for something. From her most formative years, Princess Elizabeth began to learn the meaning of being royal. For her fourth birthday, on Easter Monday 1930, her gift from Queen Mary was a set of building blocks. The royal recipient was quickly told that each block came from a different part of the Empire, thus play was tempered with learning.

Exactly four months later, on 21 August 1930, Princess Margaret was born. Princess Elizabeth was no longer to be the sole receiver of attention, and just as she has entered the record books as the only monarch to have been born in a private house, so her sister's entry into the world must rank amongst one of the most auspicious this century and portentously dramatic. Her birthplace, Glamis Castle, in Tayside, Scotland, is a fairytale castle of towers, turrets and battlements, with a stone that in certain lights can glow an eerie pink. It can boast no fewer than nine ghosts. King Malcolm the Second of Scotland was murdered there, and, more famously, Duncan in Shakespeare's *Macbeth*, after whom the old guardroom is now named Duncan's Hall. Inevitably, as with so many castles, there is an unidentified spectre known only as The Grey Lady. Most notorious of all, Glamis Castle, the ancestral home of the Earls of Strathmore and Kinghorne (the Lyon family), has the unique legend of housing a creature said to be half-human, half-monster. The monster is thought to be a former Earl and for almost two centuries now has supposedly lived in a secret chamber, the whereabouts of which is only passed on by each Earl to his heir. One Earl of Strathmore is quoted as saying: 'If you could only guess the nature of the secret, you would go down on your knees and thank God it was not yours.'

Cynics may sneer at such platitudes yet the local people in the village of Glamis have no doubts about the monster's existence. When a house party decided to search for the secret chamber, taking advantage of the then Earl's temporary absence, they went into each of the 100 rooms and hung a towel out of every window. When they then went outside they discovered seven windows that did not have a towel.

Haunted or not, Glamis Castle has such a romantic air that, given the choice Princess Margaret would probably still choose to be born there, and although she is seldom able to visit the Castle today, in earlier times she delighted in giving friends extensive tours of the rooms and pointing out the indelible bloodstain on a floorboard where murder was committed. Until recently, older villagers in Glamis spoke proudly of their memories of the young Princess running down the street 'to buy two penn'orth of sweets at Mr Buchanan's shop'. Why, however, the Duchess of York chose to have her baby, an heir to the throne and possibly a future King, in such a remote part of Scotland and did not stay in London where more advanced medical facilities would have been available in the event of complications does not seem to have been questioned at the time. Lilibet's birth had been complicated, resulting in her delivery by Caesarian section and there was nothing to suppose that the next delivery would be any easier. Only the Home Secretary, John Clynes, and the Ceremonial Secretary of the Home Office, Harold Boyd, privately expressed their irritation. Traditionally a Minister of the Crown was required to witness the birth to ensure that the royal baby was not changed for an imposter who would challenge the throne in later years. By the time of Margaret's birth, the Home Secretary was simply required to sit outside the bedroom door during the delivery. 'If there has to be a gentleman waiting outside my bedroom door,' the Duchess of York said with characteristic humour, 'I hope it's someone we know.'

Fortunately for royal mothers today, King George VI decided to abolish the unnecessary condition in 1948. A sign of progress is that royal babies are now born in hospital; it is hard to believe that when the Queen Mother as Duchess of York became pregnant with her first child in 1925 nobody other than the immediate family were told. As her condition became physically apparent, she simply withdrew from public engagements. When in 1929 the Duchess became pregnant with Princess Margaret, again it remained a family secret until 16 April, 1930, when the *Court Circular* simply announced that she had 'cancelled her forthcoming engagements and she is not undertaking any further functions during the summer'. To the discerning public this could only mean one thing.

On 4 August the political contingent of Boyd and Clynes made their way reluctantly by train to Scotland, well in advance of the birth to ensure that they would be at their post when the event occurred. If the Duchess had chosen to have the baby at home in London they could literally have left their desks in Whitehall the moment she went into labour and would have been safely at 145 Piccadilly within minutes. Instead they had a 400-mile journey and were forced to wait aimlessly for sixteen days. This they passed at Airlie Castle, eight miles from Glamis, with an army dispatch rider permanently on call to fetch them at the crucial moment. By the time the call came, the men were apparently in a state of panic. 'You haven't given us much time,' Harold Boyd is said to have fussed.

The evening of Thursday, 21 August was dramatically wild and stormy. The heavens opened, the thunder roared, a scene that Shakespeare had visualised for the first scene of *Macbeth*, and a worthy entrance for someone who would one day be dubbed the theatrical Princess. Princess Margaret was born at 9.22 p.m., and as a girl immediately became fourth in line to the throne, the wrong sex to displace Elizabeth. So convinced were the parents that the child would be a boy that no names had been chosen, and it was not until October that the Duke of York registered his daughter. The Duchess of York wrote to Queen Mary, 'I am very anxious to call her Ann Margaret as I think Ann of York sounds pretty, and I think Elizabeth and Ann go well together. I wonder what you think? Lots of people have suggested Margaret, but it has no family links really on either side.'

King George V did not like the name Ann, and eventually the Princess became Margaret Rose of York. Although there must have been times in later years when the Princess might have been preferred to have been called Ann, to avoid the corruptions of Maggie, Meg and Margo that the press have unceremoniously imposed upon her, the choice of names proved universally popular, the rose being a symbol of England and, appropriately, the emblem of York, and Margaret being a perennial favourite north of the border as the name of so many Queens of Scotland and eminently suitable for the first immediate member of the Royal Family to have been born in Scotland since the Union of the Scottish and English Crowns in 1603. For this reason alone the 6 lb 11 oz baby was the cause of much rejoicing. Beacons were lit, beer was drunk, in London the bells of St Paul's Cathedral and Westminster Abbey were peeled in her honour, and it is said that four-year-old Lilibet was allowed to stay up late to watch the celebrations at Glamis so that she would not feel excluded. When the family finally returned to London the baby was christened in the private chapel at Buckingham Palace on 30 October. The chapel itself was to be bombed ten years later during the Battle of Britain in 1940 and the loss of this ugly building was not lamented. 'A magnificent piece of bombing, Ma'am, if you'll pardon my saying so,' said a policeman to Queen Elizabeth.

Princess Margaret's official sponsors (godparents) at the christening included David, the Prince of Wales, later King Edward VIII, one of the black sheep of the Royal Family to whom the Princess has often been compared. Both were to fall in love with divorced people. David sacrificed the throne and his royal life for the women he loved; Princess Margaret had the strength to sacrifice love and marriage to continue the royal life and support the throne. When she did later marry, was it a coincidence that she called her son David?

The christening over, life began to settle down for Lilibet and Margaret Rose, who for the rest of their childhood were to lose their own identities and become The Little Princesses. Those who collected commemorative ware of the 'Empire's Darling' now had a new set of souvenirs to collect that bore the early portraits of Margaret Rose. Paragon China honoured her birth with a range of nursery ware with a design of two lovebirds, marguerites and roses, and although permission was granted for a photograph of the baby to be used on an initial range of products in the first few months, it was not long before the court photographer, Marcus Adams, produced sepia photographs of the two princesses together, and it was this image that became interminably produced on everything from jigsaw puzzles to jelly moulds.

When Elizabeth was born Mrs Clara Knight (Allah) was employed as nanny and Margaret MacDonald (Bobo) as nursery maid. With the arrival of Margaret came the addition of Bobo's sister, Ruby MacDonald. On the surface all worked in relative harmony, and their lifestyle appeared idyllic when, in January 1932, the York family moved away from the busy London streets to the peace of Windsor Great Park where King George V gave the family Royal Lodge, once the Prince Regent's private retreat. The Duke and Duchess seemed not to mind that the house was derelict as they could stamp it with their own personal style, and the location offered space and solitude for the Princesses, away from the prying eyes that they encountered as soon as they stepped outside the door of 145 Piccadilly.

Although the London house was maintained for use during the week so that the Duke and Duchess could undertake public duties and the Princesses could study, on Friday afternoons they would enthusiastically climb into a car with the ever-present dogs and drive home to Windsor. In the same year the people of Wales presented Princess Elizabeth with a miniature cottage called 'Y Bwthyn Bach' – The Little House – a child-size structure, fully furnished to scale in every detail. It was here that the children used to play in a world that they remember now as being 'always spring', vicariously playing at being 'ordinary' whilst other girls of that age pretended they were Princesses. Princess Margaret learned the intricacies of handling a dustpan and brush, a practical skill that she was never to need in the years ahead. Each had their own plot of garden in which Elizabeth grew flowers and Margaret Rose, when old enough, planted potatoes. Even in such early situations, the seeds of character are planted too and it is only in retrospect that one can see how childish games can point to adult traits. Elizabeth opted for flowers, and today she loves having blooms around her, spending in excess of £250,000 a year on floral displays throughout her homes. Young Margaret Rose, on the other hand, opted for potatoes (appropriately they were King Edwards) not simply to be different but because she has never been a great lover of flowers. Certainly they will always be displayed in her Kensington Palace home, but she returns from an engagement with a small posy and will say to a member of her staff 'Do something with those'. Perhaps also it says something about Princess Margaret's character that, as with so many gifts she receives, it is the thought that is more important. Approaching a crowd of onlookers at an engagement in Harlesden, North London, the Princess ignored the large colourful bunches of flowers that people thrust at her and headed straight for a little old lady who had one single daffodil wrapped in a piece of silver tinfoil. The elderly lady beamed with pride as Princess Margaret took the single flower, and it was this one yellow daffodil that she kept throughout the afternoon and was still holding as she entered the car for the drive back to Kensington Palace.

Throughout their childhood it was quickly noticeable that Elizabeth was methodically tidy, with her toys and her shoes meticulously arranged, whereas her sister's were haphazardly scattered, although often more out of mischief than inherent untidiness. When Margaret received a present she would tear off the wrapping paper enthusiastically; Elizabeth would undo the wrapping carefully and keep the paper for future use. When, as Queen, she was filming her Christmas broadcast of 1977, it was decided that her newly born grandson, Peter Philips, should be featured. To keep the baby alert and amused, one of the technicians suggested that a piece of paper could be screwed up and given to him; the rustle of the paper might hold his attention. Her Majesty sent a footman to fetch a piece of paper and he returned with a very inexpensive sheet of Christmas wrapping. This worked as planned, the filming took place, the baby smiled and eventually the recording was 'in the can'. As for the ball of wrapping paper, this was not to be wasted. It could after all be ironed out and used again, a member of the party suggested . . .

Life in the utopia of 1932 changed abruptly when, in April of that year, Miss Marion Crawford entered the Princesses' lives as governess. Princess Margaret was to encounter hostility for the first time in her short life. For many people today the name Marion Crawford has only one connection – *The Little Princesses*, a book she wrote in 1950 and a phrase with which she is now inextricably linked, even though it was not a term she had coined herself. For seventeen years Crawfie, as she became known, was the greatest influence in Princess Margaret's life, someone that she saw more frequently than her own mother, and the dour Scottish upbringing of Marion Crawford undoubtedly rubbed off on her young charges. Margaret was only two when Crawfie was employed so could scarcely remember a time when she was not part of the family, yet by the time of her death in March 1988 her name had become synonymous with 'traitor'. Marion Crawford died lonely, rejected and ignored.

After seventeen years of working for the Royal Family, Marion Crawford's great crime was to write about her life with the little Princesses, breaking an unwritten rule by revealing everything she had seen behind closed doors. Although the publication is harmless, it nevertheless shook Princess Margaret's faith in human nature, making her forever wary of whom she could trust. Ironically, ten years after Marion Crawford's revelations, Princess Margaret suffered again in 1960 when her then butler, Thomas Cronin, was dismissed and sold his story to a Sunday newspaper, scurrilously embellishing the lives of the Armstrong-Joneses. As a result all royal employees today have to sign a document that forbids them to reveal anything they have seen or heard in royal service, thus preventing them from writing their autobiography. When Prince Charles's valet Stephen Barry attempted to publish his life story in 1982 an injunction was taken out to prevent him from 'doing a Crawfie', even though his book was equally innocuous.

Through Marion Crawford we now have the greatest insight into the childhood of Princess Margaret and the environment in which she was raised. The greatest impression given is that Crawfie favoured Lilibet in preference to 'plump' Margaret Rose, and there were invariably clashes between nanny and governess with the young Princess caught in the middle. Progressive and ambitious, Crawfie did not suffer fools gladly, and disapproved of Allah's mollycoddling. With Lilibet now six, Allah tried to keep Princess Margaret as a baby for as long as possible, reluctant to let her grow up, spoon-feeding her long after she was capable of looking after herself. Skirmishes between nurses, nannies and governesses were commonplace at that time in any aristocractic household, yet as Lilibet was pushed further towards the throne Crawfie's tone implies that Margaret always took second place in her eyes.

After the death of King George V in 1936, for example, the

court went into mourning and it was considered inappropriate that the Princesses should continue their regular dancing classes with Madame Vacani. Swimming was thought to be more fitting and so the two were introduced to the water by Amy Daly, their instructor. So as not to be treated any differently from the other children in the class, both Princesses wore the unflattering regulation blue one-piece costume of the Bath Club. Whilst describing how 'pretty' Lilibet looked, using such adjectives as 'long', 'slender' and 'beautiful', she then goes on to say that Margaret looked like a 'plump navy-blue fish'. The attacks she makes on the Princess quite obviously did not simply evolve whilst writing the book. Constantly she refers to Margaret as 'tiresome', haughty, defiant and less dignified than her sister, whereas Lilibet is beyond reproach. If Margaret deliberately dawdled while dressing to go out, just to receive attention, Crawfie would refuse to be blackmailed and simply left her behind. It is Margaret, we are told, who even then did not like going to bed early and had to be chased around the room and transfixed with Crawfie's stony stare and firm reprimand before giving in.

During her seventeen years in royal employment, Marion Crawford was undeniably devoted to her work, so much so that she was often mawkishly in awe of royalty. She did, however, try to exert her influence on many outdated traditions, much to Princess Margaret's delight. She decried the fact that the Princesses could not walk the streets like other children and made several attempts to take them out incognito. This resulted in her having, on one occasion, to beat off a press photographer in the street, on others, to handle crowds who began staring at them when they ventured on to buses or the underground, and one day urgently to summon a royal car to take them home when they went on a 'jaunt' to the Young Women's Christian Association for tea and were recognised. More important to Princess Margaret, Crawfie took them to the theatre to see a pantomime every year. Allah, quite naturally, disapproved strongly of these outings and was not sorry when IRA bomb threats curtailed these unofficial outings. Until then, royal children had been kept shielded from public view, but Marion Crawford planted the seeds of adventure into the children, and the Duke and Duchess of York did little to stop her, rarely interfering in her work. Through her alone, Princess Margaret was able to experience the outside world, paying for a ticket on a bus, walking freely in Hyde Park, sitting in the stalls at the theatre, which would be denied her in later life.

The high regard in which Crawfie was held is shown in the way in which the Royal Family constantly prevented her from marrying in the fear that she would leave to have children of her own. For most of her time as governess she was engaged to Major George Buthlay, an employee in Drummond's Bank in Scotland, but whenever she raised the question of marriage her employers always placed an obstacle in her path. First, the Duke of York unexpectedly inherited the throne in 1936 and it was Crawfie's job to offer stability to the two Princesses, so suddenly thrust into the spotlight. When, on 17 February 1937, they took up residence in Buckingham Palace and left behind the cosy, chintzy world of 145 Piccadilly, it was she who had to help them settle into the cavernous Palace. Then came the war years, when Crawfie was needed more than ever, and a short time after the war, when Lilibet began to undertake public duties, Princess Margaret felt left out and needed her governess's company even more. After the announcement, in 1947, of the engagement of Princess Elizabeth to Prince Philip of Greece, Marion Crawford went to see the Queen armed with a photograph of George Buthlay, and complained bitterly that her own wedding had been continually postponed. The Queen was very firm. 'A change for Margaret at this stage is not at all desirable,' she insisted. The strong-willed Crawfie objected and went to the altar two months before Princess Elizabeth, tired of placing the Royal Family before her own. It was not long before she retired from service to Nottingham Cottage, a grace-and-favour home in the grounds of Kensington Palace, where to supplement her small pension she began writing about the one subject on which she was an expert, the little Princesses.

The first that the Royal Family knew of Marion Crawford's venture was when Nancy Astor gave the King and Queen an advance copy of the infamous book. Within a short time, Marion Crawford was evicted from Nottingham Cottage, her entry in Who's Who was withdrawn and the confidante of Princess Margaret and the future Queen Elizabeth II became a social outcast. Although rumours circulated that Princess Margaret kept in touch with her former governess, she has always firmly refuted the story. When Crawfie died in 1988 she left the Queen a small box of personal mementoes, including notes in their own childish handwriting, a list of Christmas presents that Princess Margaret received, an ivory elephant and a bead necklace which were gifts she had cherished from the little Princesses fifty years earlier. The box was accepted and placed in the royal archives at Windsor where its full contents remain a secret.

The importance of Marion Crawford's influence on Princess Margaret cannot be overstressed. Throughout her formative years, Crawfie taught her to read and write, was responsible for most of her education, and yet was far more than a teacher. Throughout the war years she was often the Princesses' sole companion. At Windsor Castle there were few distractions, and if they played games it was seldom with other children, and more frequently with their governess. She played at being a horse, chased the Princesses around in games of cowboys and Indians and 'sardines'. It was she who decided which radio programmes they could listen to and which books the girls ought to read. While Lilibet read *Black Beauty* and *Winnie the Pooh* it is often said that Margaret liked to read comics containing stories of blood and gore. Although their tastes were, and still are, very different, it does in reality seem unlikely that Margaret's indulgence is true. Where would she have got such comics from? They would not have been passed on via other children as they rarely met any socially, playing mostly with offspring from other branches of the family, such as the Harewoods and Elphinstones. Neither would Crawfie or Allah have obtained horror comics or even allowed such reading. Like so many fabricated stories about Princess Margaret that have dogged her since childhood, the story began when she discovered one 'penny dreadful' about pirates in an old box at Glamis Castle.

Certainly Princess Margaret enjoyed stories of adventure and was happy to hear her favourites repeated many times. Unlike Lilibet, she has always been musical and Lady Strathmore, her maternal grandmother, once told Lady Cynthia Asquith how she almost dropped her grand-daughter at the age of nine months when Margaret began to hum *The Merry Widow Waltz*. Tunes were picked up more quickly than speech. Both sisters were taught to play the piano but it was Princess Margaret who excelled, while Lilibet occupied her mind solely with horses. Both were taught to ride, but it was to Elizabeth that anything equine would become a passion. Although Princes Margaret has ridden horses often, it is as much because she is part of the huntin', shootin', fishin' set and it is part and parcel of their lifestyle. Occasionally she is seen at Badminton and always at Royal Ascot, but again because these are social events where houseparties gather, and she attends for the company rather than the horses. Watching Elizabeth at a horse-race today you can see clearly the excitement in her face, the anticipation, the anxious tension as the race begins; her fists clenched, she will jump joyfully up and down like a schoolgirl if her mount romps home. Princess Margaret remains relatively impassive, gaining more enjoyment from taking part in a Grand National Sweepstake with her kitchen staff at Kensington Palace, one year winning £10 for a 50p stake. The Queen loathes opera, whereas Princess Margaret relishes an evening at Covent Garden, taking along a cold buffet to be served during the interval to her guests.

The minutiae of the everyday lives of Lilibet and Margaret Rose as children has been meticulously catalogued in biographies for forty years since the publication of Marion Crawford's book. What seems far more fascinating, I feel, is not so much *what* Princess Margaret did as a child, but *why*. The fundamental change in her life came on Thursday, 10 December 1936.

> After long and anxious consideration I have determined to renounce the throne to which I succeeded on the death of my father, and I am communicating this, my final and irrevocable decision . . . all necessary steps should be taken immediately to secure that my lawful successor, my brother, His Royal Highness the Duke of York, should ascend the throne.

King Edward VIII announced his intentions to the House of Commons. The following evening he broadcast to the people before going immediately into exile in France. 'You must believe me when I tell you that I have found it impossible to carry the burden of responsibility, and to discharge my duties as King as I would wish to do without the help and support of the woman I love.' After a reign of 325 days the stunned nation listened to their monarch speaking from Windsor Castle, having been introduced as 'His Royal Highness the Prince Edward'. The British press had been silenced over the King's relationship with Mrs Simpson, but with the hearing for her divorce petition on 27 October came the granting of a decree nisi. The decree was to be made absolute in six months, when the couple would be free to marry. The British Government and Prime Ministers of overseas dominions were in full agreement that the King must give up the idea of marrying 'this divorced American' or give up the Crown. He chose to abdicate.

The sleeping Princesses did not hear the broadcast, but seeing a letter addressed to 'Her Majesty the Queen' lying on the hall table at 145 Piccadilly, Princess Elizabeth said intuitively, 'That's Mummy now, isn't it?' Their uncle David's decision to abdicate meant quite literally that life would never be the same again, and subconsciously Marion Crawford began to treat her pupils differently. Lilibet was special. Lilibet might one day be Queen. To Margaret this was an unwelcome change and the move to Buckingham Palace made her particularly conscious, in her child-like way, that a gulf was forming between Lilibet and herself. She took to wandering around the Palace alone; occasionally she would follow one of the two clockwinders on their sojourn from room to room, keeping each of the 360 timepieces in full working order. When her parents had moved into 145 Piccadilly it had 25 rooms. Some of the smaller rooms were either knocked into one or turned into bathrooms. Now at Buckingham Palace they had over 600 rooms. Princess Margaret would hide round corners and shout 'Boo!' as any austere official approached.

With the move, Lilibet seemed to change also. 'What are we going to do with Margaret?' and 'You *must* stop being so silly,' were phrases that the ten-year-old heir to the throne began to utter. Never one to be intimidated, Margaret retaliated with humour. She became coquettish and knew that she could win people over with her quick repartee. When Crawfie admonished her for being untidy she sighed, 'Have you ever tried to put toothpaste back inside a tube?' and if scolded she would open her eyes wide and sing 'Who's afraid of the Big Bad Wolf?' As Lilibet became more withdrawn, Margaret became more theatrical and occasionally wicked.

In her authoritative biography *Elizabeth R*, Lady Longford tells of how Princess Margaret was once taken to a children's fancy-dress party wearing the costume of an angel.

'You don't look very angelic, Margaret!' her mother laughed.

'That's all right. I'll be a Holy Terror,' quipped the young Princess, confirming Crawfie's view that she was a 'born comic'.

It was as a 'Holy Terror' that Princess Margaret enjoyed being seen, because it drew attention to herself. From the moment that she found herself pushed up a place in the order of succession, behind Lilibet, she became determined that second place was not going to mean second best.

'Does that mean you'll have to be the next queen?' Margaret asked her sister, when the realisation of the full implications of the abdication dawned on her.

'Yes, some day,' Lilibet answered.

'Poor you,' replied Margaret, later joking that she was 'heir apparent to the heir presumptive'. Although many have suggested that Princess Margaret would have liked to have been queen, this has never been the case. As she grew older and it became obvious that there would never be a brother to precede Lilibet, the pressures of being groomed for queenship seemed to weigh down upon her sister. As a child, her only concern was that Lilibet was beginning to overshadow her in importance. When the time came for the Coronation of King George VI the outfits that the Princesses would wear had to be considered. In day-to-day life the girls were frequently dressed identically, a practice that continued into their teens, but for the Coronation itself it was decided that even though they should be dressed alike in long satin dresses with an overlay of ivory lace, Lilibet's would have a train at the back as she was now first in line to the throne.

'Margaret need not have a train,' said the Queen to the designer.

'But I *must* have a train,' Margaret wailed, conscious again that she was being left out. Eventually both did have a train, although Margaret's was shorter. She was consoled with the explanation that this was only because she was physically shorter than eleven-year-old Lilibet, but once again she felt that she had needed to fight for her rights.

In Marion Crawford, Princess Margaret saw a woman who enjoyed a sense of the theatrical. She admired the way her governess could make history lessons seem 'highly dramatic', and in turn the young Princess developed a very lively imagination. Whereas Lilibet always appeared very disciplined and down to earth, Margaret sought escapism. For psychological reasons she has sought comfort in fantasy whenever she has been unhappy. In adult life she has turned to alcohol and nicotine in the past to blot out her concerns. In childhood she invented imaginary characters, 'Cousin Halifax', 'Pinkle Ponkle', and 'Inderbombanks' on whom she blamed any misdemeanours that she might have committed herself. If she was late, it was because 'Cousin Halifax' had kept her waiting; if she was awake at night it was because *he* had been unable to sleep. It was she who initiated the now famous Windsor Castle pantomimes that took place during the war years, enabling her to immerse herself in another character, and half a century later she still delights in fancy-dress parties, recently dressing herself up as Marie Antoinette for a society ball, complete with a plastic cake and a fan, given to her by Princess Marina, the late Duchess of Kent, that once belonged to Marie Antoinette herself.

Allah always insisted that Princess Margaret was highly strung. As she grew older she began to suffer from severe migraines, and even as a very young child she constantly chewed her nails. To cover up the tension Princess Margaret characteristically put on a false front, using humour as a weapon. One day she noticed that the Prime Minister, Neville Chamberlain, chewed his nails. 'If he can, I can!' she announced victoriously.

In 1937 discussions were held that could have made a dramatic difference to Princess Margaret's future. As the Princesses were relatively close in age, legal theorists began to debate as to whether they should be co-heirs to the throne and reign jointly when the time came. Eventually age won, and it was decided that Elizabeth should have priority over Margaret in the line of succession. After Elizabeth's Coronation in 1953, the Regency Act was amended in favour of Prince Philip, with no provision of any kind for Margaret to become Regent. If anything happened to Elizabeth, it would now be Philip who would take control until Prince Charles was old enough. It seemed like the end of any possible responsibility or power, although she did still remain a Counsellor of State, appointed in October 1951, enabling her to act in many respects as a 'deputy monarch' if ever the King, and later the Queen, were out of the country. On a practical level, this has occasionally involved Princess Margaret in representing the Queen at investitures when abroad. It is perhaps some measure of Princess Margaret's mellowing that two years ago she relinquished her role as Counsellor of State in favour of the Queen's youngest son, Prince Edward, conscious, possibly, that he has received adverse criticism for his lack of royal duties and may feel overshadowed by his brothers and sister.

It would be unfair to suggest that Princess Elizabeth consciously intended to overshadow her sister. Outside influences seemed to prevail over which neither had much control, and both suffered through constantly being compared. Elizabeth's aura of seriousness and dignity seemed fitting to a girl on the first step of the throne, but only added to Margaret's problems. When photographed by Marcus Adams, the photographer ensured that Lilibet stood correctly, had her hands together elegantly, her head erect, her expression often suitably serious, never worrying if Margaret Rose appeared impish, her legs apart, her grin broad, or maybe he *did* intend the contrast. Either way, Margaret fared badly. Neither did the family help. Princess Margaret would not have seen the letter that Queen Mary wrote to Princess Alice, Countess of Athlone: 'Lilibet much grown, very pretty eyes and complexion, pretty figure, Margaret very short, intelligent face, but not pretty.'

Even so, the young Princess must have been aware of the attitudes towards her. Elizabeth has always been stronger physically than Margaret, yet it has been suggested that some of the latter's childhood ailments were possibly exaggerated to receive attention.

Both Margaret and Elizabeth suffered with the advent of war, confined to Windsor Castle for most of the duration in a fortress that was supposed to provide protection, although the Princess in recent years has expressed her doubts. When she appeared as Roy Plomley's guest on 'Desert Island Discs' she described the wartime efforts to protect the Princesses at Windsor as 'pathetic' and said they 'dug trenches and put up some feeble barbed wire which wouldn't have kept anybody out, but it did keep us in'. As a result of rationing there were fewer new dresses, and to Margaret's chagrin she was forced to wear some of Lilibet's hand-me-down clothes. Despite the war, it appears that Lilibet received many greater privileges, which must have made Margaret jealous. The future Queen received one shilling a week pocket money until the age of fifteen, yet her sister received nothing. When Elizabeth was sixteen she was given her own private apartment, with her own sitting-room. She was allowed to attend the annual ghillie's ball at Balmoral from a much younger age than Margaret, even though the latter loved dancing. As the years went by, Lilibet received her own coat-of-arms, a Lady-in-Waiting, and later her own Private Secretary.

Margaret was only seventeen when Lilibet married, which meant that during her teenage years her sister was courting and preparing for marriage, and many things that they once did together, Elizabeth now did with Philip. When Lilibet learned to drive she was given a car of her own as a birthday present by their father, but when Margaret learned she did not get one. During the war Lilibet was allowed to join the Auxiliary Transport Service (ATS) as Second Subaltern Elizabeth Windsor No. 230873, was allowed to travel daily to Camberley and occasionally to London, whilst Margaret was forced to remain a virtual prisoner in Windsor Castle to study with Crawfie. Margaret was not, however, jealous of her sister's khaki uniform!

When Lilibet reached the age of twenty-one she received a Civil List allowance of £40,000, yet when Margaret came of age she was only granted £6,000. In fact she was originally omitted from the Civil List Act of 1937 altogether and a Parliamentary sanction became necessary to grant her an income. Clement Attlee opposed the idea, but Winston Churchill pleaded for Princess Margaret with some success. After all, he pointed out, she would one day undertake public duties and would need the Civil List income to cover expenses.

It is public duty that has perhaps forced the largest gulf between Elizabeth and Margaret. On the occasion of her twenty-first birthday Elizabeth made a speech from Cape Town dedicating herself to a life of service, words that were broadcast to all four corners of the Empire:

I declare before you all that my whole life, whether it be
long or short, shall be devoted to your service and the service
of our great Imperial family to which we all belong.

It was a promise that she has lived up to, placing public duty above all else, a promise that she was to reiterate thirty years later, speaking on the occasion of her Silver Jubilee in 1977:

When I was twenty one I pledged my life to the service
of our people and I asked for God's help to make good
that vow. Although that vow was made in my salad days,
when I was green in judgment, I do not regret nor retract
one word of it.

19

This is the essential difference between the two sisters. It would be wrong to say that Princess Margaret has not enjoyed her working life, that she has not taken her royal duties seriously, but ultimately she has striven to place personal happiness first, has battled between what has been expected of her and what she wanted to do. Ultimately this turned her into a rebel at a time when Elizabeth appeared to take on a greater solemnity. As the gilded cage began to close around Princess Margaret as she approached adulthood, she kicked out and began to revel in defiance.

When, in 1947, the Royal Family embarked on a three-month tour of South Africa, Lilibet and Margaret began to plan their wardrobes. The Queen warned Margaret that her clothes should be 'lower key' than Elizabeth's, more simple, less elaborate. As Elizabeth was to celebrate her twenty-first birthday while they were there, she was not to be upstaged by her sister. Margaret complied, but was it an act of defiance that, with her less fussy clothes, she wore Schiaparelli's perfume *Shocking*, or was it merely a display of confidence? When Elizabeth was presented with a casket of twenty-one fine diamonds, Margaret received a casket of smaller diamonds, yet as much as she attempted to stay in the background, it was on the South African tour that she publicly blossomed. 'Britain's Dresden China Princess' said the headlines, and while Elizabeth worked on speeches, Margaret enjoyed herself. The simple lines of her outfits only served to emphasise her developing figure, her sensuality. She was to introduce sex appeal into the Royal Family for the first time, and the Princess was unaware that many of the sailors on board the battleship HMS *Vanguard*, on which the Royal Family travelled, displayed photographs of Margaret as a pin-up alongside film stars of the day. Had she been made aware at the time she would certainly have felt that she had scored a point over her elder sister, whose austere portrait would soon hang in many an officers' mess as anything but a sex-symbol. What Elizabeth could achieve through being royal, Margaret could accomplish through being a woman.

What nobody knew on the South African trip was the real reason why Princess Margaret sparkled more brightly than the casket of diamonds. Accompanying the family on the tour was His Majesty's recently appointed equerry, 32-year-old Peter Townsend, a former Royal Air Force fighter ace, whose gentle manner and dashing good looks were slowly beginning to attract Princess Margaret. Although she was only sixteen, this was to be no teenage crush. Well aware that his younger daughter felt oppressed at playing second fiddle during Elizabeth's courtship with Prince Philip of Greece, and conscious that when the couple married there would be a void in Margaret's life, the King actually encouraged her friendship with Peter Townsend, thinking that he would provide a stabilising influence.

Throughout the tour Princess Elizabeth appeared shy and serious to the South African press by comparison with her lively sister. This was taken to be the dignity of the heir to the throne; only the family knew that she was in love with Prince Philip and had been deliberately separated from him to offer an opportunity to put her thoughts in order. Whoever Princess Elizabeth married would ultimately have to act as her consort and the choice could never be simply for love. Although Prince Philip had the right background, was a nephew of Lord Mountbatten and offered the perfect partnership, the King and Queen wanted to make sure that their daughter entered into the relationship with her eyes wide open. Having first met Prince Philip eight years earlier, just before the outbreak of war, there were no doubts in Elizabeth's mind where her heart and head were leading.

While Princess Margaret sympathised with her sister at the parting, which was obviously causing her emotional distress, she was herself falling in love. Because Peter Townsend was twice her age, no one suspected even the possibility of an entanglement. It was a secret that she kept for five long years; her father died in ignorance, but ahead of her lay a battle for independence. She would put up a good fight for the man she loved, but ultimately she would be forced to take Lilibet's approach and place duty before personal happiness.

Looking at the photographs of the South African tour, of Margaret and Elizabeth being chased around the deck of HMS *Vanguard* during the high-spirited games, standing in the idyllic setting of the Drakensberg Mountains, riding ponies along the sands of Bona Bay or sunbathing in the Orange Free State, there is no hint of the challenge that lay ahead, which would take Princess Margaret out of the shadows and put her under the spotlight.

In 1947 Princess Margaret was falling in love. When it eventually became public knowledge she was to cast aside the 'Little Princess' image for good, increasing the gulf between one sister and the other. The greatest irony is that her secret came out on Coronation Day in 1953, a day that should have been Lilibet's and Lilibet's alone.

CHAPTER TWO

Challenge of Identity

Princess Margaret glowered across the table. The charity fashion gala at Hopetoun House, the magnificent Adams mansion, and Scottish home of the Marquess of Linlithgow, had been a great success. At dinner, however, the Princess found herself the unwilling target of attention. The late television newscaster Reginald Bosanquet, fortified with alcohol, began to make inappropriate suggestions. Conscious of Margaret's reputation at the time, uninhibited Bosanquet saw what he considered to be a like-minded drinking partner in the Princess. Eventually she left the table with selected guests and retired to a private room where she spent the remainder of the evening impersonating the drunken broadcaster with annihilating accuracy, much to her host's amusement.

In Princess Margaret, probably more than any other member of the Royal Family, there is a very marked contrast between public and private image. Conscious of the solemnity of royal duty, and equally conscious of Lilibet's persona, she has mastered the public mask that friends refer to as her 'acid drop' expression. At the Hopetoun House dinner table the Princess used what she has since described as her 'defence mechanism' and put on her best Queen Victoria face that would have silenced any sober man, yet behind closed doors she used the experience to her own advantage. Rather than be angry or embarrassed, she used humour to steal the show. At any private dinner party it is she who becomes the focus of attention. Even as a child it is said that there was always more laughter from Princess Margaret's end of the table.

In her youth, when King George VI was angry or upset, Princess Margaret had the ability to relieve the tension with a timely quip. Once, during a particularly oppressive meal, the Princess tossed a spoon over her shoulder. As it clanged to the floor the King roared with laughter and the mood changed. Indeed it was from her father that Margaret inherited her devilish sense of fun. Once when Elizabeth was working on a car engine during her ATS training the King removed a rotor arm from the distributor without her knowledge. 'What, still not got it going?' he playfully chided her sometime later. When the press began 'marrying' Margaret off to all and sundry she teasingly departed from London Airport on an official visit to Malta in 1950 wearing a scarf printed with the message 'Toujours L'Amour'. 'Disobedience is my joy,' Princess Margaret is reported to have told the French film director, artist and dramatist, Jean Cocteau, a man whose enormous versatility and originality she greatly admires and to some extent resembles. Although she seldom deliberately sets out to shock, throughout her life the Princess has frequently taken unexpected courses of action to assert her own authority and to challenge expectations. One of her greatest thrills as a child was being taken on an underground train by Marion Crawford, and thirty years after that first trip she was still suggesting that she travel on the tube to avoid heavy traffic and arrive at a film première on time. Although the traffic could have been halted, it was the sense of daring that made the four-stop journey from Knightsbridge to Leicester Square more exciting. While other members of the family were being chauffered in Daimlers, Princess Margaret bought herself a Mini. 'All sorts of people were happy to keep up with the Armstrong-Joneses,' said car enthusiast Lord Montagu of Beaulieu, after the Princess had helped popularise the world's smallest automobile.

In many ways Princess Margaret was born ahead of her time. She grew into an assertive woman long before the age of sex equality, asking men to dance in an era when girls demurely waited for the opposite sex to make the first move. She began smoking publicly purely as an act of defiance, and when Queen Mary (who smoked Woodbines in private) complained that it was an unladylike habit, Princess Margaret took to using cigarette-holders made from either ivory or tortoise shell, which only served to make her appear more flamboyant. By the time her father died of lung cancer exacerbated by smoking it was too late for his younger daughter to stop. She had become addicted.

The quality that Princess Margaret had seemingly in abundance was confidence. She would wear low-cut gowns that shocked her sister, once taking an unfinished dress to Lilibet's room and teasing her that she intended to wear the outfit publicly as it was. Only later did she reveal that the plunging neckline was missing one vital piece of material. Yet only those who really know the Princess understand that Margaret was basically insecure. The over confident manner that she assumed was frequently used to cover up her own feelings. While outwardly Elizabeth seemed the more serious of the two, one would expect Margaret to have a devil-may-care attitude, but it was the latter who was invariably sick with nerves before a public engagement. Although she enjoyed the behind-the-scenes preparation of the wartime pantomimes at Windsor Castle, Princess Margaret was literally green with fear on the day of the performance and had to be confined to bed for most of the day. Even today she seldom makes public speeches and it is in private amongst those who pose no threat that she is most at ease.

Lack of confidence, however, did not mean weakness of character and it was in personality that Princess Margaret's strength lay. Outward aggressiveness in later life stemmed from insecurity, but her basic sense of humour and charisma enabled her to make her mark. On Thursday, 10 July 1947, the speculation about Elizabeth's engagement to Prince Philip ended with the announcement that they were betrothed. That same afternoon there was a garden party at Buckingham Palace and although the skies were gloomy, the weather showery, those present noticed that Princess Margaret sparkled. While congratulations were heaped upon Elizabeth it was as if she were being upstaged. Whether intentionally or not, Margaret attracted attention. As the Royal Family walked back to the Palace at the end of the afternoon, Princess Margaret was arm in arm with Queen Mary and as the Princess chatted animatedly her grandmother, renowned for her austere countenance, roared with laughter. Behind Elizabeth and Philip walked glumly, a gap of some four feet between them, neither apparently enjoying the occasion.

While Elizabeth preoccupied herself with the wedding preparations that were to be completed in just sixteen weeks, Princess Margaret embarked on her first solo engagement. For many members of the Royal Family one of the first assignments is the launching of a ship, a daunting but innocuous task, at which little can go wrong. Princess Margaret's initial launch was performed in her own characteristic style. She flew to the Harland and Wolff shipyard in Belfast accompanied by her newly appointed Lady-in-Waiting, Jennifer Bevan, a friend she had made during madrigal lessons a year earlier, and a detective. Making up the third member of her small entourage, although it seemed insignificant at the time, was the King's equerry Peter Townsend. Although nervous, the seventeen-year-old Princess visibly relaxed when she was greeted at Belfast airport by her Aunt Rose, the Countess Granville. She named the ship with aplomb and was then presented with a bouquet of roses by the youngest shipbuilder, Tommy Smith. Flirtatiously, Princess Margaret pulled out one of the roses and placed it in his buttonhole. The boy blushed and the crowds went wild. The Princess began to enjoy the attention of being centre stage. Having named the liner *Edinburgh Castle*, she then listened intently to the technical information offered by the experts and received it earnestly. The ability to appear interested even if bored rigid was a quality that she would need in abundance in the years that lay ahead. Suddenly in the crowds she spotted the Mayor and Mayoress of Cape Town, her hosts for part of the South African tour earlier in the year, and instantly offered them an invitation to visit her at Buckingham Palace. The liner she had launched only moments before was bound for the Cape and she revealed to them that instead of the customary champagne, she had actually broken a bottle of South African wine against its hull.

This first solo engagement in October 1947 was a turning point in Princess Margaret's life. With Lilibet about to be married and soon retitled the Duchess of Edinburgh, Margaret came into her own. Having cast off the 'Little Princess' tag once and for all she was now able to prove her maturity by undertaking responsibility within the Royal Family and it was a prospect that she relished. It gave her a function, a purpose in life. She was no longer a privileged daughter in an ivory tower, but someone who could benefit the nation in her own right. Offers began to come in from various charitable organisations. With the war only recently ended the popularity of the Royal Family was at its height and their presence at any function was still good for morale. With Princess Elizabeth's wedding dominating the headlines, attention inevitably focused on Margaret as the only eligible female member of the Family, and her ultimate marriage partner was the subject of much speculation.

By the age of eighteen she was everyone's idea of a fairy-tale Princess and those who remembered the once dumpy child looked with renewed interest at Britain's 'Porcelain Doll'. She was, quite literally, 'five foot two with eyes of blue', and was extremely proud of her petite figure and eighteen-inch waist. Cecil Beaton had photographed the two Princesses as children, but had six solo sittings with Margaret between 1949 and 1960 and it is during this period that the development of her character along with her appearance can be clearly monitored. In his diaries he describes her as witty and amusing with piercing blue eyes, noting how her expression could change from solemnity to laughter in an instant, with no 'semi smile'. Beaton's photographs show more clearly than any words how the Princess experiments with her appearance to find her own identity and it is no coincidence that the look she ultimately achieves is very different from Lilibet's. As teenagers, the sisters were almost like twins, usually wearing identical dresses and with identical hairstyles, the only obvious difference being Margaret's left-hand hair parting and one row of pearls less than her counterpart. Beaton remarked in March 1945 that Princess Margaret's dresses frequently looked homemade and her hair seemed lank, but by the time he came to photograph her again in June 1949 the transformation had begun. Margaret continually experimented with make-up, highlighted her eyes with mascara and her cheeks with blusher and accentuated her full sensual lips. Against a romantic backdrop of Watteau's *Pleasures of the Ball*, the resulting portraits were a mixture of sophistication and sexuality. Her face unworldly, the bareness of her shoulders complimented by the Hartnell ballgown made up of yards of white tulle and embroidered with sequins, Princess Margaret posed like a Winterhalter painting of her ancestors. As usual, the demure expression belied her thoughts. 'I like the embroidery on this dress,' she commented, 'it looks like pieces of potato peel.'

Over the next decade Cecil Beaton was to witness many changes in style, and by February 1958, when he came to photograph the Princess at Clarence House, the severe classic image was just a memory and before him stood an elfin faced woman with a short, fringed haircut, looking somehow more youthful yet worldly wise, her wide eyes colder, as if hardened by that decade's bitter experience. The celebrated photographer and royal favourite was to have two more sittings with Princess Margaret, first as a bride and later as the mother of two children in 1965, and on each occasion there are subtle but distinct changes in her appearance. Always there seems to be a relentless searching for an identity and for new experiences. Her sister and mother, in line with many members of the Royal Family, adopted a style with which they felt comfortable and which came to be identified with them. From Queen Victoria to Queen Mary, Princess Marina to the Queen Mother, all presented an instantly recognisable form, a hat, hairstyle or persona that remained reassuringly the same. Easily bored, Princess Margaret has sought constant change and even now, in her sixties, her hairstyles and fashions continue to vary.

It was common belief that when Elizabeth married Princess Margaret would feel a sense of anti-climax, that having never known a time when her sister was not easily accessible she would suffer loneliness. On the contrary, her life changed for the better, and although today the Princess looks back upon her childhood with great fondness, most of her early life suffered as a direct result of the war and the inevitable restrictions imposed upon her. Consequently, not until her eighteenth year did life really begin. In her family life she now felt a greater sense of importance and responsibility. 'Papa and Mummy need me to keep them in order,' she joked, 'What would they do without me?' Socially she was now of an age to enter the fray of nightclubs and country house weekends. On VE night, King George VI wrote sadly in his diary of his two daughters, 'Poor darlings, they have never had any fun yet,' and so he and Queen Elizabeth raised no objections to their lively daughter's nightlife. Always accompanied by eight or twelve friends, with a detective discreetly in tow, one favourite haunt was a club called '400' in London's Leicester Square where the Princess held court, enjoying the anonymity. Sometimes it would be the Milroy Club, occasionally a West End restaurant, and frequently the theatre. Almost every weekend she would stay with friends in the country. If she had never had any fun before, she certainly grasped the opportunity with both hands now. Lilibet was married, quickly became pregnant, and as Heir Presumptive was already firmly set on the path that was to be a life of duty, but for Margaret there were no such restrictions. She was young and fancy free.

These were the years when the Princess could legitimately lie in bed until eleven, having sometimes not returned to the Palace until 4a.m., without receiving criticism. Her engagement diary was steadily filling and she began to tour schools and colleges, open exhibitions, presented colours to Royal Airforce Cadets; she became Colonel-in-Chief of the Highland Light Infantry, launched two more ships, attended charity galas, and made solo royal visits throughout Britain before her eighteenth birthday, so nobody could accuse her of shirking her duties. Her energy, enthusiasm and glamour caused Princess Margaret to become newsworthy in her own right. 'She is Britain's No. One item for public scrutiny,' declared the American press under a headline 'The Blooming of Princess Margaret Rose', and continued, 'People are more interested in her than in the House of Commons or the dollar crisis'. Although some news reports bordered on the scandalous, few stories were total fantasy, and newspaper editors seldom printed sensational stories merely for the sake of increasing their sales, as the Princess was to experience later in life.

One of the most significant events in the late 1940s was the moment Princess Margaret began official overseas travel in her own right. Although she had whetted her appetite for foreign lands when in South Africa, she had been only part of the King's entourage, which lacked the thrill and fear of solo travel where the success or failure of the visit would rest squarely on her shoulders. Early reading during the war years, while entombed at Windsor Castle, had kindled the Princess's desire for adventure and when the opportunity to travel abroad 'on duty' arose, she welcomed the prospect. It was to begin a lifelong love affair with travel. Whereas the Queen now takes her holidays at Balmoral Castle in Scotland or Sandringham House in Norfolk (where she revealed to Labour Minister Richard Crossman that she felt more remote than anywhere else in the world) and never goes abroad to lie on sun-drenched beaches, for Princess Margaret, escape to a warm climate is her idea of heaven.

As Princess Margaret was not to receive an official Civil List income of her own until she was twenty-one, she undertook her foreign visits at this time as the King's representative, and they were therefore financed by His Majesty. The first solo trip was to Amsterdam to attend the Installation Ceremony of Princess Juliana as Queen of the Netherlands. Much to Queen Mary's disgust, Juliana's mother, Queen Wilhelmina, had abdicated at the age of 58, just as Juliana would herself renounce the throne in 1980 in favour of her daughter, Beatrix. Although the very thought of the function caused 'a sick feeling . . . just as before our pantomimes', Princess Margaret was equally excited about the attention and the responsibility, particularly when Queen Mary loaned her a diamond tiara to wear at the investiture banquet. It was like receiving a crown. (Recent writers have claimed that Queen Mary gave her grand-daughter a *pearl* and diamond tiara, but the diadem was in fact loaned, and Queen Mary had had the pearls removed from it two years earlier.) It was to rankle later in life that when Princess Margaret needed a tiara she had to borrow one from Lilibet, and it is no mere coincidence that when she eventually came to purchase one of her own at a Sotheby's auction in 1959, the Poltimore tiara for which she paid £5,500 is deeper and more crown-like than any that her sister owns.

The 1948 visit to the Netherlands was a personal triumph for Princess Margaret. On 6 September, just two weeks after her eighteenth birthday, she had become a fully-fledged British royal, representing the monarch, inspecting a guard of honour at the royal palace in Amsterdam and finding herself principal guest at Juliana's investiture banquet, receiving an almost embarrassing amount of media attention that put her in danger of overshadowing the new Dutch queen. Her entourage included Lady Margaret Egerton, an experienced Lady-in-Waiting who was able to advise the Princess in times of difficulty, and once again Peter Townsend, who was beginning to find himself increasingly captivated by the vivacious teenager. For four days the Princess was the centre of attention. Despite the fact that clothes rationing was still in force in Britain, which affected the Royal Family just as much as the general public, she had been left £20,000 in the will of Mrs Ronald Greville in 1942 which enabled her now to buy stylish evening gowns. It was to 'Maggie' Greville that Princess Margaret owed her financial independence at this time. From her £1^1/$_2$ million estate she left all her jewellery to Queen Elizabeth, nothing to Lilibet, and what then seemed like a fortune to Margaret, perhaps because they shared the same christian name. Had the eccentric Mrs Greville lived longer she would certainly have enjoyed watching her beneficiary's character develop.

Princess Margaret returned from the Netherlands with her

confidence boosted. It had been her good fortune that Lilibet was seven months pregnant and out of the public eye, otherwise the whole visit would certainly have been denied her. 'How composed, how dignified,' wrote the British press. 'So beautiful and charming,' said her Dutch hosts. Even Queen Mary, who had not always been complimentary about her grand-daughter, was impressed by her performance.

Margaret seemed not only to have boundless energy but a definite *joie de vivre*. With Elizabeth close to giving birth, Princess Margaret was able to deputise for her on many long-standing engagements that she was now unable to fulfil herself. As the health of King George VI began suddenly to fail, starting with an unexplained numbness in his left leg, once again Princess Margaret was required for public duty. In the 1990s we are now used to having a large contingent of royals to fulfil engagements around the world, but in 1948 there were fewer than ten members of the family regularly engaged in public life. Once over the initial nerves, the Princess looked upon the work as an opportunity rather than drudgery.

With a hectic social life on top of an ever-increasing official role, combined with concern for her father's health, there were inevitably occasions when Princess Margaret's own welfare suffered. Susceptible to sudden and debilitating migraines, she sporadically had to cancel engagements. Today, as Patron of the Migraine Trust, she is aware of the causes of the condition and seldom if ever suffers, but forty years ago research was not advanced, and the Princess was forced to succumb. At one time she caught measles, the effects of which were more severe than if she had been infected in childhood. Dogged by bad luck, this was quickly followed by acute fibrositis in the neck, and a series of colds, the combination of which have resulted in what has been a lifelong belief that she continually suffers from poor health. Although her ailments have been fewer than those of the average person over the years, they have been highlighted, not just because of her position but because they have been measured against Lilibet's robust constitution. Seldom has the Queen ever had to cancel engagements. She continues her public duties with a cold, and when the public are told that the Queen has 'a chill', as during her 1989 visit to Singapore and Malaysia when the Duke of Edinburgh had to deputise for her on one particular morning, it is in fact a euphemism for a stomach upset.

For some time the prospect of a tour to Australia was in the offing, which not only would provide the Princess with a chance to travel further than ever before, but also offered three months in pleasant temperatures, warmth that suited her temperament and constitution, as she detests the damp, cold English winter. As the King's health deteriorated, however, and severe cramp developed in both legs, sparking fears that one leg might have to be amputated, the tour was cancelled. The possibility of gangrene necessitated an operation, and arteriosclerosis was the eventual diagnosis. With the operation successfully completed, His Majesty began to undertake less strenuous duties in Britain, resting his foot upon a stool at investitures, riding in a carriage for Trooping the Colour (as the Queen does today) rather than on horseback as was customary, and once again his younger daughter offered her services for overseas duties.

In April 1949 Princess Margaret embarked on a month-long European tour, not as the King's representative this time, but in her own right as a Princess of the United Kingdom. Visiting Naples, Capri, Sorrento, Pompeii, Salerno, Rome, Florence, Siena, Bologna, Venice, Stresa, Lausanne, and finally Paris, the Princess appeared to have limitless energy and captivated the crowds wherever she went. In Italy she was *la bella Margherita* and was followed by hordes of enthusiastic onlookers wherever she went. From Princess Margaret's point of view, this was her first major encounter with the world's press, who dogged her every footstep. So eager were they for stories that they went to exorbitant lengths to photograph her swimming – just as the media today train their lenses on the Princess of Wales – and one journalist even went to the extent of bribing a chambermaid to reveal details of Princess Margaret's hotel room. Sensation! The great revelations were that she wore 'Peggy Sage Nail Varnish' and sprayed herself with 'Tweed' perfume.

Although such insignificant details seem very tame to us today, in 1949 the Royal Family were still highly revered. A press report of a royal function told only what the individual concerned was doing, not who designed the dress. If a member of the Royal Family purchased a gift, the retailer remained mute. Yet, in the 1990s, if the Princess of Wales buys a jokey costume jewellery brooch for a friend, not only do we all know about it within hours, you can be certain that a tabloid newspaper will have 5000 identical brooches

to give away as prizes the next day. The interest that had begun
to develop around Princess Margaret in Italy marked the change
in attitude to royal reporting. This was twenty years before the
royal walkabout, four years before television sets became widely
available (the 1953 Coronation doing much to boost sales), and a
time when much of the mystique remained. So, to discover that
Princess Margaret was reading *Busman's Honeymoon*, or the brand
name of her favourite perfume really was a revelation. Margaret
mania reverberated throughout Europe, the Princess experiencing
the kind of adulation that was not even lavished upon pop stars.
'Our visitor is all that we have dreamed in our childhood of a
fairy princess,' wrote *Le Figaro*, 'All France is now nostalgic for
a princess.'

'Look into my eyes,' she later told a dancing partner, 'Do you
realise that you are looking into the most beautiful eyes in the
world?' Then Princess Margaret roared with laughter, revealing
that she was quoting a recently written article. Although the tour
did much to inflate the Princess's ego, two specific events continued
to influence her long after she had returned to England. Because
of her deep religious convictions, her most significant meeting was
with Pope Pius XII at the Vatican. Although obviously private, her
audience with the Pontiff had a marked effect, and she returned
home with the gift of a crucifix, which stands on her desk at
Kensington Palace to this day. The second significant encounter
was the opportunity to attend fashion shows at Jean Dessès and
Christian Dior in Paris. For a girl with a perfect figure, who
had until recently often been forced to wear her older sister's
hand-me-down clothes and even some of her mother's adapted
evening dresses, the visit to Paris to see the home of *haute couture*
was to influence her wardrobe in the future. Hence Cecil Beaton's
comments on her transformation by June 1949, just a matter of
weeks after her return.

There was no doubt that by this time Princess Margaret had
firmly established her own identity on the public. Lilibet was now
a wife, mother, and heir. Although Princess Margaret attacked the
newspapers for making her 'the gay one' and Elizabeth 'the dull
one', she must have secretly enjoyed the glamorous image that was
gradually being carved out for her. Although occasionally irritated
by the more outlandish gossip columnists, she nevertheless revelled
in the stimulating social life that resulted from the publicity. Had

the press cast her as a boring stay-at-home, she would never have found herself the life and soul of every party. Equally this image had a 'knock-on' effect in her public life, for people turned out to see her *en masse* at each engagement, spurred on to see if she were as exciting as her reporters would have them believe. Seldom did she let them down.

Although these were apparently carefree years for Princess Margaret, there were underlying pressures that the public did not see. Her life was dominated by concern for her father. Parents should not have favourites among their children, but the bond between the King and his younger daughter was especially strong. Perhaps the empathy stemmed from their both being the second born. Maybe he feared that one day something might happen to Lilibet that would place Margaret in the terrifying position in which he had found himself, as monarch without training. Then, as Lilibet had children of her own, he equally feared that Margaret might feel pushed out, and he showered her with love to prove that second place did not mean second best. Elizabeth's future role was assured, Margaret's was less certain.

On Thursday, 3 May 1951, King George VI opened the Festival of Britain on the south bank of the River Thames. He looked pale and drawn, the first public indication that all was not well. Obviously aware of his condition, he began wearing make-up at evening functions to restore a healthy colour and avoid gossip, but an X-ray that same month revealed what he had most feared, a patch on the lung. A short time later, he had an attack of influenza from which recovery appeared exceptionally slow. Eventually a leading chest surgeon, Clement Price Thomas, examined the King and made a firm diagnosis – cancer.

Although the King probably suspected his condition, the true nature of the disease was kept from him and he was told simply that there was a blockage in his left lung which would necessitate its removal. The operation was carried out on 23 September at Buckingham Palace. 'I've never heard of a King go to hospital before,' he had grumbled when it had been suggested that the operation might be carried out away from the Palace. Anxious crowds stood silently outside the Palace railings waiting for news. Eventually a framed bulletin was hung outside: 'The King underwent an operation for lung resection this morning.

Whilst anxiety must remain for some days, His Majesty's immediate post-operative condition is satisfactory.' What the bulletin did not say was that some of the nerves of the larynx had also to be removed, which meant that the man who had suffered a severe stutter for most of his life might only ever speak in a faint whisper. Nor did it say that on that day Princess Margaret was appointed a Counsellor of State in case her father did not survive the operation.

Recovery was slow, but the operation had been sufficiently successful for Lilibet to embark on a tour of Canada and the United States two weeks later. Because of the frailty of the King's health, however, amongst her luggage was a draft Accession Declaration, but by the beginning of December he was well enough to warrant a national day of thanksgiving for his recovery, which was held in churches throughout Britain. The King celebrated his fifty-sixth birthday quietly with the Queen and the two Princesses, and a week later, on 21 December, travelled by train to Sandringham House to spend a traditional family Christmas. He recorded his Christmas Day message in advance, to avoid the stress of a live broadcast, and because of speech difficulties recorded it a section at a time. It was a particularly affectionate Christmas for the Royal Family, although they shut from their minds the thought that it might be their last together. The King, in high spirits, looked forward to revisiting South Africa in March 1952, confident that the warm sun would speed his recuperation.

On returning to London in the New Year, the King was given a thorough medical examination and was pronounced fit enough to wave Elizabeth and Philip off at London Airport (now known as Heathrow) where they were to board the BOAC Argonaut airliner *Atlanta* that was to take them to Kenya on the first stage of a tour to Australia and New Zealand. On 31 January the King stood in the bitter cold with Queen Elizabeth, the Duke of Gloucester and Princess Margaret to wave what turned out to be a final farewell to his elder daughter.

Princess Margaret returned with her parents to Sandringham on 1 February. It was a cold but sunny month, and the King seemed fitter than for many weeks. He enthusiastically read daily news reports of his daughter from abroad, and laughed at a story of baboons eating the lampshades at Treetops Hotel just before Elizabeth's arrival. On 5 February the King felt fit enough to participate in 'Keepers' Day' at Sandringham, the end-of-the-season hare shoot. Never happy about bloodsports, Princess Margaret drove with her mother to Ludham, just east of Norwich, to see the artist Edward Seago. They returned that evening in time for dinner and afterwards eagerly showed the King pictures that they had brought back. At 10.30p.m. Princess Margaret kissed her father goodnight as he retired to bed, weary but content. There was no sense of foreboding. The following morning it was her mother who calmly broke the news that at some time during the night King George VI had passed away peacefully in his sleep.

'During these last months the King walked with death,' said Winston Churchill, the then Prime Minister, 'as if death were a companion, an acquaintance, whom he recognized and did not fear. In the end death came as a friend.' Although this was how Princess Margaret wanted her father's days to end, painlessly and without fear, this was the first time that anyone close to her had died, and as she went to her father's bedroom to say her final fond farewell, an aching void opened up within her. Though she had not experienced loneliness when Lilibet married, she certainly felt it now, in the silence of Sandringham House, that same house where the life of her grandfather, King George V had moved 'peacefully towards its close' when she was too young to understand the loss. Naturally, all the Royal Family suffered deeply from the King's death, but few realised the depth of Princess Margaret's grief. She kept up an outwardly bright appearance for her mother's sake, but while friends and family fussed around the widowed Queen, the distraught twenty-one-year-old Princess had few people to whom she could unburden herself.

Lilibet returned to London Airport the following day as Queen Elizabeth the Second. Despite her obvious grief, there was much to occupy her. Many demands were made of the new sovereign, and before she could even return to Sandringham House, she had first to make her Declaration of Accession at St James's Palace, and discuss the state funeral with the Lord Chamberlain and Earl Marshall of England. This burden of responsibility eased the immediate sadness, but for Princess Margaret there was nothing. She spent much time alone with her thoughts and memories, just yards from where her father's body lay.

In distress she turned first to her ever increasing faith and religious beliefs, and then to the man she now needed more than ever, someone who could replace the father figure that she had now lost. It was the late King's equerry, Peter Townsend, who provided the shoulder for her to cry on. With his own marriage on the verge of disintegration, the two sought solace in each other's company. Princess Margaret's once secure world was about to be turned upside-down as a result.

CHAPTER THREE

The Hinge of Fate

In October 1988 I gave a talk to the Cambridge Union about the Royal Family and when I had finished speaking I invited the students to ask questions. The first took me by surprise. In passing I had briefly mentioned Princess Margaret and her relationship with Peter Townsend, automatically assuming that everyone present would understand my reference. Then came the question from a nineteen-year-old student. 'Please, could you tell us who Peter Townsend was?' From then onwards, many in the room heard the story of a momentous happening in Princess Margaret's life for the very first time. Not until that point did I realise that the episode I recounted had happened forty years ago and meant nothing to today's younger generation.

Peter Townsend. The name must still haunt Princess Margaret. A man, twice married and now seventy-six years old, with whom she will always be inextricably linked in the minds of many despite the passing of the years. An incident that she neither regrets nor would wish to forget. The only change today is that she can look back upon the legend without pain, as if it were someone else's story.

On 16 February 1944, Group Captain Peter Wooldridge Townsend then aged just twenty-nine, visited Buckingham Palace for the first time. With a distinguished record as a fighter pilot for the Royal Air Force, having been honoured with DSO and DFC medals, but physically and mentally scarred by battle, he found himself recommended by the Air Ministry for the post of equerry to King George VI. One of the many changes brought about by war was the appointment to the Royal Household of staff chosen for their abilities rather than their social connections. On that fateful Wednesday afternoon, Peter Townsend not only had an audience with the King, but, more significantly, after leaving the King's presence, while being taken down the corridor by Sir Piers Legh (the then Master of the Household), he met Princess Margaret for the first time. Contrary to popular belief it was not love at first sight. The Princess was, after all, still six months away from her fourteenth birthday and Peter Townsend had been married barely two and a half years. In fact, Townsend described the Princess as 'unremarkable'. The two Princesses giggled to themselves at the sight of a dashing young man in uniform, but he was not even the object of a teenage crush. Princess Margaret was to mature a great deal before she became drawn to her father's handsome equerry.

When Peter Townsend began his duties at Buckingham Palace in March 1944 the war was in progress, Princess Margaret's life still centred around Windsor Castle and the two rarely came into contact. What did register with the Princess, however, when she saw the new equerry, was his youthfulness compared to the staid courtiers of the 'old school' who surrounded her father. Peter Townsend was from a new mould, handsome, gentle, and a military hero.

It is common knowledge that Peter Townsend, as he gradually came to know the King's daughter, quickly came to appreciate her qualities; her generous nature, the ability to change her expression from saintliness to one of hilarity, her coquettishness. Most telling is that he pinpointed how Princess Margaret had what he called 'a dazzling facade' and apparent self-assurance, that often belied the gentle, caring nature that she really possessed. At just fourteen this characteristic of putting on an act to cover up her true feelings was quite clear. As she grew up this trait was to be an adversary. If her critics had witnessed her sincerity rather than an apparent coolness, they would have warmed towards her. Peter Townsend's heart warmed.

The very idea of a relationship between the two seemed inconceivable to all. There was the social gulf between an equerry and a Princess, and an age difference of some sixteen years. Nevertheless, Peter Townsend found himself increasingly drawn to the young Princess Margaret's vivacious personality, and circumstances were to bring them closer together. In each case it was the loss of a loved one.

Peter Townsend was a dreamer, an adventurer, yet in July 1941 he married Rosemary Pawle, the daughter of an army brigadier and a down-to-earth realist. It was she who had helped restore him to health and renew his confidence, lost after being shot down by a German bomber a year earlier. Her commonsense and patience pulled him from the brink of a nervous breakdown, yet she lacked her husband's sense of daring. Peter Townsend later confessed that theirs was a marriage that would probably not have happened in peace time. Amid the horror of war is an acute awareness of the frailty of human life, and many entered into relationships before time ran out. Peter Townsend and Rosemary Pawle had known each other just six weeks when they married.

A devoted mother of one son, and a nest builder, Rosemary Townsend was ecstatic when her husband was appointed equerry to the King. It was a step up on the social ladder and appeared to offer security for life. The war had already meant continual partings, separations that had caused friction, and she was unprepared for the equally unsocial hours that any career in the Royal Household inevitably entails. Rosemary assumed that time would be divided between Windsor Castle and Buckingham Palace, and with a grace-and-favour cottage in Windsor Great Park they could settle down to a 'normal' married life. It was not long before the unpredictability of royal duty started to take its toll and Rosemary began to wonder which family came first, the Townsends or the Windsors. As love died, the contrast between Princess Margaret's sense of fun and Rosemary's air of despair must have seemed great and Peter Townsend began to enjoy Princess Margaret's company more and more. Yet for several years he saw her only as a release from his marital problems, never as a replacement for Rosemary.

In Peter Townsend, many feel that King George saw the son that he never had, and certainly theirs was more than a mere working relationship. As the King's health failed, he relied on his equerry and confidant more than ever. In the summer of 1945 the King had happily consented to be a godparent to the Townsend's second son, Hugo, and looked upon them as a perfect family. Ironically, it was also the King who knocked one of the final nails into the coffin of the Townsend marriage when he requested that Peter accompany the Royal Family on the South African tour. Twelve weeks away from the bitter winter of England meant not only that he left Rosemary behind with two small sons to care for in a cottage that proved impossible to heat, but also placed him in the warmth of a beautiful country with Princess Margaret. From there, Fate was to take a hand. The Princess fell in love with Peter Townsend. Peter Townsend fell in love with South Africa.

Brimming with enthusiasm for the country, Peter wrote home to Rosemary of his feelings, suggesting that a whole new life awaited them there. If they, as a family, emigrated permanently, they could perhaps make a fresh start in a vibrant and exciting environment. On Saturday, 15 March 1947 Britain was experiencing the worst floods ever recorded, and Rosemary Townsend was in no mood for dreams. She replied by telegram that she had no intention of uprooting herself and the children to South Africa. Some time later she wrote a letter reiterating her thoughts, which were immovable. As Rosemary, thousands of miles away, shattered his ideals, Princess Margaret seemed to epitomise everything that was different and unconventional. Had she not been born to a life of royal duty, she would quite happily have settled in a country away from England. Travel and new experiences appealed to her and Peter Townsend began to enjoy being in her company.

By the time they returned from South Africa, Princess Margaret had fallen in love with Peter. Perhaps at that time it was still a teenage crush; possibly it was part of her nature to desire the unattainable. Peter was married, a member of the King's staff, and therefore forbidden fruit. Yet Princess Margaret undoubtedly found him attractive, and while Lilibet had pined for Philip when they were abroad, it amused her that she had her own secret love. At this age she was coquettish, and teasingly flirted with members of their party, and nobody noticed any difference in her familiarity towards Peter. After all, was he not the man that her father treated like a son? Back home, the couple exchanged photographs of the tour and shared memories that were gradually building up a special bond between them. While Princess Margaret's feelings deepened towards Peter, there was no question yet that those feelings were reciprocated. It fits very neatly into historical legend to suggest that the Townsend marriage ended because Peter fell in love with the Princess, but in fact he had separated from Rosemary before he began to consider Margaret romantically.

Whether it was fortunate for Princess Margaret or not, the collapse of Peter's marriage coincided with her maturity and blossoming into womanhood. Had the marriage ended earlier, the Princess would still have been a plump teenager and not then desirable to the mature Townsend. Had Peter and Rosemary married later, maybe he could have persuaded his new bride to start a life with him in South Africa. As it was, the marriage began to fall apart at a time when Princess Margaret was most concerned about her father's health and needed a mature person to confide in. Peter Townsend stood out from the friends of her circle because of his age and experience. The very fact that he was different made him all the more attractive.

The return from South Africa coincided with Princess Margaret's embarkation on royal duties and Peter Townsend became part of her entourage, which meant that they spent a great deal of time with each other. Accompanying the young Princess Margaret on her highly successful début engagements was more like fun than work for Peter Townsend. An added bonus was that he equally enjoyed the company of Jennifer Bevan, the Princess's Lady-in-Waiting.

In 1950, at the time of Princess Margaret's twentieth birthday that August, the King promoted Peter Townsend to the position of Assistant Master of the Household, one of the highest positions among the staff. The job meant being deputy to the Master of the Household on whose shoulders rests the responsibility for all interior and domestic arrangements in every royal residence. It requires diplomacy and enterprise in order to solve every Household crisis, however small. He is royal confidant, mentor, Jack-of-all-trades and above all has to satisfy and anticipate the Royal Family's every need. In the Household of Queen Elizabeth II some 189 permanent staff come under the Master of the Household's supervision; this can swell to over 300 when temporary staff are employed for a state banquet. In the 1950s the staff of King George VI's Household was considerably higher. The job provided variety and greater responsibility for Peter Townsend, involving far more than simply dealing with catering arrangements. The 600 rooms at Buckingham Palace alone required constant attention. If a bulb had to be replaced, a painting restored, upholstery repaired, the Ballroom floor polished or a carpet cleaned, he had to organize it. Under him were a large team of carpenters, plumbers, electricians, french polishers, upholsterers and clock-menders. From approving the duty roster of the housemaids to arranging for the drains to be unblocked, even arranging for wreaths to be sent on the King's behalf, all came under the jurisdiction of the Master and Assistant Master of the Household. From Princess Margaret's point of view, the advantage of Peter's upgrading was that he travelled continually with the Royal Family to Windsor, London, Sandringham and Balmoral. He was now like a permanent member of the Family. At Adelaide Cottage, Rosemary Townsend now rarely saw her husband and sought solace in the arms of an export merchant, Mr John de Laszlo.

In 1951 Princess Margaret celebrated her twenty-first birthday at Balmoral. It was a hot summer and although the King's health was poor, there was a mood of optimism that the relaxing atmosphere combined with the Scottish air would somehow be beneficial. In the month of August Peter Townsend realised that he was in love with Princess Margaret, although neither revealed their inner feelings to each other. In his autobiography *Time and Chance* he writes of one specific memory. After a day's grouse shooting at which the female members of the houseparty had joined the men for a picnic lunch, he lay asleep in the heather. Suddenly he was conscious that a coat was being laid over him and he opened one eye. Just a few inches from his face was Princess Margaret's. As he opened the other eye he was aware that the King was watching them. For a second Princess Margaret gazed deeply into Peter's eyes, then giggled and walked away with her father. For Peter Townsend it was a moment of realisation.

When he eventually returned home to Windsor that autumn, Rosemary Townsend revealed that she had fallen in love with John de Laszlo. It offered Peter the escape he needed from a stagnant marriage, despite the anguish that the separation was to cause him. For a time they stayed together, for the sake of their children, for the sake of appearances in an age when divorce was still an ugly word. (Until 1955 no divorced person was allowed into the Royal Enclosure at the Ascot Races, being ranked alongside bankrupts and ex-convicts). Divorce was to be the inevitable conclusion, and Peter knew that he would be free to remarry, but still completely unaware of Princess Margaret's feelings, he did not at that time even consider her as his future wife. When Princess Margaret's world fell apart on 6 February 1952 with the untimely death of her father, she felt able to share her grief with Peter. With Lilibet now Queen there were inevitably changes that were to affect them both; firstly, Princess Margaret's home, secondly, Peter's job. Initially it was suggested that the Queen might retain Clarence House, which had been her marital home since 1949, turning Buckingham Palace into a government department for use as a venue for constitutional duties and affairs of state. The Prime Minister, Winston Churchill, was fiercely opposed to this suggestion. For 115 years Buckingham Palace had been the home of the monarch; four kings had followed Queen Victoria into this gloomy mansion and for Queen Elizabeth II there was to be no escape either. In a life that would be dictated by tradition, she was forced to retrace the footsteps of her predecessors. As Queen she should be seen to live in a palace. The obvious solution was the one eventually adopted. Elizabeth and Philip would take up residence at Buckingham Palace, doing a direct swap with the Queen Mother and Princess Margaret who would move into Clarence House.

Not only was Princess Margaret then grieving her lost father, she was confused about her feelings for Peter, worried about her status within the Family now that Lilibet was Queen, and on top of it all had to uproot herself from Buckingham Palace which had been her home since she was six years old. She divided her time between Windsor Castle and Sandringham until Clarence House was made ready for them. Invariably Peter went too. Conscious that he seemed to be a stabilising influence on the Princess, and knowing the affection that the late King had held for Peter, the Queen Mother (after consulting Lilibet) invited him to be Comptroller of her household at Clarence House. This was a position especially created for him. Once again, a situation that was out of Princess Margaret's control had pushed her closer to Peter; had he remained Assistant Master of the Household at Buckingham Palace they would seldom have met. Now he was to run Princess Margaret's new home.

As far as senior members of the Royal Family knew at this time, the Townsends were a happily married couple. It was an impression that Peter and Rosemary worked hard to create. Just six months before they were divorced the Queen and Prince Philip had dinner at Adelaide Cottage, unaware of the situation. Princess Margaret was invited too, although was noticeably restrained, desperate not to give out any wrong signals to Rosemary. On 20 December 1952 Group Captain Peter Townsend was granted a decree nisi on the grounds of Rosemary's 'misconduct' with John de Laszlo, whom she later married. Peter Townsend was, therefore, the innocent party in the dissolution, a point that was to weigh heavily in his favour when his life became a matter for public scrutiny. Depressed by the situation, he turned that winter to the one person he now felt close enough to pour out his heart to – Princess Margaret – just as she, a year earlier, had needed his shoulder to cry on. Thus, one afternoon in the red drawing-room at Windsor Castle in the spring of 1953 he finally revealed his love for her. To his surprise, the Princess was neither angry nor shocked. She looked at him with the same expression that had been on her face when she had gazed down on him asleep in the heather. 'That's *exactly* how I feel,' she said.

This was no longer a passing fancy or teenage crush for the Princess. Some six years had passed since the seeds of love had been planted in South Africa and we can only guess at the agonies that she must have suffered during that period. Conscious of the age difference, the social barrier, and above all else the fact that he was, for most of those years, a married man, it was a heavy burden for one so young to bear. Had Peter Townsend not divorced, or, having freed himself from the unhappy marriage, not confessed his love for her, it is unlikely that she would ever have made an approach herself. Otherwise she would have at least hinted much sooner. Instead it was he who would have to make the first move. Meanwhile she threw herself into a hectic social life to keep her mind occupied. She enjoyed the attention and was amused by the possible suitors, possibly hoping too that a boy might come along and capture her heart, but no one stood a chance.

Now certain of each other's passion, the couple naïvely felt that, as they were both free, marriage was the obvious goal. Princess Margaret was prepared for a few eyebrows to be raised among the general public because of the large age gap, but felt safe that the family's acceptance would be total. It was not as if she were introducing them to a stranger. Peter was universally liked amongst the whole Royal Family. What the Princess had not bargained for was the fact that, as her sister was Queen, she would need Her Majesty's permission to marry, under the Royal Marriages Act of 1772, just as anyone under twenty-five years of age in the line of succession to the throne needs her authority today. This appeared to be no problem. Surely Lilibet would not deny her own sister the chance of happiness. It would be a mere formality for the Queen to concede. Elizabeth the Second is, however, Head of the Church of England, Defender of the Faith, whose ecclesiastical law forbids divorcees to remarry in Church. As Head of the Church it would be impossible for her to agree to Princess Margaret's marrying a divorced man. She had to put her position as Queen before that of sister. Whereas it might have been better to have offered the cruel truth, Elizabeth opted for kindness and chose not to tell her sister this at the time. Princess Margaret wrongly assumed that because Elizabeth was Queen she would agree to the marriage; it seemed like an advantage rather than a stumbling block.

Possibly the Queen knew that if she had raised the Church's position at that emotional time, Princess Margaret might well have thrown back at her, 'Well you're Head of the Church, change the rules. If you can't, who can?' Elizabeth would have gently pointed out that she was also *Defender* of the Faith. It was not her role to change God's laws. When Peter Townsend had married twenty-year-old Rosemary Pawle in the Hertfordshire village of Much Hadham they had taken vows, 'forsaking all other so long as ye both shall live'. The Queen knew the Bible and Christ's words, 'Whosoever shall put away his wife, and marry another, committeth adultery against her.' But this was not the time for confrontations, in her opinion, and so when Princess Margaret broke the news to her that she wished to marry Peter Townsend, the Queen's only proviso was that the couple should wait twelve months.

This also gave the Queen time to consider the situation with her advisers, and secretly she may have believed that their ardour would have cooled down after a year, or that someone Princess Margaret's own age might come along and vie for her affection. Either way Princess Margaret suffered. She had loved Peter for a long time, so one more year was not too difficult to bear. What was far worse was the eventual dawning that she would encounter stiff opposition because of the Church's viewpoint on divorce. If the Queen had explained this critical point at the outset it would have been easier to come to terms with. Instead, Princess Margaret believed for a long time that she and Peter would be able to marry in the end, even if it ultimately meant waiting until she were twenty-five and then free to wed without Her Majesty's consent.

Once the hurdle of telling the Queen had been effectively jumped, Peter Townsend approached one of his colleagues, Sir Alan Lascelles, the Queen's Private Secretary. He had assumed that this would be a mere formality, but 'Tommy' Lascelles was enraged, railing at Townsend that he must be 'either mad or bad'.

Unlike Peter Townsend, Sir Alan Lascelles was of the 'old school'. He began royal service as Assistant Private Secretary to the Prince of Wales, later King Edward VIII, in 1920, but disapproved of the Prince's lifestyle and lack of commitment and so eventually resigned. He later returned as Assistant Private Secretary to King George V, and went on to become Private Secretary to King George VI in 1943. So, by the time Elizabeth ascended the throne and inherited him as her Private Secretary he had served under three monarchs and had thirty years' experience. Unlike the majority of the Household he had never warmed to Queen Elizabeth the Queen Mother, who had always posed a threat to his influence over George VI, and equally held Princess Margaret in low regard. He had respect for the sovereign only and preferred the days when royalty were remote from the general public. Princess Margaret appeared to be too frivolous for his liking, and to him youth was no excuse, hence his horror at Peter's announcement of his desire to marry the Princess. Like the Queen, however, Lascelles gave no hint that the path to the altar would be blocked.

With neither Peter's nor Princess Margaret's knowledge, Sir Alan went to the Prime Minister and together they came up with a solution. Peter Townsend should be sent abroad immediately. It would be little short of banishment. Fortunately for Princess Margaret, the Queen took a more sympathetic view. Conscious that her sister's health and happiness were at stake she insisted that Peter retain his post as Comptroller at Clarence House. There were two reasons for this. To take him away for his job would inevitably incite interest. The press quickly learned of comings and goings at the Palace and knew of all appointments. Why, they would ask, has Townsend been removed? This would not only then result in press speculation, which might turn out to be worse than the actual facts, but it would cause consternation amongst the Household staff who were still ignorant of the situation. Although backstairs gossip was rife, the only people who legitimately knew of Princess Margaret's love were her own immediate family, the Private Secretary and the Press Secretary, Richard Colville. Secondly, the Queen felt that to separate the couple would only deepen their feelings. Perhaps if they remained under the same roof and saw one another every day, the relationship might cool off.

It is popular belief that the Princess's secret remained a

private matter until June 1953, but even she did not know at the time that within days of her telling the Queen that she wished to marry, European papers were naming Peter Townsend as her future husband. It is a sad fact that has dogged Princess Margaret throughout her life that there have always been staff who overhear conversations and are unscrupulous enough to 'do a Crawfie'. Peter Townsend later suggested that the Buckingham Palace Press Office *must* have known what the foreign papers were saying, yet they too kept quiet.

Throughout the matter, Princess Margaret seems to have been kept in ignorance. Perhaps those close to her thought that they could shield her from the facts of the Royal Marriages Act, the facts of the Church's stand on divorce, the fact that she was the subject of public gossip abroad. All would have been far easier to cope with had she continually been kept informed, but she was allowed to live in limbo, still believing that one day it would be acceptable to marry Peter.

As is now legendary, it was on Coronation Day itself, 2 June 1953, when Lilibet became the forty-second monarch since William the Conqueror to be crowned, that Princess Margaret herself unleashed the whole can of worms. It was unfortunate timing that, when chatting animatedly to Peter after the Coronation ceremony, Princess Margaret brushed the tiniest piece of fluff from his jacket in full view of the press contingent. It was the most innocuous, most innocent of gestures, yet to the eager journalists this simple action confirmed what the foreign press had been saying for weeks. Princess Margaret went to bed that night completely unaware that she of all people had turned her romance into scandal.

Scarcely had Elizabeth's head been anointed with holy oil than she was faced with the most delicate of situations. Whatever solution was adopted it would mean either a constitutional embarrassment, or heartbreak for Princess Margaret. As in all things as Queen she placed her duty before personal desire. Sir Alan Lascelles twittered that if only Group Captain Peter Townsend had been sent abroad when he suggested then the crisis would never have arisen. The young monarch was forced to agree. The Prime Minister and the Cabinet met, all staunchly opposed to the union, and it was decided that the Air Ministry would find him a post overseas immediately. Eventually he was given a choice of three locations and opted for Brussels because of its proximity to Britain.

From then onwards the situation was totally out of Princess Margaret's control. Peter was speedily removed from his post at Clarence House and appointed equerry to the Queen until arrangements were completed for his assignment in Belgium. To his horror, when he eventually accompanied the Queen in public on an engagement in Belfast (which unfortunately coincided with the official announcement of his foreign posting) the press contingent aimed their lenses at him rather than the royal visitor, but it was the Queen's way of showing her acceptance of him.

Princess Margaret had been looking forward to a visit to Rhodesia from 29 June to 17 July and Peter Townsend had originally been included as part of her entourage. That was now out of the question, but Sir Alan Lascelles saw the visit as fortuitous as it successfully placed the Princess out of the limelight. The Princess was angry and upset. Her time with Peter was so short, she wanted to spend every moment with him before he was banished, but like her sister she would have to place duty first and would count the days until her return. On 15 July, two days before she flew back to Britain, Sir Alan Lascelles arranged for Peter Townsend to be flown to Brussels. More than a year was to pass before he saw Princess Margaret again.

At her lowest ebb, Princess Margaret contracted influenza while in Rhodesia and was confined to bed with a temperature of 103°, although she cancelled only a few of the fifty-four engagements planned, a gruelling schedule for someone in low spirits.

In Britain the national press were now having a field day. 'It is high time for the British public to be made aware of the fact that scandalous rumours about Princess Margaret are racing around the world. Newspapers in both Europe and America are openly asserting that the Princess is in love with a divorced man . . .' revealed the *People*. 'Group Captain Townsend was the innocent party in the divorce proceedings . . . but his innocence cannot alter the fact that a marriage between Princess Margaret and himself would fly in the face of Royal and Christian tradition.' The *Daily Mirror* even held a poll among its readers, 'Should Princess Margaret be allowed to wed Peter Townsend?' Of the 70,142 members of the public who took the trouble to vote, an incredible 67,907 people felt that she should, resulting in a newspaper headline of the single word 'YES'. To this climate of intense speculation and unhealthy interest in her private life, Princess Margaret returned, shattered to discover that Peter had been deliberately sent away before she got back. The Princess scarcely spoke to Lascelles again, even though, for nearly thirty years, until his death in 1981, they were practically neighbours, he having been given a grace-and-favour apartment at Kensington Palace which was to become the Princess's home too. Was it pure coincidence that Lascelles opted to retire from royal service as soon as Princess Margaret returned from Southern Rhodesia?

Four days before the Queen and Prince Philip embarked on a six-month tour of the Commonwealth in the autumn of 1953, the Regency Act of 1937 was amended to exclude Princess Margaret in favour of the Duke of Edinburgh. The inevitable process of being pushed further away from the throne had begun. Until the amendment, even though Lilibet's children were now ahead of her in the line of succession she could still in theory be 'deputy Queen' for a time as Regent. Now she had gone down to third in line of succession and would gradually be pushed down by Lilibet's children and grandchildren. Even though Princess Margaret has never had any desire to be Queen, and obviously did not want her sister to die, it was the very fact of being made to feel less significant that seemed painful at the time. Again, was it coincidence that this should happen in the wake of the Townsend affair?

When Princess Margaret had informed the Queen of her desire to marry Peter, Her Majesty's command had been to wait one year. Yet the spring of 1954 came and went, as did the spring of 1955, and still the situation remained unresolved. Conscious that Edward VIII had to renounce the throne to marry a divorced woman, Queen Elizabeth the Queen Mother was only too aware of the implications of that ugly word 'divorce' amongst the Royal Family. The Queen remained relatively aloof, hoping that the longer the matter remained in the background the greater the probability that Princess Margaret would fall in love with some-one else. This was not to be the case and the depth of Princess Margaret's love is shown in her faithfulness to Peter for more than two frustrating years apart. During this time they must have been in touch either by letter or telephone, secretly, even under assumed names which the Royal Family often use when desiring anonymity. She and Peter did meet once during those years. In July 1954 Peter Townsend flew from Brussels to London using the pseudonym 'Mr Carter'. Like a scene in an espionage film, he then went to the book department of Harrods. Princess Margaret had arranged to have waiting for him there one Brigadier Norman Gwatkin. The many shoppers in one of the world's most exclusive stores took no notice of the two men walking casually out into the Knightsbridge street. Equally casually they entered the waiting car and drove the five-minute journey to Clarence House where Princess Margaret was waiting excitedly. To her, the plan of arranging the clandestine meeting was almost as exciting as seeing Peter again after so long, and she was thrilled when Peter returned to Brussels to discover that she had actually been able to do something without the knowledge of the press.

Peter Townsend spent two hours with Princess Margaret alone in her private sitting-room. Their conversation was naturally private and unrecorded, but both knew that Princess Margaret was just one year short of her twenty-fifth birthday, a milestone which placed her outside the confines of the Royal Marriages Act of 1772 that was haunting them like an ancient spectre. They would be free, so they believed, to marry at last. Their parting was made less painful by this apparent light at the end of a very long and dark tunnel. A parting kiss and then Peter had gone, back to Brussels for what was to be another fourteen months.

Princess Margaret had taken a huge gamble in setting up the meeting. As it happened, one Sunday newspaper discovered that Peter had travelled under a false name and criticised him for pretending to be like royalty, attempting to journey under an alias. The resulting article attacked what it considered to be his pretentiousness. Amusingly, they did not question his destination. Had they discovered then that he had met Princess Margaret in secret, there would have been a further scandal.

The suppression and frustration that Princess Margaret felt at this time often caused her to be rebellious and unconventional. She was building up an image that was to dog her for the next forty years. By surrounding herself with friends and enjoying a busy social life, she was able to keep her sanity. Having written all that they possibly could about Peter Townsend, the gossip columnists now turned their attentions to the Princess's escorts, constantly speculating that she was about to get married. Had the circumstances been different, the Queen might have curtailed her sister's social life. Even now, the Queen carefully monitors the Royal Family's publicity to ensure that no one member of the family is receiving too much adverse criticism and if they are, she will set about changing it. Equally the public relations machinery would have worked on Princess Margaret, had it not been felt that gossip about her harmless social activities were infinitely preferable to potentially damaging reports about Peter Townsend. In fact it almost seems as if the Princess revelled in any publicity that took people's minds off the subject. It was considered to be an outright act of defiance when she went to see a show called *The Moon Is Blue* which had been condemned by the Church because of its repeated use of the word *virgin*. Apparently this was the first time the word had been used on the English stage, but it turned out to be a light comedy and scarcely the immoral production that had been suggested. The Church's condemnation today seems strange, but it only serves to show the depth of feeling that Princess Margaret was up against. If they objected to a single word, and not even a blasphemous one at that, they would never accept her marriage to a divorced man.

Even up to her twenty-fifth birthday in August 1955, Princess Margaret still firmly believed that some way would be found around the problem. But within a short time of that all-important birthday, the truth was spelt out for her at Balmoral by Sir Anthony Eden, who was now Prime Minister. Ironically Eden was the innocent party in a divorce and was married for a second time to Clarissa Churchill, but his news was grave. Princess Margaret might now be free to marry without the Queen's consent, but the Cabinet was still opposed to the union. So strong was the feeling, that members of the Government had threatened to resign rather than allow a Bill through Parliament consenting to the marriage.

As far as Princess Margaret was concerned she was back to square one. She had waited an interminably long time for nothing and blamed the Queen and Sir Alan Lascelles for not pointing out the clear facts from the outset. The only way in which the Princess could marry the man she loved now was to give twelve months' formal notice to the Privy Council of her intentions, and to renounce her titles and place in the line of succession and all her rights as a member of the Royal Family including her Civil List income. To add insult to injury, one prominent clergyman pointed out that if she did go ahead with the marriage it would not be recognised by the Church. This meant that any children they might have would be considered illegitimate.

We can only imagine the depth of Princess Margaret's feelings at this time. For possibly the first time in her life she must have cursed the fact that she had been born royal. That title 'Princess' brought many privileges, but equally many restrictions. Because of love, she had the Church, the Government, the Establishment against her. 'Palace Circles Say Meg Will Wed' declared the *New York Post*, 'Come on, Margaret!' screamed the *Daily Mirror* in Britain. Some 300 pressmen gathered around the perimeter of the Balmoral Estate, waiting for an announcement, hoping for a photograph, writing stories regardless. Her life no longer seemed to be her own.

On 12 October, Princess Margaret returned from Scotland to Clarence House. At the same time Peter flew back to Britain. At precisely 6.20p.m. the following day they met for what the press believed to be the first time in over two years. They were both emotionally exhausted; there was so much to say, so many decisions. By then both knew in their hearts that Fate was against them. Princess Margaret is a strong character and usually gets what she wants, but this one battle had lasted so long, the fight had been tough, but now she had to admit defeat. Ten days of agonising, talking, crying, now took place. 'No announcement concerning Princess Margaret's personal future is at present contemplated,' came a press statement from Buckingham Palace, but the world waited with baited breath.

On 24 October the couple met at Clarence House, both now resolute in their minds that marriage was out of the question. Peter poured out his thoughts to the Princess, who replied, 'That's exactly how I feel'. They were the same words she had spoken when Peter first declared his love for her. On a piece of paper he had jotted down a statement for her to make publicly, the same statement that she made with little alteration. Three days later, Princess Margaret went alone to see the Archbishop of Canterbury. The popular myth, quoted by every 'authority', is that the Archbishop, Dr Geoffrey Fisher, was prepared for the Princess. Supposedly, he had numerous books on marriage and divorce in his study at Lambeth Palace open at the relevant passages, and as the Princess entered the room she is reported to have said 'You can put away your books, Archbishop, I am not going to marry Peter Townsend'. Princess Margaret has in fact never revealed her exact words, but Dr Fisher, who was not likely to lie and had no reason to, made a point of telling his biographer: 'I had no books of any sort spread around. The Princess came and I received her, as I would anybody else, in the quietness of my own study. She never said "Put away those books" because there were not any books to put away.' Princess Margaret spoke with calmness of her decision, one that came as a relief to the Archbishop whose resignation had been demanded from certain quarters over his handling of the situation.

Even though Princess Margaret wanted to release her statement immediately to put an end to speculation and to start her own life anew, Buckingham Palace advisers, rightly or wrongly, decided to withhold the statement until they felt that the timing was right. This gave the Princess and Peter time to spend one final, farewell weekend together in Sussex in the house of mutual friends, the Nevills, in Uckfield. The finality of it cannot have made it an enjoyable weekend, especially as the house was surrounded by the press as a constant reminder.

On Monday, 31 October they both returned to London, separately. That night they met in the Princess's sitting-room at Clarence House for a 'stiff drink' and to say goodbye. As Peter drove out of London at 7.00p.m. that evening, Princess Margaret's statement was released. Her words have become as familiar and as poignant as Edward VIII's abdication speech:

> I would like it to be known that I have
> decided not to marry Group Captain Townsend.
> I have been aware that, subject to my renouncing
> my rights of succession, it might have been possible
> for me to contract a civil marriage. But mindful of
> the Church's teachings that Christian marriage is
> indissoluble, and conscious of my duty to the
> Commonwealth, I have resolved to put these considerations
> before others. I have reached this decision entirely
> alone and in doing so I have been strengthened by the
> unfailing support and devotion of Group Captain Townsend.
> I am deeply grateful for the concern of all those who
> have constantly prayed for my happiness.
>
> (Signed) MARGARET

All who read her statement knew how difficult the decision must have been and Princess Margaret's reputation was enhanced as a result. As a member of the Royal Family she had been seen to do her duty, and had her grandmother Queen Mary still been alive she would have been prouder of her than she had ever been. It was to give many British subjects a lasting sympathy for the Princess, of whom many still say, 'If only they'd let her marry Peter Townsend . . . ' We can only speculate as to whether it would have worked. Had she not been forced to make sacrifices, certainly the marriage would have stood a greater chance. After all, they had weathered some very rough storms together. But if Princess Margaret had relinquished everything to become plain Mrs Peter Townsend, with no income or state of her own, then the onus on him would have been too great for the marriage ever to have survived.

In Princess Margaret's library at Kensington Palace today, next to a leather-bound volume of *Peter Pan*, are the writings of Sir Winston Churchill. One book with a particularly worn dust-jacket bears the title *The Hinge of Fate*. Although about war, the title aptly sums up the Princess's position at this time. At the end of the day, she had to console herself with the harsh fact that marriage to Peter Townsend was never meant to be. The couple met three more times in 1956 in the hope that their friendship could continue, but while friends may become lovers, it seems much harder for lovers to become friends. Once the press became aware that they had met, it was not long before reporters began to suggest that they had become secretly engaged. Just as journalists had hounded them for much of their relationship, so they finally closed the door on the last vestiges of love. Peter Townsend married again, in 1958, to Marie-Luce Jamagne from Brussels, a marriage that has lasted over thirty years. He and Princess Margaret have not met again during that time.

Across the English Channel, in their exile in the Bois de Boulogne, Princess Margaret's aunt and uncle, the Duke and Duchess of Windsor, followed their niece's decision with interest. They, perhaps more than anyone, understood just what the Princess had suffered. They too had faced the same agonizing decision. In the end, the Duke gave up the throne to marry divorcee Wallis Simpson, and renounced all his rights for love. He left England with his honour scarred, his public esteem destroyed. Princess Margaret, in contrast, did as her sister would have done and put duty first. She received nothing but admiration, her reputation remained relatively intact.

Talking about her favourite pug dogs one day, the Duchess of Windsor revealed 'We did have one called Peter Townsend.' Then added wistfully, 'But, of course, we had to give the Group Captain away . . . '

CHAPTER FOUR

The Margaret Set

On a shopping expedition to the Berkshire town of Hungerford with her old friend Sunny, the eleventh Duke of Marlborough, during the winter of 1989, Princess Margaret decided to invest in an attractive antique clock. Having paid £750 for the timepiece, the Princess asked for the clock to be packaged so that it could be taken away safely. Removing the clock's pendulum the dealer looked at her without the least sign of recognition and asked, 'Do you have a little man at home who can adjust this for you?' Princess Margaret stifled a laugh as the Duke drily replied, 'Yes, I think she *does* have a little man at home . . . ' The couple roared with laughter when out of earshot and it became a story that they told with relish to friends for weeks afterwards.

If there has been one characteristic that all of Princess Margaret's friends have had over the years, it has been the ability to enjoy a joke, especially when it has been at their own expense. Queen Elizabeth the Second has been described as one of the loneliest women in the world, having few close friends, and as she seldom accepts evening engagements she often dines alone in front of the television at her Buckingham Palace apartment. By comparison, Princess Margaret has more friends than probably any other member of the Royal Family and knows that she can command their loyalty.

One of the greatest drawbacks of being royal is knowing exactly who to trust. Who is a true friend and who is cultivating friendship as a social climber. Perhaps Princess Margaret has been lucky in her choice; many of her friends are of long standing and few have ever been banished from her circle through indiscretion, although one or two have occasionally been given the cold shoulder. Unlike her sister's horsey set, Margaret's is drawn from a more bohemian sphere. Actors, authors, dancers, playwrights, all have received friendship as a result of the frequent invitations that she issues. While I was researching this book, one of the Princess's friends said, 'Oh, she'll probably invite you to lunch'. Although the prospect was unlikely, the remark was meant seriously in the knowledge that Princess Margaret loves entertaining. Gregarious by nature, if the Princess meets someone whom she likes, or sees a performance on the stage that she admires, then an invitation to lunch or dinner is frequently forthcoming. Like the Queen Mother, Princess Margaret dislikes eating alone and often her personal secretary, Muriel Murray Brown, will have to telephone around in the mornings to see who might be free for lunch and will herself sit at the royal table on occasions as a valued friend as well as employee. Princess Margaret's chef consequently is never surprised if the number of guests for lunch increases at the last minute, and he has learned to stretch out many a meal. It is always noticed that Princess Margaret eats very little herself, while encouraging her guests to eat more.

As a result of the restrictions on the two Princesses during their childhood, Princess Margaret has grown to appreciate the company of others and through building up friendships from all walks of life she is able to keep in touch with the real world. The more fun a person is to be with, the greater degree of friendship they will receive.

Today, Princess Margaret's after-theatre parties are legendary. Members of the cast of a ballet or musical are frequently invited back to Kensington Palace at the last minute and are often surprised at the informal atmosphere. At one such party, in 1986, the Princess persuaded a male ballet dancer to partner her in a duet from Tchaikovsky's *Swan Lake*, much to the gathering's amusement. The Princess of Wales has received much publicity for her private dance routines with Wayne Sleep, and as Princess Margaret was lifted high into the air in this mock ballet, it must have amused her that although she is more than thirty years older than Diana, she can still compete on equal terms. It has often been said that Princess Margaret could have been an actress and such private performances are a great release. The painter Claude Muncaster revealed that in 1947, at a Balmoral houseparty, the Princess

From a very early age Princess Margaret was conscious that she ranked below her sister Lilibet. (Hulton)

Above: At five months Princess Margaret posed with her sister for an early official portrait which was later used on commemorative china. (Camera Press)

Right: A sortie into the outside world. Accompanied by 'Crawfie' (far right) and Lady Helen Graham, the little Princesses travelled on the London underground for the first time to visit the Y.W.C.A. in May 1939. (Camera Press)

Above: Princess Margaret at play with her family, and numerous dogs, outside 'Y Bwthyn Bach' in 1936, blissfully unaware of events which later that year would change their lives. (Popperfoto)

Below: Incarcerated at Windsor Castle for the duration of the war, Princess Margaret occupied much of her time in a fantasy world of books. Here her corgi Jane is in attendance. (Hulton)

Princess Margaret, alias The Hon. Lucy Fairfax, in the alternative pantomime *Old Mother Red Riding Boots*, the family's final wartime production. (Hulton)

A formal twenty-first birthday portrait taken in the White Drawing Room at Buckingham Palace by Cecil Beaton, who noted how mature and sophisticated Princess Margaret had suddenly become. (Camera Press)

Above: Colin Tennant, now Lord Glenconner, attends a charity dinner with the Princess and is instantly tipped to be a prospective husband. (Popperfoto)

Below: The Princess with 'Sunny' Blandford, now the Duke of Marlborough, at a charity ball in 1949. He has remained one of her many loyal friends. (Popperfoto)

Neither Princess Margaret nor Billy Wallace seem to be enjoying the last waltz. Their unofficial engagement in 1956 was short-lived. (Popperfoto)

Left: Peter Townsend keeps a discreet distance behind Princess Margaret as they return from an early morning ride in South Africa, 1947. (Popperfoto)

Below: A smiling Princess Margaret looks on as King George VI holds an investiture during the Royal Family's 1947 South African tour. Less relaxed is Group Captain Peter Townsend, holding the cushion. (Popperfoto)

performed a complete Gracie Fields act, and at her forty-eighth birthday party impersonated Sophie Tucker, the last of the Red-Hot Mamas, in full costume. In 1965, Princess Margaret played the role of Queen Victoria in a spoof film directed by the late Peter Sellers, which was presented to the Queen as a birthday present; sadly this has never been given a public showing. The Princess insists that although she is an excellent mimic, like her sister, she is better at performing 'types', in the style of Victoria Wood, rather than imitating actual people.

It is Princess Margaret's sense of fun that draws her to certain people. She dislikes pomposity and fawning, and is prepared to ignore protocol if she enjoys a person's company. When actor Rupert Everett was invited to dinner at Kensington Palace, after the Princess had admired his performances in the films *Another Country* and *Dance With a Stranger*, as he did not possess a suit he decided to dress casually. Princess Margaret neither commented on, nor did she feel insulted by the lack of formality. When visiting the theatre with friends in the 1950s she would always shun the royal box in favour of the stalls, wanting to see rather than be seen, and still prefers the anonymity. This was denied her in April 1989, when attending an early performance of Andrew Lloyd Webber's musical *Aspects of Love* at the Prince of Wales Theatre in London, a performance which was also attended privately by the Princess of Wales. Princess Margaret was sitting unrecognised in her seat when Diana arrived and embarrassingly discovered someone else sitting in her place. The House Manager rushed in to resolve the problem, saying very loudly to an usherette who had reported the mix up, 'Don't be silly, we've got Margaret in tonight, not Di'. The cover of both Princesses was immediately blown.

Although Princess Margaret visited the theatre frequently with her parents (even a week before her father's death the family went to see the musical *South Pacific* at Drury Lane) it always seemed to be in a mood of formality. If royalty wanted to see a favourite comedian or singer then they had to wait for the Royal Command Performance when they had some say in who should be called upon to entertain, or else a private production at Windsor Castle had to be organised. It was Princess Margaret who was to introduce a note of informality into royal social life.

In 1949 she had the good fortune to meet Sharman Douglas, daughter of the American Ambassador, Lewis Douglas. Sharman was two years older than Margaret, a gregarious fun-loving girl, and was invited to ride in the Princess's carriage at the Derby. The two girls struck up an instant rapport and soon Princess Margaret was invited to parties at the Douglas home in Princes Gate. Sharman was in awe of royalty and enjoyed the social connection; Princess Margaret equally admired Sharman's confidence and freedom. So began the makings of what was to be termed by the press 'The Margaret Set', the name applied to the group of young socialites who became the Princess's friends. Most were originally introduced to her by Sharman Douglas, so in theory they were an adopted set of friends, but eventually Sharman had to return to the United States with her father, leaving Princess Margaret as leader of the pack.

It was with Sharman Douglas, known to the Princess as Sass, that informal theatre outings began. If they were to see American performers, Sharman did not hesitate to rush Princess Margaret backstage after the show for an introduction. Strangely starstruck, the Princess enjoyed meeting celebrities almost as much as they felt honoured by the royal visit. Several of the Princess's friends today are from the world of showbusiness, not only because she still enjoys hearing the backstage gossip and revels in the theatrical atmosphere, but because they share something in common. They too are in the public eye. They know what it is like to be hounded by the media and they respect the Princess's privacy in exactly the same way that they want to keep their private life private.

Through one of these theatrical excursions to the London Palladium the Princess met the entertainer Danny Kaye, who had become a favourite through his film career, and soon became a friend, receiving an invitation to dinner at the Palace. It was noticed by those present that he called the Princess 'Honey' rather than 'Ma'am', a lack of protocol that she found endearing then, but would certainly find less so now. Today if anyone refers to 'your sister' she is quick to point out 'you mean the Queen', but in her late teenage years and early twenties, away from the stuffy court, the Princess was amused by the American lack of etiquette and, finding Danny Kaye fun to be with, she would have forgiven him anything. He was to appear in royal variety performances, and once coached the Princess in performing the can-can. The dance was performed with seven other friends at an American Embassy ball, at which the Queen and Prince Philip went dressed as a waiter and a parlour maid, and was a very tame version of the Folies Bergères, only knee-high kicks and yards of petticoat, though naturally reports of the cabaret embellished the performance to such an extent that Princess Margaret might just as well have performed a striptease. It later amused the Princess that when the show *Call Me Madam* transferred from New York to London, the Lord Chamberlain's Office censored the line, 'Even Princess Margaret goes out with Danny Kaye'. The Princess and the Showman seemed too immoral for a 1950s audience. Once again, fuel was added to the fire of Princess Margaret's 'unconventional' image; unwittingly, the Lord Chamberlain had put the suggestion into people's minds that there could be something more than just friendship with the American star. By now she was becoming the butt of people's humour, and even top comedians were making snide jokes. 'Tinker, Tailor, Soldier, Group Captain . . . '

Although 'the Margaret Set' was equally made up of both sexes, it was her male companions in whom there was most interest. Princess Margaret was, after all, still the most eligible girl in Britain and was surrounded by an entourage of equally eligible young men. Her social life was bound to become an obsession. Few could seriously believe that her relationship with Danny Kaye was anything more than platonic, but other members of her circle came under very close scrutiny. There was never any shortage of male escorts, but if you study the newspapers of the early 1950s, it is astonishing to see the sheer number of men with whom Princess Margaret's name was linked. All were just friends, and many are still close friends four decades later, sharing the distinction of being 'married off' to the Princess by the press. Heading the list of favourites were always Johnny, the Earl of Dalkeith, today the Duke of Buccleuch and Queensbury, of whom the *Star* wrote on 10 October 1950: 'People close to Court circles are saying that Princess Margaret's engagement to the Earl of Dalkeith will be announced before the end of the year . . . ' followed closely by Sunny, the Marquis of Blandford, now the present Duke of Marlborough. Frequently Colin Tennant, now Lord Glenconner, was mentioned, as was Viscount Hambledon.

Princess Margaret found herself paired off by the press with Prince George of Denmark, Prince Nicholas of Yugoslavia (Princess Marina's nephew, killed in a car crash in 1954), Prince Bertil of Sweden and Prince Christian of Hanover. There was Simon Ward, son of the Earl of Dudley (supposedly seen on a bus with her),

Lord Ogilvy (because he once took her to a fox hunt), Michael Tree (who accompanied her to a church service), Julian Fane (an escort to the opera), even King Michael of Rumania (a guest at Lilibet's wedding, nine years older than Margaret and at that time still a bachelor). Member of Parliament, Hugh Fraser; Mark Bonham-Carter, the grandson of former Prime Minister Asquith, the first Earl of Oxford, himself created a Baron in 1986; Simon Phipps, the clergyman cousin of the late Joyce Grenfell, who went on to become the sixty-ninth Bishop of Lincoln and remained a bachelor until he was fifty-two; Henry Porchester, known as 'Young Porchie', now Earl of Carnarvon and the Queen's racing manager; Dominic Elliot, whose grandmother had been one of Queen Mary's Ladies-in-Waiting; playwright William Douglas-Home; television producer Derek Hart; the son of King George VI's racing manager, Tom Egerton; magazine publisher, Jocelyn Stevens, whose uncle Sir Edward Hulton founded *Picture Post*; Patrick Plunkett, David Naylor-Leyland . . . the list is seemingly endless and inexhaustible. When Princess Margaret arrived at a Dorchester Hotel 'Red, White and Blue' ball with no fewer than seven of the above, royalwatchers must have been extremely confused. In fact, her crowded entrance was probably quite cleverly calculated, based on the theory that there is safety in numbers. So ludicrous was the media matchmaking that the Princess cannot have been seriously upset by it. As so many of these speculations were rife at the time when she was desperately and secretly in love with Peter Townsend, there must have been times when she relished the fact that the press were widely off the mark. When she had dinner one evening in a Bloomsbury restaurant with two brothers, James and Robin McEwan, she reportedly joked, 'Am I supposed to marry both of them?' Her love life had become a national pastime.

For many years Princess Margaret was said to be about to become engaged to Billy Wallace, son of a former Conservative Cabinet Minister, Captain Euan Wallace. Princess Margaret used to stay with the family at their home in Lavington Park, on the edge of the Sussex Downs, a county that frequently offered her a retreat from the limelight, except when Billy went to play polo at Cowdray Park and photographers trained their lenses on a certain newsworthy young lady amongst the spectators. Billy Wallace has been described as one of the 'chinless-wonders' who were part of the Princess's set, yet his life had an element of tragedy. His father and four brothers all died within a very short space of time, three of the brothers being killed in action, leaving him as the only surviving child. He himself suffered from a lifelong liver complaint and was to die of cancer in 1977, still in his fifties. Rumours abounded for years about Princess Margaret's relationship with him, and although writers strayed on to other 'possibles', in the hope that if they introduced the names of every eligible aristocratic bachelor in London they would be bound to be right eventually, they always came back to Billy Wallace. In the 1950s he shared a flat in Chesterfield Street with a friend called Peter Ward. After a party one summer Princess Margaret was driven home in the early hours of the morning, apparently by Peter Ward. The next day, newspapers were 'revealing' that the Princess's latest boyfriend was indeed Peter Ward. The Buckingham Palace Press Office insisted that Her Royal Highness had used a 'royal car', but it was later revealed that her escort had been none other than the party's host, Billy Wallace.

In Billy, Princess Margaret saw a like-minded spirit. She felt sorry for him because of his failing health and she knew from personal experience what it was like to lose a loving father; they both shared a love of the theatre and a great knowledge of art. Billy's grandfather was Sir Edwin Lutyens, President of the Royal Academy of Arts, designer of the Cenotaph in London's Whitehall, and creator of Queen Mary's celebrated dolls' house, now on permanent display at Windsor Castle. From his grandfather Billy Wallace inherited a sense of humour that Princess Margaret so admired. In Queen Mary's Dolls' House a pillow on one of the beds was embroidered with the initials 'MG' and another with the letters 'GM'. Princess Margaret laughed uproariously when she was old enough to understand the joke. The initials stood for, 'May George?' 'George May'.

Although Billy Wallace's name became linked with Princess Margaret's, readers did not seriously believe that they might marry. What the general public did not realise was that Billy actually proposed to the Princess several times. She jokingly rebuffed him, but he continued to enthuse about the good life they could have together; his inheritance from his father had been considerable, which meant that he could keep her in style even if he were a commoner. For a long time the Princess did not realise how deeply his love ran, and it must have been painful for him whenever he was used as a cover-up to hide the fact that she was seeing Peter Townsend. Later he was heard to say how relieved he was that the Townsend affair was out in the open and he could stop being a decoy. He continued to bounce back, but probably nobody was as surprised as he when Princess Margaret accepted his marriage proposal. The year was 1956. She had been forced to resign herself to the fact that Peter Townsend was out of her life once and for all; many of her friends were getting married, and of her so-called suitors, Billy seemed the most reliable. Perhaps, at the age of twenty-six, she worried that she might be left on the shelf, although this seems unlikely for someone so eligible and an obvious magnet for admirers. Sunny Blandford married in 1951, Johnny Dalkeith in 1953, now Colin Tennant and Jocelyn Stevens were both marrying in 1956. Her set was breaking up and there was a danger that she would be left alone. Billy Wallace had stood by her and although there was no question that she was in love, she was nevertheless very fond of him. Part of her heart still remained with Peter Townsend and she knew that their emotion could not be repeated, so she prepared herself to settle for loyalty rather than love.

She told Billy that, subject to the Queen's approval, she would be his wife. In this context, it is important to remember the pain that Princess Margaret had suffered in the preceding years and the bitterness she felt for what had happened. It was almost as if she agreed to Billy's proposal simply because she no longer cared what happened. She had not been allowed to marry the man she wanted, so she agreed to marry Billy on a whim, perhaps feeling that if it didn't work out, everyone would feel guilty for not letting her have her own way in the first place. Once again Fate was to take an unexpected turn. Billy took a holiday in the Bahamas, a rest that was needed from time to time for the benefit of his health, and uncharacteristically had a brief affair – nothing more than a holiday romance, a fling that he did not consider would affect his future with Princess Margaret in any way, or so he said. What seems amazing, however, is that as soon as he returned he told the Princess exactly what had happened. Was he really so besotted with her that he believed she would forgive him a little indiscretion? Or, more realistically, did he perhaps have second thoughts now that Princess Margaret had actually accepted him? Did the full impli-cations of marriage to the Queen's only sister suddenly dawn on him in the tropical heat? Meanwhile, had Princess Margaret also had time to ponder on the enormity of the step she had taken? If she needed an excuse to cancel the engagement, Billy Wallace offered it to her on a plate. He was immediately ostracised from her circle, and Princess Margaret did not speak to him again for nearly five years. When he did become part of her circle once again it was only when she was herself married and there could be no danger of Billy pressing his attentions on her. Once more she appeared to flaunt the man in her life in front of Billy, who was still unmarried, but when he did eventually become engaged to the daughter of a diplomat, Elizabeth Hoyer-Millar, the Princess was one of the first to offer her congratulations, and she attended the wedding in 1965. As she sat in the small church at Lavington Park as one of the honoured guests, the same church where she had often worshipped with Billy in earlier years when staying at Beechwood, the family home, it must surely have crossed her mind that before her was a scene in which she might have been involved. She seems to have had no regrets, however, and Billy took to farming – a lifestyle that Princess Margaret would not have enjoyed. Sadly, twelve years later, Princess Margaret had to attend the funeral of Billy Wallace, who died of cancer.

Although in the 1950s Princess Margaret seemed to be having little luck in the marriage stakes herself, she was not averse to acting as matchmaker to others. Once when she visited a restaurant with Robin McEwan, accompanied by the Queen Mother's Private Secretary Oliver Dawnay and the Earl of Essex's grand-daughter, Iris Peake, it was automatically assumed that Princess Margaret and McEwan were the romantic couple. Yet it was not long before Captain Dawnay's marriage to Lady Margaret Boyle was to end in divorce and he took Iris Peake as his bride. They are still married today. Princess Margaret is credited with bringing together various of her friends. Lady Anne Coke, daughter of the Earl of Leicester, had long been a friend and had even been one of the Queen's Maids of Honour at the Coronation in 1953. She was to marry Colin Tennant, with a little bit of influence from the Princess. Other of Margaret's friends, Susan Hornby, Rachel Brand and Jane McNeill, married Sunny Blandford, William Douglas-Home and Johnny Dalkeith respectively. It is even believed that Billy Wallace was introduced to his future bride at an Invalid Children's Association event, by the charity's President, Princess Margaret.

With so much rumour, gossip and speculation regarding Princess Margaret's future husband, the general public received the impression that her circle of friends consisted only of men. Naturally this was not the case. Her first group of friends consisted only of girls. Early female friends were usually relatives, such as Margaret Elphinstone, a cousin on the Bowes-Lyon side of the family (the Queen Mother's sister, Mary, having married the 16th Baron Elpinstone). She became one of Princess Margaret's closest friends. There is an early photograph that typifies their childhood games, with Princess Margaret sitting in a childsize cart which is being pulled by Princess Elizabeth and Margaret Elphinstone who are pretending to be horses. Other friends included Libbie Hardinge who had occasionally undertaken school lessons with the Princesses during the war, and family friends, Mary Morshead and Alethea Fitzalan-Howard. Later the Brownies and Girl Guides increased Princess Margaret's social circle and there were always plenty of friends to make up the cast of the Windsor Castle pantomimes. Occasionally local children were roped in. In the 1943 production of *Aladdin*, with Princess Elizabeth in the title role and Princess Margaret as Princess Roxana, a young boy from the Supply Department at Windsor Castle played Widow Twankey, with inevitably many jokes about the quantities of laundry at the Castle.

Childhood friends with whom Princess Margaret was to remain in contact were Rosemary Spencer-Churchill, Lady Elizabeth Cavendish, and Laura and Katharine Smith (of the stationery/bookselling family W.H. Smith), daughters of Lord and Lady Hambleden from Henley-on-Thames, just a few miles from Windsor. Through Laura Smith the Princess met Rachel Brand (Laura later married Rachel's brother), whom Princess Margaret introduced to her future husband, William Douglas-Home. The friendship with Lady Anne Coke, now Lady Glenconner and one of Princess Margaret's Ladies-in-Waiting, developed because her family home was Holkham Hall, a short distance from the Norfolk coast and her ancestors, the Earls of Leicester, had been on intimate terms with the Royal Family and guests at Sandringham since the reign of Queen Victoria.

Thus, the close knit circle became more and more intertwined as the years progressed. New friends were introduced and occasionally romance blossomed. Two women became particularly close to Princess Margaret. One was Johnny Dalkeith's sister, Lady Caroline Montagu-Douglas-Scott, who had joined the Princess as a bridesmaid at Lilibet's wedding along with Margaret Elphinstone and various cousins. At one time the Princess described Lady Caroline as her 'very best friend'. Coming a close second was Judy Montagu, daughter of a former Secretary of State for India and grand-daughter of Lord Swaythling. She was five years older than Princess Margaret and became a role model for her to follow. Many feel that Judy in some ways took the place of Lilibet once she had married, and certainly the Princess and Judy appeared to act like sisters. The friendship lasted even after Judy married the American writer and art critic Milton Gendel and went to live in Rome. They saw less of each other, but it gave Princess Margaret an excuse to visit one of her favourite countries, which to date she has visited thirty-eight times. The Princess was devastated when Judy was killed in a car crash.

Although Princess Margaret has had many female friends in her life, and has consciously guarded their privacy, she has always enjoyed the company of the opposite sex more. Amongst a group of men it is she that stands out, she who becomes the centre of attention. Some of her closest friends, such as Lady Elizabeth Cavendish, Lady Glenconner, and the former Jane Sheffield, ex-wife of Jocelyn Stevens, have become Ladies-in-Waiting to accompany the Princess on public engagements. They have learned the art of blending into the background so that they are almost unobtrusive when Princess Margaret is on show. Rarely, however, is Princess Margaret seen out socially with a group of girlfriends. It may seem old-fashioned now, but when Princess Margaret goes out to the opera, to a concert or (much more rarely these days) to a restaurant, there is still a sense of occasion. She enjoys putting on the glamour and cocks a snook at fashion experts who insist that long evening dresses are out of date, opting for traditional elegance rather than the dictate of modern designers. Along with the traditional evening wear, Princess Margaret prefers a male escort. In public life she is accompanied by one of her friends as Lady-in-Waiting and, as someone who enjoys being a woman, she prefers the company of men in private.

In London her escorts have included Derek Deane, a principal dancer with the Royal Ballet, and Guy Munthe, a Swedish bachelor, but two of her closest friends are long-term escorts. Chairman of a small Canadian film company, old Etonian Norman Lonsdale is four years older than the Princess and first met her when they were both teenagers. Their friendship reformed in 1981 after the death of Lonsdale's wife, at a time when Princess Margaret was herself a free agent once again following her divorce from Lord Snowdon in 1978.

Like most of Princess Margaret's friends, Norman Lonsdale has had his finger in a great many pies. He has been a banker, became the pioneer of mail-order language courses, has run a chain of restaurants and once worked on a ranch in Montana, and therefore has a wealth of experience and anecdotes to keep the conversation lively. Depending upon which gossip column you read, he is often either 'about to propose to Princess Margaret' or he has 'deserted her in favour of his Filipino millionairess girlfriend, Minda Feliciano'. Neither, of course, is true. The relationship between the Princess and Mr Lonsdale has only ever been on a friendship basis, the rumours of possible marriage stemming from an article in the *Sun* in 1982 after the Princess had been seen with what journalists thought was an engagement ring. 'When a fifty-one-year-old woman puts a twenty-five-year-old ring on her finger, it does not mean she is going to get married,' the Princess told author Christopher Warwick. Rumours of impending marriage have continued to dog the couple ever since. Norman Lonsdale's relationship with Minda Feliciano is of more than five years' standing, but neither will be drawn on whether they will eventually marry. Either way, this has not prevented Princess Margaret's continued platonic friendship with Norman Lonsdale, and the very fact that each can retain their independence is part of the attraction. He still holidays with the Princess in Mustique and can be seen escorting her to Covent Garden, and she has dined at his home by the river in Fulham. There is no reason to believe that the friendship will not continue in the same vein.

Whenever Norman Lonsdale is otherwise engaged, the Princess always has property owner Ned Ryan to accompany her. Like Norman Lonsdale he has had a varied career, from selling carpets to driving a number 19 bus. He once had a stall on the Portobello Road selling antique silver, and he has been spotted very early in the morning taking Princess Margaret on a shopping expedition for antiques – obviously a favoured pastime amongst her friends. Ned Ryan is three years older than Margaret and has been dubbed her 'Court Jester', with his Irish wit reducing the Princess to fits of uncontrollable laughter. Those on the periphery of today's 'Margaret Set' have accused the Princess of being haughty and making sure that her position is respected. She often asks friends to call her 'M', supposedly an abbreviation for Margaret, and yet it sounds uncannily like 'Ma'am'. But her closest friends would certainly dispute that, and just as Danny Kaye was permitted to call her 'Honey', so Ned Ryan is able to tease her mercilessly. Not only does he get away with it, the Princess revels in it. At a Rolling Stones concert at Wembley – not the most obvious event that you would expect the Princess to patronise, yet Ryan persuaded her to go – a naked man streaked across the arena. Ned Ryan immediately put his hands over his eyes.

'You're supposed to clap a hand over *my* eyes!' said the Princess with mock ferocity.

'I did think about it,' replied Ryan cheekily, 'but I thought you'd be disappointed if I did.'

There are only a handful of people who can give as good as they get to the Princess, and be encouraged to do so. The Princess has visited Ryan's Knightsbridge home and she is well aware that he has been the escort of many society ladies, but once again there is no commitment, no jealousies. Ned Ryan introduced the Princess to former actress, now hotelier and fashion designer, Anouska Hempel, who has since become one of the newer members of Princess Margaret's ever increasing circle. Practically neighbours, the Princess is happy to visit the recently elevated Lady Weinberg (to give Anouska Hempel her official title since her husband's knighthood in 1987) just down the road from Kensington Palace at Holland Park, and has also visited the Weinbergs at their Wiltshire home.

It is interesting that the Queen's small circle of close friends has remained almost unchanged for three decades or more. Lord 'Porchy' Porchester, Lady Mickey Nevill, the Countess of Airlie, the Countess of Westmoreland and the Duchess of Grafton – they are all from aristocratic backgrounds, and most have known the Queen since childhood. Although Princess Margaret has a fair smattering of aristocrats amongst her friends, which is only to be expected as a member of the Royal Family, many others come from widely differing backgrounds and are mostly achievers – people who have made their own money and created their own lifestyle.

As a girl, her friends inevitably developed out of the upper-class set because they were the people she was allowed to mix with socially, but in adulthood, when she has been able to select her own companions, her friends are always people who have led an interesting life, individuals who can not only amuse and entertain, but keep Princess Margaret in touch with the real world outside her golden cage. Anouska Hempel, for example, arrived in Britain from Australia in the early 1960s with a degree in psychology and very little else; she and her first husband (sadly killed in a car crash) bought a run-down hotel in Earl's Court, and with drive and ambition she is now a millionairess. Ned Ryan was the son of a Tipperary farmer. When he first came to London he sold carpets in a department store, yet today he is a self-made millionaire. It is not the fact that they are the *nouveaux riches* that attracts Princess Margaret to certain people, more that they are *bons viveurs* and have used their talents to their best advantage to achieve their desired lifestyle. Bored by the chinless wonders of her youth, who had the world at their feet financially, the Princess admires those who have the guts to create their own position in life. She admires them, but she envies them too, because she was never in control of her own destiny. Had she been born thirty years later when, like the Duchess of York, she could perhaps have had a career in publishing, or, like the Queen's youngest son, Prince Edward, have gone into the theatre, then her life would have been much more content.

Despite her great love of music and drama, Princess Margaret's only sortie into public dramatics came in 1954 when Judy Montagu suggested the 'Set' – although they never actually called themselves that – could put on a play to raise money for charity. Princess Margaret jumped at Judy's suggestion. It would be an event she would enjoy and the Invalid Children's Aid Association could benefit from the proceeds. As usual, Princess Margaret had to get the Queen's permission first, which was granted, although it was felt that the Princess should not appear in person. Instead she took on the position of Assistant Director. The play chosen was an Edgar Wallace thriller called *The Frog*, a plot concerning terrorists and the planting of bombs. A professional director, Alan Jefferson, was engaged and is reputed to have elevated Princess Margaret to Associate Director.

The fact that this was an almost entirely amateur company with the exception of two professionals seemed to be no bar to getting a West End theatre in which to perform. The Scala Theatre was booked for a week in June and the cast list alone ensured sufficient publicity to put seats in demand. The Princess herself spent much of her spare time designing costumes, assisting with the directing, making astute observations, and at the beginning she and Judy Montagu undertook the casting. It must have been the most illustrious cast ever to hit the West End stage, with Colin Tennant in the leading role of the villainous Frog, Lord Porchester was a Police Sergeant, Billy Wallace the Detective, the Duke of Devonshire a Prison Governor, and various parts played by Lord Norwich, the Earl of Carnarvon, Lord Brooke, Lord Plunkett, with the added bonus of Douglas Fairbanks Jnr and Elsa Maxwell. The heroine was played by Barbara Cartland's daughter, Raine Legge, now the Countess Spencer, the Princess of Wales's stepmother, wickedly dubbed 'Acid Raine'. Her role was that of nightclub hostess and was a part that Princess Margaret chose to understudy, which meant that if Raine had been indisposed then Princess Margaret really would have performed on the London stage. As it was, Raine was never off. During a cabaret scene, however, Princess Margaret decided that Elsa Maxwell should impersonate Sophie Tucker, and it was an act that the Princess kept in her own repertoire for private performances. To the aristocratic actors, the whole production was a fun fund-raising event, but the theatre critics of the day nevertheless savagely criticized the production. Most of them were aggrieved that a bunch of amateurs could put themselves on the West End stage, and expressed their disapproval in print. Even Noël Coward slated the performance, writing in his diary that the actors were incompetent, conceited and impertinent, with no talent whatsoever.

Princess Margaret nevertheless enjoyed the whole experience and made a curtain speech revealing that in excess of £10,000 had been raised for her charity, which was, after all, the main point of the exercise. She was not dissatisfied. Naturally she had no idea what Noël Coward had written in his diary, and he later became a much valued friend. She was one of the principal guests at his 70th birthday celebrations in 1969 and attended a charity midnight 'matinée' in London at the Phoenix Theatre as the climax of the celebrations. Noël's date on that occasion was the actress Merle Oberon, who revealed that when she walked into the theatre with 'The Master', Princess Margaret stood up and encouraged the entire audience to applaud. It was a magical moment, and later every actress and actor who had worked with him lined up on stage. It was the kind of theatrical experience Princess Margaret adored. Noël Coward, who was knighted by the Queen the following year, revelled in the Princess's friendship, and at his house in Switzerland had a signed photograph of her permanently on display. When he died, amongst his many treasured possessions was a charming photograph of a smiling Princess, with himself on one side and the legendary Marlene Dietrich, with her head resting on the table, on the other – a memory of yet another magical evening at the Café de Paris. It was with a wry smile that the Princess had watched Dietrich's performance in 1954 singing 'Falling in Love Again'. The lyrics seemed to sum up the media image of herself.

Although many thought the song could become her theme tune, it was not to be too long before she really was falling in love again. She went with her close friend Lady Elizabeth Cavendish to watch the rehearsal of a new review called *Cranks*. Although it did not register with Princess Margaret at the time, there was also a young twenty-six-year-old photographer there, taking pictures of the show. His name was Antony Armstrong-Jones.

CHAPTER FIVE

A Marie Antoinette Aroma

When the late lamented actor Richard Burton stood up on the stage at the Odeon Cinema, Leicester Square, to introduce the royal film première of Zeffirelli's *The Taming of the Shrew*, his words struck a chord with Princess Margaret. 'My name is really Richard Jenkins,' he proclaimed, then gestured up towards the circle where the glitter of Princess Margaret's tiara instantly located her. 'Up there is a lady who is really Maggie Jones.'

Although the Princess smiled, she was not amused. But in Burton's shrewd way he had, no doubt unintentionally, hit upon the very crux of her marital problems. As a Princess of the Royal Blood who had married a commoner, she was continually trying to equate 'Princess Margaret' with 'Maggie Jones'. At heart, she wanted the freedom to enjoy being a wife and mother, yet at the same time she enjoyed the privileges of being a Princess and all that it entailed. In earlier generations, royalty married within their own circle; if not royalty, at least someone titled. Typically, Princess Margaret married a man she had herself chosen, part of the attraction being that his life had been so very different to her own. In some cases this works. In all cases there are problems. Lady Diana Spencer, albeit from an aristocratic family, had known freedom before her marriage to Prince Charles in 1981. When thrust into the international spotlight that her husband had always lived with, she found it difficult to cope. The marriage of Princess Anne to Captain Mark Phillips suffered because of the inherent differences. It was horses that had brought them together, and like her aunt, she found her husband's non-royal upbringing attractive. But ultimately the differences can lead to a rift, and it is as difficult

73

for the royal to cope as the non-royal partner. Lady Diana had lived on the fringes of the royal circle and was young and pliable enough eventually to adapt to the new role, especially when she became a mother, but neither Antony Armstrong-Jones nor Mark Phillips ever really came to terms with marriage into the Royal Family. The two men both tried desperately to continue with their own careers and interests, hoping to retain their own identity, yet dipped into royal engagements when it suited them. The marriage of Princess Alexandra to Mr Angus Ogilvy (knighted in 1989) has worked because he consciously chose to stay out of the limelight completely.

When Princess Margaret first met Antony Armstrong-Jones has been a source of conjecture as neither she nor Tony have the same story. Some writers suggest that they met in the St Martin's Theatre and it was love at first sight. Untrue. Tony remembers meeting the Princess in Norfolk at Lady Anne Coke's family home, Holkham Hall, when he took the official photographs at her wedding to Colin Tennant. The Princess has said in recent years that she cannot even remember who took the pictures on that day. Had Princess Margaret not been on a foreign tour of East Africa during the autumn of 1957 she would certainly have met the young photographer who, by sheer coincidence, was chosen by the Queen to take pictures to mark the eighth birthday of Prince Charles. One released from the session is particularly dramatic, showing the Prince with his sister in profile, studying a large globe; a far cry from the usual formality of royal portraiture. Tony had worked for Prince Philip's favourite photographer, Baron, who had recently died and so his assistant's work was considered.

When the artist Simon Elwes painted a portrait of Princess Margaret, he gave a party to show off the work at his home in St John's Wood, which the Princess attended. One of the guests was the noted designer Oliver Messel, who took along his nephew, a young photographer called Armstrong-Jones. Again, neither the Princess nor her future husband remember meeting, yet fate seemed to be continually placing the opportunities before them. The first definite meeting, on which they are both in accord, came on 20 February 1958 at the Chelsea home of Lady Elizabeth Cavendish (one of Margaret's Ladies-in-Waiting since 1954), a mutual friend. By all accounts they got on well, having so much in common. They both enjoyed the theatre, indeed Tony's uncle, Oliver Messel, had designed sets for ballets that the Princess had seen. They shared a love of art. Yet the conversation that evening was of social pleasantries and there was no indication that the photographer and the Princess would ever meet again. Indeed, exactly one month later, Peter Townsend came back into her life.

The Princess and Peter Townsend had agreed to remain friends, and as two years had passed since they had last met there was plenty of news to catch up on. Possibly the Princess still harboured a secret desire that they might get back together again one day, but as they drank tea quietly in her sitting-room at Clarence House he told her of his love for Marie-Luce and that they intended to marry. He wanted to tell the Princess personally, rather than have her discover the news through the press. This effectively put an end to any real possibility of friendship, and when he departed that day in March 1958 it was literally for the final time. Less than two years later, Princess Margaret was engaged to be married. She had kept a torch alight for Peter for more than a decade, yet when she walked down the aisle with Tony Armstrong-Jones it was after a two-month engagement.

After Elizabeth Cavendish's dinner party, the Princess met Tony again at the Fortune Theatre in London where they had gone to see the successful Flanders and Swann review *At the Drop of a Hat*. This was Princess Margaret's third visit to the show. Sitting down at the piano to perform a comic song was something she could identify with and she enjoyed the witty lyrics of the talented duo. If any kind of romance was in the air, it was as a result of Lady Elizabeth, who has been credited as the matchmaker and was the hostess on both occasions that the couple met. Even she had not visualised a possible relationship, inviting Tony only because he and the Princess had seemed to get on well at her dinner party. The late Michael Flanders was a victim of polio and performed on stage from a wheelchair. It was at the Fortune Theatre that the Princess learned by chance that Tony Armstrong-Jones had contracted polio as a teenager and had spent more than twelve months confined to a wheelchair. Expert medical treatment and sheer determination to get well led to an almost total recovery. He has been left with one leg slightly shorter than the other as a result, a deformity that is no longer noticeable. When she knew of Tony's affliction, the Princess felt an immediate sympathy towards this good-looking young man, just six months older than herself and only six inches taller. Like so many people who have suffered a debilitating illness, he had a renewed zest for life, as if given a second chance. Margaret was impressed by his energy and enthusiasm, combined with a very gentle and extremely polite manner – qualities he has retained. Despite the end of his relationship with the Princess now, he has always refused to sell his story to the press and has remained totally discreet about her, declining any request to speak to authors about her.

A month or so later, to Princess Margaret's delight, Tony asked her advice about the layout of an exhibition of his work. Royalty, of course, visit so many exhibitions of all types throughout their working life that they, better than anyone, know what makes a good display. Tony's exciting and novel ideas for photographs appealed to Princess Margaret's sense of the unusual. She liked the way he dressed informally when other men wore white collar and tie. He respectfully called her 'Ma'am' and bowed formally whenever they met. She could not ignore his boyish good looks either, and before they had known each other very long they were chatting like close friends. Tony would have liked to have the Princess open his new exhibition, but that was asking too much of someone he hardly knew, and so the actress Leslie Caron did the honours. Princess Margaret did not visit the exhibition at all.

At this time, in 1958, Tony had a flat in the Pimlico Road, London, sandwiched between an antique shop and the Sunlight Laundry. Previously it had been an ironmonger's but now became his studio, and home. It was here that Princess Margaret was to visit, in strict secrecy, for a private view of Tony's photographs once the exhibition was officially over. The 'cloak and dagger' approach to relationships certainly seemed to appeal to the Princess, knowing that even the slightest hint of gossip would quickly make its way into the newspapers. Whether true or not, it is said that the Princess often drove up and down the Pimlico Road for ten or fifteen minutes before visiting Tony, to be sure that she was not seen.

Soon she invited Tony to dinner and, as no journalist was on the look-out for anything in particular, nobody noticed his arrival or departure from Clarence House. If they had – well, he was after all a photographer. He had taken portraits of the Duke of Kent, Princes Charles and Princess Anne, and before long was taking pictures of the Queen and Prince Philip; there was no reason for him not to be visiting. He could have had a photographic sitting with the Queen Mother or Margaret herself. The Queen remarked that she enjoyed being photographed by Armstrong-Jones because he was extremely well organised and knew in advance the poses he required, and the session was over more quickly than any she had experienced in the past. As he did take the official twenty-ninth-birthday portrait of Princess Margaret, in preference to the tried and trusted Cecil Beaton, there was the proof that his visits were purely business. The portrait of the Princess was as dramatic as ever, the Princess apparently emerging in the darkness between two of their childhood horses. The very fact that Tony was a photographer created the perfect cover for them when they did become emotionally involved. No one considered that the Princess could marry an untitled photographer any more than she was allowed to marry a former equerry and Comptroller of the Household. When Princess Margaret went to see films such as *Gigi* (starring Tony's friend, Leslie Caron), Hitchcock's *Witness for the Prosecution* and *West Side Story* nobody expressed any surprise that a photographer was amongst the party. By this time Tony had established himself as a top photographer anyway; he had published books, and worked on magazines run by the Princess's friend Jocelyn Stevens, so was an accepted member of 'the Set'. What the public did not yet know was that in private, at Clarence House the Princess and Tony watched *The Wild Ones*, a then banned Marlon Brando film and *held hands*! This piece of scandal was eventually revealed by a footman who sold his story to the press. Although angry that she had once again been betrayed by those in whom the Royal Family place their trust, Princess Margaret must have laughed that such an innocent gesture was even thought newsworthy. The simple sign of affection, nevertheless, did indicate that they were more than just friends.

Occasionally, Princess Margaret would cross the River Thames privately by ferry, but more often by car and frequently one driven by Tony, to visit 59 Rotherhithe Street, London SE16, an end-of-terrace house which looked out over the river towards Tower Bridge, near Cherry Garden Pier. This was a new and exciting adventure to Tony's haven and retreat from city life. The Queen would have been concerned had she been told, as would modern security men if the same thing was to happen to the third in line to the throne in the 1990s. The house, now demolished, belonged to a friend of Tony's, a journalist called William Glenton. He rented out the one-roomed ground floor to Tony and lived upstairs himself. It is strange in retrospect that Viscount Linley, Princess Margaret's son, should now have a business interest in London's dockland, an area that has nostalgic memories for his mother.

Princess Margaret's visits to Rotherhithe were strictly occasional. Too often would arouse suspicion, not least from William Glenton himself, who for a long time was completely ignorant as to the identity of Tony's new girlfriend, until one day he spotted Lady Elizabeth Cavendish leaving the house and recognised her to be a certain royal personage's Lady-in-Waiting. Later his suspicions were confirmed when he saw the silhouette of the Queen's sister in 'Tony's Room', which became the title of a book about the royal romance that he later wrote, after the relationship had become public knowledge. Although writers look upon the small white room as a love nest, Princess Margaret actually used Rotherhithe much more as a retreat when married than while courting. The attraction was that it was the absolute antithesis of the houses in which she herself lived. It was a single 12' x 12' room, simply furnished with pieces Tony had bought from antique markets or made himself. He had painted the walls, built cupboards and shared his lavatory with the landlord. It looked out over the Thames with no prying eyes other than those of ducks and swans. Princess Margaret was enthralled at seeing how the other half lived. Apart from her games in 'Y Bwthyn Bach', the little thatched cottage she had shared with Lilibet as a playhouse when they were children, the Princess, at the age of twenty-nine, had not had the opportunity or the desire to cook or wash up. Here, at number 59, she could imagine herself as 'ordinary' and play at being a housewife. Tony would invariably cook and the Princess would help with the washing-up, although one wonders to what extent her domesticity stretched. On the occasion that William Glenton met Lady Elizabeth leaving number 59, she revealed that she had simply come to tidy up. It might have been simpler to have said that she had come to collect something, or was a friend of Tony's but she spoke what we presume to be the truth. Does this perhaps mean that Princess Margaret, who is known to be untidy, asked Lady Elizabeth to go along and put the room straight? If so, this implies what one might suspect, that the Princess enjoyed playing her game of normality, but at the end of the day still needed someone to pack her toys away.

Whatever the situation, 1959 was one of Princess Margaret's

happiest years for as she gradually got to know Tony she began to like him more. They shared an artistic streak and even sat designing clothes together. The Princess is able to draw, a skill that might have been developed to good use had she been born in other circumstances, and even today will make the occasional sketch to help her clothes designers. Just as Tony had asked her advice about his photographic exhibition, so the Princess drew on his expertise to help her with dress designs. At Rotherhithe, or in her rooms at Clarence House, they listened to records, watched television, talked and talked to discover more about each other's past lives, and after all the drama that surrounded her relationship with Peter Townsend it must have been refreshing for the Princess to share her leisure hours with someone her own age, who lacked the complications she had previously encountered. An added bonus was that the Queen and the Queen Mother both liked Tony and found him an eminently suitable friend who obviously made the Princess happy. He had that essential quality that Princess Margaret demanded. He could make her laugh.

For the New Year in 1960 Antony Armstrong-Jones was invited to Sandringham, not apparently as a guest but in a working capacity to design an arbour for an area of the garden. He duly arrived complete with plans, even a model, to give the Queen an idea as to how the finished structure would look, and was eventually shown into the library to discuss it with her. Behind closed door, once the footman was out of the way, Tony asked the Queen for her sister's hand in marriage, which was granted. This was, of course, a mere formality by this time, but it still had to be done and so the clandestine plan was hatched, to make sure none of the staff knew what was happening. Margaret was given a ruby and diamond engagement ring, which Tony had designed himself.

The official announcement of the engagement was delayed until the end of February, for two reasons. The Queen was pregnant with her third child, and as public interest centred around the new arrival, Princess Margaret did not wish to steal Lilibet's thunder or indeed compete with a baby. Secondly, the Royal Family try to avoid long engagements in the knowledge that the resulting wedding fever builds up to an almost irreverent pitch. Prince Andrew was born at Buckingham Palace on 19 February, 1960, and once the furore and initial interest in the child who had pushed Princess Margaret down from third to fourth in line of succession had died down, the official announcement was made. On 26 February the following announcement came from Clarence House:

> It is with the greatest pleasure that Queen Elizabeth the Queen Mother announces the betrothal of her beloved daughter The Princess Margaret to Mr Antony Charles Robert Armstrong-Jones, son of Mr R.O.L. Armstrong-Jones Q.C., and the Countess of Rosse, to which union The Queen has gladly given her consent.

For Princess Margaret, the Queen's consent, and that of the Privy Council, must have come as a relief. It must equally have been a relief to her family that the Princess was finally to be settled. It also pleased the Princess that she had managed to conduct her courtship without major press speculation. Maybe her experiences in the past had taught her the pitfalls; even after the engagement was announced and press interest was high, she and Tony still managed to escape into the country without being followed.

Margaret's and Tony's first public appearance together came shortly after the engagement had been announced, at the Royal Opera House in Covent Garden for a gala ballet performance. When Princess Margaret later appeared as a guest of the late Roy Plomley on BBC radio's *Desert Island Discs*, she gave as her favourite piece of ballet music the waltz from Act Two of Tchaikovsky's *Swan Lake*. When Tony had been guest on the same programme, he gave as his single favourite piece of music the waltz from Act One of the same ballet. Did they share the same taste in music and therefore both chose Tchaikovsky, or did they deliberately opt for different pieces? Princess Margaret has often told friends that Tony's apparent love of music was in fact only superficial, and his knowledge was not as great as she had originally thought.

By the time of her engagement in 1960 Princess Margaret had matured into a beautiful woman with poise and a very forthright approach, which gave the impression that she was brimming with confidence. Yet although she was certainly in love with Tony, she surprisingly had nagging doubts about the relationship. At the time of Princess Anne's engagement in 1973, Princess Margaret said tellingly of her niece 'Anne's much more positive than I was, so I think she'll be all right', the implication being that Anne seemed to know that she was doing the right thing, whereas Margaret had obviously had doubts. It is ironic that both marriages were to last exactly sixteen years (Princess Margaret's, 1960–1976; Princess Anne's 1973–1989), and both were a marriage in name only long before they became legally separated.

When Princess Margaret and her fiancé stepped into the royal box at Covent Garden on that first public appearance, already the Palace machinery was in operation. What had attracted Margaret to Tony was his unconventional approach to life, the fact that his lifestyle seemed somewhat bohemian and anti-establishment, but now here he was in public wearing white tie and tails, dressed like any other male member of the Royal Family. He trotted respectfully behind the Princess, as he was to throughout their married life, and had already adopted the typical hands-behind-the-back pose that Prince Philip, Prince Charles, the Dukes of Gloucester and Kent, all seem to use. Perhaps the Princess was unaware of the subtle changes that were to take place in Tony; he was even given an office in Buckingham Palace to work from once they were engaged. Although he was to rebel against playing second-fiddle to his wife, there were certain advantages of being royal that he enjoyed. The non-royal air that so attracted the Princess to him was slowly to change.

From a commercial point of view, Tony's career had an obvious boost through his regal connections. He hastily released selections of his own royal photographs which brought in many hundreds of pounds in royalties and copyright fees. To his credit, when he worked later as a commercial photographer for newspapers and magazines, he insisted that no celebrity being featured could actually request him to take the pictures in preference to another photographer, and many a person being interviewed for a Sunday colour supplement was surprised when they suddenly recognised the cameraman. There is the story of a certain Duke who was being interviewed and told the journalist that his photographer could 'wait in the pub until we're ready for him'; when he saw who the man with the camera was, he invited him to lunch at his own table.

For once, Princess Margaret began to enjoy the press coverage that she was receiving, most of it written in a romantic vein and inevitably calling her a 'fairytale Princess', a tag which she was not happy to adopt. Yes, she had been born in a castle, had a royal title and occasionally wore diamonds and rubies, but as she had descended a coalmine as part of her working itinerary, received years of criticism for loving a divorced man, and detested the kowtowing of certain courtiers, there were times when life seemed anything but a fairytale. And, like the spectre at the feast, stories soon abounded that an 'unprecedented number of wedding invitations' were turned down. There actually seems little evidence to substantiate this; few people turn down the honour of being present at a royal wedding whether they approve of the union or not. The rumour began because invitations *were* declined by a number of European royals. Invitations had naturally been sent out of courtesy to Princes and Princesses that Margaret and Tony in many cases neither had met nor knew. Some felt that Princess Margaret should not be marrying a commoner but should be forming an alliance with a European country by joining one of their royal families to the House of Windsor, just as Queen Victoria and Prince Albert married their children off to various countries for reasons of politics. The rumour also spread, not from people who had refused the invitation, but from those who had not received one. Notorious socialites Lord and Lady Docker, for example, were omitted from the guest list. On the day preceding Margaret's wedding they boarded the *Queen Mary* and sailed across the Atlantic to New York. There they did not disembark, but simply sailed straight back again. It was so much better to say 'out of the country' than 'not invited' when asked if they had been to the wedding.

The ceremony itself has been well documented. Needless to say, the Princess did not escape hostility for there were always those who criticised the cost of the wedding, estimated to be in the region of £25,000. It was not helped by the fact that, on marriage, Princess Margaret's Civil List allowance automatically increased from £6,000 a year to £15,000. As this is intended to be used entirely for public duties, and as Tony was continually to insist that he was *not* a member of the Royal Family, just married to one, questions were asked as to why the Princess should need more than double to carry out her duties as before. The main reason was that in the past she had shared expenditure with the Queen Mother as both operated from Clarence House and used some of the same staff, but now she would have a home of her own to run and would require her own chauffeur, butler, maids and private secretary to carry out her duties. This also meant upkeep of official cars, paying for the use of a helicopter from the Queen's Flight if she needed it, and a fee to British Rail should she ever require use of the Royal Train.

There is little doubt that marriage to Tony was a love match. It was not an arranged marriage; Princess Margaret had not agreed to spend her life with him because of his social connections or to please her family, but quite simply because at the time she loved him. Equally he loved her. Six years before they had even met, Tony is quoted as having said that he would like to photograph the Princess because of her vivacious personality. The physical attraction between the two was intense and they were highly passionate. Suggestions of early rifts and clashes of personalities were inevitable, but it is true to say that the early years of marriage were extremely happy, despite the teething troubles that any newly married couple encounter. It is one thing being in love, but however long you know someone or think you understand them, you have actually to live together to *really* know them. The added difficulty, for this particular couple, was not just that of learning to live with each other, but having to merge two completely different lifestyles. Tony had always been a free spirit, able to come and go whenever he pleased; for many years he had been answerable only to himself and in private he could be master of his own life. As soon as he had married Princess Margaret, this changed. They moved, not to his Pimlico studio, now sold, or to Rotherhithe, but to her suite of rooms in Clarence House. From the outset he was living in his mother-in-law's house and on his wife's territory. This was not a new home built together, starting from scratch, but one which had been Princess Margaret's home for eight years, and he was an outsider.

Coupled to that, Tony was unused to royal servants. Princess Margaret had grown up in an environment where she had very little privacy in her own home. There were staff to serve meals, staff to take care of the laundry, staff to clean, and at all times it was known where she was. Even if she went to the bathroom someone knew. To her it was a way of life, to Tony it was all new. While we might feel that it would be nice to have an entourage of 'servants' (a word the Royal Family never use) to do everything, it becomes wearing when first encountered. On top of that, Clarence House staff gave a look of disapproval if Tony sat down to dinner without a tie or with his shirt sleeves rolled up.

The newly married couple were offered a small apartment at Kensington Palace, number ten, once belonging to the Marquess of Carisbrooke. The last surviving grandson of Queen Victoria, he had died just two days after Princess Margaret's engagement had been announced, somewhat conveniently it would seem. 'Drino' Carisbrooke had been described by the Duke of Windsor as an 'affected ass', yet Princess Margaret liked him. He always dressed immaculately, wore many rings and bracelets, enjoyed music and society gossip. When he died it was the end of an era, and it did not upset the Princess to be taking over his old home. As for Tony, the preparations in getting the apartment ready could not be completed soon enough, and he supervised much of the simple redecoration himself – simple because the rooms were small, and the move could only ever be considered temporary. Of the utmost importance, however, was that it was a home of their own. When they did take up residence in July 1960, it was with a butler, Thomas Cronin, housekeeper, Nora Foley, a cook, footman and chauffeur, plus a personal maid for Princess Margaret, Ruby Gordon. She had been with the Royal Family since Margaret was a child, and was sister to the Queen's long-time dresser, Bobo MacDonald.

Perhaps initially they felt that life would be as it had been in Rotherhithe, where they still managed to escape in the first years of marriage. But the magic did not rub off. Not only was Kensington Palace their home, it was also an official residence, which meant that occasionally receptions needed to be held there, and quite simply there wasn't the space. This was not an easy start to married life. On a personal level, the couple were extremely happy with each other. It is said that Princess Margaret felt more fulfilled than ever before now that, at long last, her emotional life was in order. No longer was she haunted by press reports of her latest lover, the only irritation being that they now referred to her as 'Mrs Jones'. Princess Margaret's dislike of this tag is shown in the fact that she remained officially 'Her Royal Highness The Princess Margaret', the royal equivalent of a wife who continues to use her maiden name. Princess Anne, for example, until her elevation to Princess Royal was always known as 'Her Royal Highness The Princess Anne, Mrs Mark

Phillips' on all official notices, wall plaques that she unveiled, court circulars and all legal documents. Was it coincidence that, when her marriage was breaking up, she finally agreed to become Princess Royal which effectively abolished the public use of 'Mrs Mark Phillips'? Princess Alexandra, after her marriage in 1963 and until her husband's knighthood in 1989, added the suffix 'the Hon. Mrs Angus Ogilvy' to her title. Princess Margaret, however, did not actually use a suffix until Tony's eventual elevation to the peerage. Perhaps she found 'Mrs' incongruous with 'Princess'.

The only real bone of contention between Margaret and Tony in the first years was a wedding present. Her old friend Colin Tennant gave the Princess a piece of land which, in 1960, was said to be worth around £15,000, a generous gift by any standard considering that the money would have bought several large houses in Britain at the time. Tennant had purchased the island of Mustique the year before, and what he actually gave the Princess was a ten-acre plot of land on which to build a villa. He also gave her a choice of location, and she eventually decided on a piece overlooking the spectacular Gelliceaux Bay, which had privacy combined with magnificent views – eventually building a villa there, *Les Jolies Eaux*, literally 'The Pretty Waters' (see Chapter Nine). The Princess visited Mustique with great excitement for the first time on Thursday, 26 May 1960 – a significant date in her life as it was to mark the beginning of a new love affair, this time with the Caribbean island that was to become her paradise on earth. This was part of their honeymoon tour, and is equally significant in that it was the one and only time Tony was to visit the island. Considering the great importance Mustique was to hold in Princess Margaret's life, it is surprising that he did not share her love, especially as he was never averse to lazing in the sun and sand. Those close to Tony say that he did not like the way Colin Tennant's gift was a two-edged sword. It was a glorious present for the Princess and she was to be eternally grateful for it, but at the same time what a commercial boost her patronage gave to the island. When it became public knowledge that the Princess holidayed there, the small island (3 miles long by 1 mile wide) soon became a millionaire's haunt. Today it has forty-five homes owned by the rich and famous who wanted to rub shoulders with royalty. The Princess proved to be an excellent investment, for in 1977 Colin Tennant sold the island for undisclosed millions, and went on to buy a £3,000,000 coconut plantation on the neighbouring island of St Lucia and turn that too into a holiday paradise. His initial investment in Mustique had been a mere £45,000.

Tony may have objected to Colin Tennant's apparent commercialism, but more likely he was jealous of his wife's closeness to her old friend. Colin had known the Princess for more than a decade longer than Tony, and so there were memories from which he felt excluded. Already he felt an outsider to the Royal Family, and wanted to share friends with his wife, not tag on to her set. Even though he was now a successful photographer, he could not afford to give his wife a £15,000 gift to match. This was bound to evoke a feeling of inadequacy, and if he really did feel that his wife was being exploited by Tennant then he must also have felt hypocritical when selling his royal photographs. This may be why he soon began to throw his energies into worthwhile projects, such as his highly acclaimed documentary *Don't Count the Candles*, highlighting the problems of the aged and infirm, followed by other films on similar areas of social concern such as *Love of a Kind* and *Born to be Small*. Like a fully-fledged member of the royal family he began to accept Presidencies and Patronages of his own. He went on the committee of Mental Health Trust, became a Member of the National Fund for Research for the Crippled Child, and backed causes to help the disabled. It was not until he could carve a niche and fulfil a function in his own right that he relaxed into his role. His great fear was that of being known only as Princess Margaret's husband.

Inevitably the question was to arise as to whether Tony should receive a title. Although in the 1970s Princess Anne was to stand her ground and insist that her husband remain a commoner and, therefore, her children should not have titles, in 1960 it still seemed unacceptable for the Queen's sister to be Mrs Jones. Having been criticised for most things, Princess Margaret hoped to avoid any controversy by refusing to have a title given to Tony for no better reason than that he was marrying the Queen's sister. At a time when titles and the Honours system really were an honour, she did not wish to debase the mark of distinction.

When Princess Margaret became pregnant in February 1961 the question of Tony's title became more pressing, as her children would immediately enter the line of succession. Could a plain Mr or Miss Armstrong-Jones really end up as fifth in line to the throne? Naturally the Queen was keen to honour her brother-in-law and would have done so sooner. Now came the problem, however, as to what that title should be. Many people felt that Princess Margaret's husband should be made a Duke, as Princess Elizabeth's had been. At heart there was a question of protocol. Royal Dukes are either born to the title or at the very least have blue blood in their veins. Could this commoner really be expected to rank alongside those with the highest of pedigrees? Eventually it was agreed that he should be granted an Earldom, an Earl ranking just below a Duke. Princess Margaret's feelings on this are unrecorded at the time, but did this not once again smack of 'second best'? 'I know my place!' the Princess said to biographer, Christopher Warwick, but was this not said with more than a touch of sarcasm? After much deliberation Tony opted for the title Earl of Snowdon, after the highest mountain in England and Wales, a compliment to his Welsh ancestry. As his subsidiary peerage he chose the title Viscount Linley of Nymans, which would be passed on to his first-born son. Tony chose the name Linley as a tribute to his maternal grandfather, Linley Sambourne, a famous cartoonist for *Punch*. Nymans had been the Messel family home in Sussex. Tony's choice of titles was announced on 3 October 1961, exactly one month before Princess Margaret gave birth to their son, David.

Now a wife and mother, Princess Margaret's life seemed completely fulfilled. The only blot on the horizon was that their apartment was too small for the new Earl and Countess of Snowdon, their baby son, and household staff which now included a nanny, Verona Sumner. Work began early in 1962 on making another part of Kensington Palace habitable. Apartment 1A in Clock Court, once the home of Princess Louise, Duchess of Argyll, the fourth daughter of Queen Victoria. Her great legacy to the Palace is the statue of Queen Victoria that she carved herself, which stands overlooking the Round Pond. Princess Louise died at Kensington Palace on 3 December 1939, at the age of ninety-one since which time the twenty-one-room apartment had been left empty and allowed to decay. Twenty-two years of neglect had taken its toll on the four-storey wing of Kensington Palace and it is surprising that the Royal Family ever allowed it to get in such a state. Little had been done to the apartment in the last years of Princess Louise's life; some rooms had not in fact been redecorated since the early 1890s, and as she had actually died in the apartment, there were few who wanted to live with her ghost. Princess Margaret instantly saw the vast possibilities that could make Number 1A a decent family home, and if Princess Louise did come back to haunt, that would only add to the excitement. She has not, incidentally, put in an appearance in the last fifty years, but if she did Princess Margaret could scarcely worry. A succession of royal ancestors had lived in the rooms in its 300-year history. Queen Anne died here, William III, Mary II, George II, and more recently Princess Alice, Countess of Athlone in 1981; the ghosts must be legion. Who could worry about one more? What was to haunt the Snowdons was the eventual cost of the restoration programme before they could move in and the ensuing criticism.

Not only had Number 1A been neglected for more than two decades, there was a certain amount of wartime bomb damage still to repair, there was crumbling plaster, dry rot and a dank musty smell of decay. The only solution was to gut the inside totally and begin again almost from scratch, a task that was to take nearly two years. The original estimate for the work was in excess of £70,000. As Kensington Palace is technically a public building, like Buckingham Palace and Windsor Castle which are the nation's heritage and not the Queen's own property, the repairs came under the jurisdiction of the Department of the Environment. Because of this, the Princess was given a £55,000 grant from the Government, and as costs began to escalate the Queen donated £20,000. For any critics of the Royal Family here was a certain target for attack. Public money was 'being wasted' said some Members of Parliament, and the notorious Willie Hamilton referred to Margaret as 'a kept woman'. From the Princess's point of view, the furore came at a bad time for when her critics looked back over her engagement diary for 1961, it was very slim. The Princess had spent most of the year pregnant with Viscount Linley and had practically withdrawn from public view. Whereas now it has become acceptable for the Princess of Wales and the Duchess of York to continue their duties almost into the last month of pregnancy, and we are shown pictures throughout, in 1961 expecting a baby still meant *confinement*. Photographs of the mother-to-be in that condition were strictly forbidden, and so no pictures are available of either the Queen or Princess Margaret in maternity wear. Yet again Princess Margaret was a victim of her age, and had medical opinion been different, or had she been born later, then the situation that she unwittingly found herself in would not have arisen.

The furore over the cost of their new home coincided with Tony's acceptance of the offer of a job. He was invited to be Artistic Adviser to the *Sunday Times* and as the salary was £10,000 a year it was assumed that once this was made public it would show that he and his wife were not spongers but were actually earning an income and could contribute to the costs. Unbeknown to the general public, Princess Margaret had already paid nearly £2,000 of her own money for the new kitchen at Kensington Palace. There was to be no truce in this battle, however, for once the news of Tony's job was released there was an outcry that a member of the Royal Family should work for a newspaper. Now it would be politically biased. Others said that Tony would never have been offered the job if he hadn't married the Princess. One tabloid even suggested that Princess Margaret should begin writing a gossip column just to even things out. On the whole, his decision was seen as debasing the family into which he had married. So exhausted had Princess Margaret been by her pregnancy that once baby David was born and safely under the supervision of Nanny Sumner, the Snowdons escaped for a short holiday to Antigua, a dose of Caribbean sun being the quickest reviver Princess Margaret knows. Here again is evidence of Tony's attitude towards Mustique which would have been the obvious place to visit. As far as the Princess was concerned, David was too young even to notice that she was not there, but obviously she was to meet with yet another outcry for neglecting her son. The episode was mirrored, twenty-seven years later, when the Duke and Duchess of York flew to Australia leaving Princess Beatrice with her nanny. The fairytale image that had been created for Princess Margaret at the time of her marriage was beginning to show cracks. That is not to say that her marriage suffered in any way at this time. Any criticism was now more bearable for the Princess because she had Tony. No longer was she fighting alone, but had someone with whom to share her fears and concerns, a shoulder for her to cry on, and because of contentment in her personal life she felt able to put on a much harder front to the press. Some said it was contempt, but it was much closer to resilience. At the age of thirty-one, she was building up a shield, a public mask to hide behind.

Early married life for the Snowdons coincided too with the swinging sixties, an age of sexual freedom and expression, a new generation that was kicking back at old traditions and the Establishment. For fashionable young people the Snowdons became a glamorous couple. They were seen singing together at parties in restaurants, Tony had a motorbike on which the Princess would sometimes ride pillion, some of their friends were known to be homosexual and even their first choice of best man, Jeremy Fry, was forced to step down when it was revealed that he had a homosexual conviction from eight years earlier. Princess Margaret enjoyed the mixture of friends from the artistic and theatrical world whom Tony introduced her to, and as a married couple they could invite guests more easily to drinks or a party. When she had been single, it was not so easy for the Princess to throw out invitations so openly, but as one of a pair it was socially acceptable. Had they been from any other family, Margaret's and Tony's lifestyle at this time would have seemed fashionable and typical of many in the sixties, but they suffered through no other reason than that they were royal. Princess Margaret could still influence fashion, and when the length of her skirts decreased as the mini skirt became shorter she was seen as 'trendy' by the younger generation, but raised the eyebrows of the old school. Her mini skirts were extremely respectable compared to many, but it was during this time that she gained the tag 'unconventional'. She smoked in public, was known to drink, her social circle as usual dominated the gossip columns and when measured agains the Queen and other women in the family, Princess Margaret stood out as the black sheep. She now felt liberated. When she had been growing up there had been no such thing as a teenager. The pressures on Princess Margaret, a teenager in the 1940s, had been great and with the liberation of the late 1905s, followed by the even more relaxed '60s, she began to live out her missed teenage years. She and Tony sought diversions and new experiences, which kept them happy but knocked the conventional dignity of the Royal Family. Because, thirty years on, she still has artistic friends, and is known to join in beach parties when holidaying on Mustique, she will now always have to suffer being thought unconventional even though events have overtaken her, giving her lifestyle in the 1990s an air of respectability and conventionality that was never considered before.

In 1963, the new apartment at Kensington Palace was nearing completion and Princess Margaret hoped to be settled by the time of Tony's birthday party in March. Two months before that deadline a workman in the apartment one day smelt smoke. A fire had started in the next-door attic and was spreading across the roof. Within seconds, firemen were on the scene, but it took an hour to put out the flames as the Princess watched her dream going up in smoke. Although only the upper storey was damaged by fire, water soaked down to the rooms below, creating a need for further restoration and more expense. It seemed as if the Gods were against them. A member of staff secretly wondered if the bad luck had occurred because Lord Snowdon had not carried the Princess over the threshold when they moved into their first home together at Number 10. Tony had intended to, but Princess Margaret somehow arrived before him and walked around the building by herself first. When Tony did arrive he carried her in, but maybe it was too late. A frivolous thought, perhaps, but they did seem to encounter more than their fair share of ill fortune.

Princess Margaret's happiness seemed complete when Apartment 1A was finally ready to occupy. Much of the work she and Tony had undertaken themselves, not only to cut costs, but as much for the fun of literally building a home together. They acquired a door and some ornamental pillars for £15 in Bristol, they shopped early in antique markets mostly unrecognised, picking up pieces of the Princess's favourite blue glass to display in some of the larger rooms, and various items of furniture that would be in keeping with the period of the house, resulting in an interior that is suitably impressive as a royal residence yet still a comfortable family home. Princess Margaret has now spent nearly thirty years at Kensington Palace, as long as her years at 145 Piccadilly, Royal Lodge, Buckingham Palace and Clarence house combined, and has naturally stamped her own personality on the building (see Chapter Nine). It is a country house in the very heart of the city.

In 1964 the Snowdon family was completed when Princess Margaret gave birth to Lady Sarah Armstrong-Jones on May Day, this time in her own home rather than at Clarence House where Viscount Linley had entered the world. On the surface they gave the appearance of a perfect couple with the equally perfect combination of children, a boy and a girl. Living in a Palace with no real financial worries, it would seem to be everyone's ideal. The love that Margaret and Tony felt for each other shone out even in public. It was noted that they often touched each other and he openly called her 'ducky' or 'pet', but when talking *about* her always referred to his wife as 'Princess Margaret'. Staff who worked for the Snowdons at the time knew too that it was an intensely physical relationship in private. By 1966 there were rumours of rifts, impending divorce, separations, all manner of marital problems were bandied about. Although most of the speculation was unfounded and invented, hairline cracks in the partnership were beginning to appear.

As the early years of their marriage were so blissful, what then went so devastatingly wrong with the relationship in the end? There is no single answer as to why the marriage ended in divorce, but a whole host of contributory factors that led to incompatibility. Although the rumours of divorce began more than ten years before the couple were legally separated, astute observers began to notice changes in the mid-sixties. The reasons were cumulative, starting in 1964 when 59 Rotherhithe Street was demolished, much against Princess Margaret's wishes. A compulsory purchase order had been served on William Glenton, forcing him to vacate the premises so that the entire area could be pulled down and redeveloped in the name of progress. Some of Princess Margaret's most happy and carefree times had been spent in the 'Room' and it was as if part of her life were being demolished by modern architects. It was still somewhere to retreat from the pressures of royal life, and it was Tony's only means of escape. Without it, he was forced to remain at Kensington Palace where he now had four rooms as his office and studio. If Princess Margaret had tried to prevent the demolition she would have been accused of wielding her royal position to her own advantage. They just had to accept the finality.

The loss of a building may seem a trivial matter, but royalty value their stability and privacy above all else. Prince Charles once wrote an angry note to his staff when somebody removed his favourite tooth mug from his bathroom. Just a small thing, but he needed the security of familiar items around him. The demolition of number 59 symbolically marked the end of the first stage of Margaret and Tony's relationship. To make up for it, Tony's uncle, Oliver Messel, having set up home in a house called 'Maddox' in Barbados, let them have the use of one of his homes in England. Called 'Old House', near Nymans in Sussex, it was part Tudor, part Georgian and had once been three cottages. Once called 'Little Beeches', Princess Margaret is said to have jokingly referred to this new retreat as 'Little Bitches'. Intentional, or just the Windsor accent? Although this became a weekend family haunt, it was not like Rotherhithe where Tony could escape easily when he needed solitude and quiet.

This he was certainly to need in January 1966 when his father died suddenly. He and Tony had always been close and, just as Princess Margaret had suffered when King George VI died, so now there was an aching void in his life. There were feelings of guilt that he had perhaps not done all that he could, said all that he should. The grief was immense, and as so often happened in periods of great stress, Tony suffered problems with his leg and had to visit a specialist in hospital. In a typical press report at the time it was recorded that Lord Snowdon had spent two whole days in hospital and Princess Margaret had not visited her husband once. Tony was actually in hospital for less than one hour having his leg examined.

Not long afterwards, the Snowdons visited Northern Ireland where Princess Margaret received death threats from the IRA which naturally added to their anxiety. Back home at Kensington Palace, they suffered the trauma of a burglary. The thief was caught, the stolen items returned, but Princess Margaret was shocked that such a thing could happen in what were assumed to be secure surroundings.

The first years of Princess Margaret's marriage had been ones of sharing experiences. In the first three years of marriage they had three homes, and getting the Kensington Palace apartments in order had occupied much of their spare time. By 1966 Apartment 1A was complete, and unlike most married couples who are continually saving to buy something new or have plans to make eventual improvements, this house had everything they needed. With no house to concentrate on, they suddenly had to take stock of themselves. Here they were. They had a home, two children, this was their life. Perhaps Princess Margaret sometimes felt trapped. Yes, they had lots of friends, they had a hectic social life, but this was it. This was how she seemed destined to live out the rest of her life, involved in the same routine of official engagements, year in, year out, and when not working she and Tony still had to live out their private life in the constant glare of the spotlight. Pressure was beginning to build up with Tony's work, which meant that they soon began to spend less and less time together as he threw himself into new projects.

Although Princess Margaret had a nanny to help with the two

children, she remained a good mother. Like Princess Anne, she was never particularly maternal but spent every spare moment with David and Sarah. They were part of her, the only two people in her life who had no understanding of the word royal, could not care less whether or not she was a Princess. She was first and foremost their mother. Spending time with the children meant that sometimes she began to neglect Tony.

After the death of his father, Tony threw himself into his work, not only to overcome grief, but as a way of reconciling himself to the rituals of royal life. He detested the protocol, those who tried to buy friendship, some of the seemingly petty points of etiquette. 'We both hate black tie,' he once said, and reacted badly when people criticised his own flamboyant choice of clothes. When necessary he put on the conservative uniform expected of him at official functions, but his discomfort was obvious. Because Princess Margaret wished it, he often partnered her on suitable engagements to act as an escort and to support her generally, but this meant always being in the background, walking behind her, with no worthwhile task to perform. There are many photographs of him sitting next to the Princess at an event looking so completely bored that it cannot have escaped anyone's attention.

One aspect of working for the *Sunday Times* that Tony most enjoyed was the opportunity it offered for foreign travel. The assignments obviously made no provision for this journalist's wife to travel too – besides Princes Margaret had her own full schedule – but it was during these periods of enforced separation that rumours of marital rifts first began to be printed in the press. The couple occasionally met up when foreign venues for Princess Margaret's overseas visits coincided with Tony's business trips, and they spoke constantly over the telephone even when aware that on occasions the equipment was bugged and journalists eavesdropped on their conversations. The situation was not helped when Tony seemed to be photographed frequently with beautiful girls, appearing to enjoy the pleasure of business. At times there were reports that Princess Margaret had sought male company elsewhere, but there is no concrete proof of this, only hearsay. Princess Margaret alone knows the truth, and why should she allow that to be revealed? Whatever the situation, she would agree that the reports of her love life over the last forty years have been far more exciting than the boring facts. It has been a two-edged sword, resulting in a glamorous image, but denting her dignity.

What has angered Princess Margaret is that men can build up a macho playboy image and not only was it not frowned upon, in the pre-AIDS world, it was almost encouraged. Yet a woman with a number of male escorts was immediately branded a tart. 'Diamond Lil' was a nickname that Princess Margaret once acquired as she swept into a film première in vivid evening gown and sparkling jewels, nothing worse than the sixties equivalent of her mother's extravagant crinolines and furs that added glamour to the immediate post-war years. No one would have dared criticise the Queen in the same way as they insulted Margaret. Whether or not Tony was ever seriously linked with anyone else during their marriage, he had certainly had his fair share of girlfriends before meeting the Princess, and was even rumoured to be bisexual, but after their engagement Margaret was intensely jealous of any female who tried to monopolise him at parties or flirted with the handsome photographer. She did not hesitate to let any starry-eyed girl know when the party was over, time to call it a day.

'Are you enjoying yourself?' Princess Margaret gently asked one girl who had spent most of the evening dancing with Tony at a ball in the Docklands.

'Very much,' replied the girl, with a bob, honoured that Her Royal Highness had actually spoken to her. This was an evening to remember.

'Good,' said the Princess, fixing her firm blue eyes on the hapless creature who seemed too close to her husband for comfort, 'Then that's enough for one evening. Run along home.' An equally cold look in Tony's direction ensured that no other girl flirted with him that evening, as his dancing partner fled from the ball faster than Cinderella at midnight.

As always, Tony retained a dignified silence in public, but once behind closed doors sparks flew if he ever felt that his wife had humiliated him. Princess Margaret's body language when they were out together instantly said, 'This is mine. Touch at your peril'. Tony had once known freedom in a way that she had never experienced and there were times when he felt as trapped by her possessiveness as Princess Margaret did by the golden chains of her birth. Although those who met Lord Snowdon officially saw him as a shy, nervous man who gave off an air of uncertainty that many found endearing, his temper was as volatile as Princess Margaret's. In times of peace and harmony their relationship worked well, but during periods of discord, quarrels quickly erupted. Both considered themselves the dominant force.

One of the main attractions in Tony was that he was the total opposite to the Princess. He had a vivid imagination and fantasies, whereas the Princess was down-to-earth and more materialistic. It is said that she appreciated the 'gypsy' in him, but needs security and stability herself. Whereas most members of the Royal Family have a London residence and a home in the country, Princess Margaret has just one base with all her prized possessions around her. To escape she goes to Royal Lodge or Windsor, to other people's homes, and even *Les Jolies Eaux* on Mustique is rented out to others when she doesn't need it. It is not another home, just a place of refuge. Princess Margaret felt seduced by Tony's unconscious charm, and made to feel dominant while he was really in control. When she became aware of this, feelings of insecurity came to the fore.

As in childhood, Princess Margaret managed to give an appearance of strength, but became the cowardly lion when faced with rejection. It surprised many when she once revealed that she cries easily. Her relationship with Tony worked initially because he was a good listener and had a natural charm that made him easy to talk to. They were both artistic and creative, preferring play to exercise. Princess Margaret enjoyed being admired, and appreciated his compliments. She has a warm heart but an ego that needs to be gratified, and although she always appeared to flirt in the company of men, it was merely to feed her ego rather than for any sexual overtones. Tony enjoyed it when she showed interest in his work and dreams, but when eventually she became bored by it, he became introspective. The Princess was irritated that her husband's inherent insecurity made him secretive about his work so that he often barred her from his study. Under pressure, he became moody, hypersensitive and anxious not to reveal his vulnerability. Princess Margaret has always liked to make snap decisions, often without practical considerations, and felt let down when Tony did not always automatically fit in with her plans. It was a battle of contrasts between two strong characters, and eventually the couple began to drift apart. 'This is the first meal we've had together in more than six weeks,' the Princess surprised guests at a dinner party by revealing, and as their worlds became more alien so Tony became increasingly moody and uncommunicative. He was selfless in his devotion to work and helping others, but in doing so he made his wife feel rejected. By the early seventies she felt that she was no longer the main priority in her husband's life. In March 1973 she flew to Mustique to holiday with friends just four days before Tony's birthday. A decade earlier she would not have dreamt of being apart on that day. It was a clue that something was seriously wrong. The early romance had gone, superseded by reality. Princess Margaret needed to feel that she had total devotion, and became frightened when Tony seemed to be living a life of his own.

As the Snowdons spent more and more time apart, Princess Margaret naturally turned to the support of her friends. One in particular was to add to the marital problems. Robin Douglas-Home, the nephew of the former Prime Minister, was someone with whom the Princess had a great deal in common – a love of classical music and poetry, and, naturally, a shared sense of humour. They attended concerts together. Robin even stayed with the Snowdons at Old House – a retreat which the Princess grew to detest as it lacked the cosy homeliness of the 'Room' it had replaced. The Princess was seen dancing with Robin at the Travellers' Club in Pall Mall, and they jokingly wrote poetry together. Tony was as jealous of Princess Margaret's friends as she was of his, but did he seriously believe the rumour that she and Robin Douglas-Home were lovers? This rumour has become one of those unproven myths which seem to dominate Princess Margaret's life, and is based on the fact that some highly suspect love letters from Douglas-Home to the Princess were once offered for sale in America. The so-called affair was innocent enough, but caused ructions with Tony not because of any infidelity, but because his wife was sharing the company of another (and younger) man.

In 1972 Lord Snowdon met Lucy Lindsay-Hogg, who was later to become his second wife; a year later Princess Margaret met Roddy Llewellyn, a young man with whom she was to form a close friendship. Neither was the cause of the final collapse of the Snowdon marriage, but unconsciously Margaret and Tony began to realise that there was a life and a chance of happiness outside the charade of their once-happy marriage. By 1975 they were living virtually separate lives, occasionally appearing in public together in a vain attempt to act out their role of happily married couple.

In April 1978 Tony secretly moved out of Kensington Palace to a house less than five minutes' walk away. It was impossible to drive anywhere without coming face to face with Kensington Gardens and his former home in front of him.

On 10 May 1976 a statement had been released to the media:

> Her Royal Highness The Princess Margaret, Countess of Snowdon, and the Earl of Snowdon have mutually agreed to live apart. The Princess will carry out her public duties and functions unaccompanied by Lord Snowdon. There are no plans for divorce proceedings.

For the sake of the children, the couple stayed apart under the same roof, unable to face the finality that their marriage had failed. The royal and the commoner could not actually live together because of the fundamental differences of their backgrounds. When Tony finally moved out in 1978 it signified the end of the relationship once and for all, and they had to face what they had shied away from for so long. Divorce. A word that, ironically, had put an end to Princess Margaret's relationship with Peter Townsend. Now it reared its ugly head with Tony. 'Mindful of the Church's teachings that Christian marriage is indissoluble . . . ' How her words from 1955 must have haunted her as Kensington Palace released a second statement on 10 May 1978, that had been long expected by so many:

> Her Royal Highness The Princess Margaret, Countess of Snowdon, and the Earl of Snowdon, after two years of separation, have agreed that their marriage should be formally ended. Accordingly Her Royal Highness will start the necessary proceedings.

The statement was tantamount to admitting failure. It was with regret rather than relief that the decision had been made. As she lay in her hospital bed suffering the effects of hepatitis, while the world press raked up her past once again, Princess Margaret must have reflected over her life and achievements as her fiftieth birthday loomed. For Lord Snowdon there was a future. Exactly five months after the decree absolute was granted in July 1978 he quietly married Lucy Lindsay-Hogg – no state landaus, world-wide television broadcasts nor waving from the balcony of Buckingham Palace, but a quiet ceremony in a registry office and a return to their home just a stone's throw from Kensington Palace. What the Princess, at her lowest ebb, did not appreciate at the time, was that she had been handed on a plate the one gift she had never had in almost half a century – total independence. Ahead lay a new and inviting world.

CHAPTER SIX

Charley's Aunt

On 4 August 1988, Queen Elizabeth the Queen Mother celebrated her birthday surrounded by close members of her family at Clarence House. The occasion is the one day in the royal year when even the Queen is prepared to blend into the background and let someone else take centre stage. The Queen Mother collected flowers and cards from well-wishers, listened to choruses of 'Happy Birthday' and smiled benignly at her assembled family, but she must have been conscious that her younger daughter was missing.

It was not the first family celebration from which Princess Margaret has been absent and it will not be the last. As the Queen sipped a dry Martini before the birthday lunch at Clarence House, her only sister was 500 miles away in Scotland, giving comfort and support to her close friends Lord and Lady Glenconner, who were in the midst of a family crisis. This year had proved to be one of personal devastation for the Glenconners. Their youngest son Christopher, then aged twenty, suffered horrific injuries in a motorcycle accident, which left him paralysed in a wheelchair; their eldest son Charles had become addicted to heroin (now thankfully recovered) and their second son, Henry, discovered in March that he had contracted AIDS (sadly, he died on 2 January 1990). Faced with a family celebration in London or the chance to provide much needed support in Scotland, Princess Margaret had no doubts as to where her duty lay.

Experience taught her to anticipate criticism from the press, but with the tide now turned in her favour, no one drew attention to her absence from Clarence House. By now the press had their gun barrels firmly aimed at the Duchess of York instead, who in

1988 was attacked over her abilities as a mother, her choice of clothes, the fact that she went abroad leaving her newly-born baby behind, the question as to whether she was working hard enough and providing value for money, all of which must have caused Princess Margaret some amusement. The sniping she had received in the 1960s over her children, wardrobe and work, were exactly the same.

Princess Margaret has much to thank the new generation of royals for. In the 1950s and '60s the Royal Family had been smaller, and although the gentle Princess Alexandra was beginning to undertake duties and Katherine Worsley entered the ranks as the new Duchess of Kent, it was Princess Margaret who was the senior Princess and the obvious target for criticism. By 1986, the Princess of Wales, Princess Michael of Kent and the Duchess of York had higher profiles and shielded Princess Margaret from the firing line. But though she may be thankful to the new breed of royals, she has not totally accepted them. At times she is distressed that they steal media attention on a frivolous level, casting a shadow over the more serious work that the Royal Family undertakes. From her own point of view Princess Margaret is happy that the harsh spotlight has been taken off her, allowing her now to lead a more peaceful life in private, but she has been angered that much of her public life has passed almost unreported throughout the 1980s. Equally she still looks upon them as outsiders, not true blue-blooded royals, and therefore never part of the inner clique. Although the frequent reports that Princess Margaret never speaks to Princess Michael of Kent are untrue, there is an obvious coolness between the two ladies. Living under the same roof at Kensington Palace, Princess Margaret has been known to complain about the noise made by Princess Michael's cats.

Joined together by a single bond of status, the Royal Family are an enigma. Although they present a united front, and turn out in force for jubilees and weddings, they remain remote from each other, despite the fact that many branches of the family live very close together. Princess Margaret's home at Kensington Palace is a prime example. Once a single royal home for one family, it is now divided into a number of self-contained units. Princess Margaret has the equivalent of a four-storey, twenty-one roomed house, once needed to house herself and Lord Snowdon, two children and the necessary staff. Hers is one of the larger apartments, consistent with her role as a senior member of the family, but she shares the building with no fewer than fourteen members of the family. Apartment 4 is the home of the present Duke and Duchess of Gloucester and their three children. It is also occasionally the London residence of Princess Alice, the Dowager Duchess of Gloucester, who spends much of her time now in the country at Barnwell. Another of the larger apartments, Numbers 8 and 9 is the London home of the Prince and Princess of Wales, with the Princes William and Harry, housing also Diana's office and official wardrobe. In Princess Margaret's former home at Number 10 now live Prince and Princess Michael of Kent and their two children. Apart from the state apartments which are on permanent display to the public, the remaining units are grace-and-favour homes for members of staff and less well-known members of the family, such as Lady Mary Clayton, the Queen Mother's cousin.

This division into apartments occurred at the beginning of the nineteenth century, George II having been the last monarch to use the whole building. One was occupied by the then Duke and Duchess of Kent (Queen Victoria's parents) and various other sons and daughters of George III. What differed almost two centuries ago was that this royal building housed a much more sociable world in which the occupants mixed freely and sociably. In the royal family of the 1990s the community seldom integrates, and only formally when it does, by gilt-edged invitation. When they leave Kensington Palace en masse for a state occasion, they depart from this private home in order of succession, with Princess Margaret leaving after the Prince and Princess of Wales, but always before the Gloucesters and the Kents. Although they live just yards apart, for most of the year they could live at opposite ends of the country for all they actually see of each other. Partly this is because each has a full engagement diary, and if Princess Margaret were to tap on the Wales' door, the chances are that they would be out. The situation, however, is unlikely. There is a certain rivalry that exists between the families, each aware of their own importance. Even if the Queen visits Princess Margaret for afternoon tea it is carefully organised, a call being put through from Buckingham Palace at the exact moment Her Majesty drives out of the forecourt for the five-minute journey, so that the Kensington Palace butler can open the door to coincide with the Queen's arrival. The door must be open as the monarch approaches. Non-royal guests would have to ring the bell. The strange protocol that exists between them also means that if the Queen calls to see Princess Margaret, she would not also call and see her son, Princes Charles, unless it had been formally arranged beforehand. At least Diana knows in advance when her mother-in-law is going to call, and Princess Margaret can entertain guests to tea in her sunny garden room without having to worry about the last-minute unexpected guest, but non-royals would find the situation strange.

One of the few occasions when Princess Margaret mixes with her Kensington Palace neighbours is Christmas, and in her sister's home. On 21 December 1989, the houseparty set off to Sandringham in Norfolk for the Christmas festivities. All childhood Christmasses had been spent at Sandringham until 1964, when the Queen, Princess Margaret, Princess Alexandra and the Duchess of Kent had all given birth to babies during the year, necessitating a move to Windsor Castle where there was more room. It was, therefore, a nostalgic return to Sandringham for Princess Margaret when, in 1988, Christmas once again was celebrated in Norfolk owing to urgent repairs to Windsor Castle. In 1989 Princess Margaret joined the Queen and Prince Philip, the Queen Mother, the Prince and Princess of Wales with William and Harry, the Duke and Duchess of York with Beatrice, Princess Anne (now without her husband) and Peter and Zara Phillips, Prince Edward, plus Viscount Linley and Lady Sarah Armstrong-Jones. Princess Alexandra and Sir Angus Ogilvy did not join the main party but stayed with the Duke and Duchess of Kent at nearby Anmer Hall. Missing from the guest list altogether were those who had once always been included at Windsor Castle: Princess Alice, the Duke and Duchess of Gloucester, the Earl of Ulster, Lady Davina and Lady Rose Windsor, Prince and Princess Michael of Kent and their offspring, Lord Frederick and Lady Gabriella Windsor. While Princess Alexandra's son James and his wife Julia, stayed at Anmer Hall, Marina Ogilvy did not join her parents.

Diminished though it may be in recent years, the gathering at Sandringham is the one occasion in the year when most of the Royal Family are together. There is a passing nod of acquaintance as they attend Trooping the Colour, pass each other in the Royal Enclosure at Ascot, or face the throng across a State Banquet table, but Christmas is the closest they ever get to relaxing in each other's company. For Princess Margaret this is seldom her favourite celebration of the year and it is noticeable that while the Queen plays the perfect hostess, circulating with her guests throughout, personally checking each room to make sure that everything from the Bronnley soaps and Floris toiletries to the fresh flower arrangement are all in order, the Princess is less comfortable with some members of the family than others. While the Queen plays with Princess Beatrice or her two grandsons, Princess Margaret will be chatting to the older members of the family. Being great-aunt Margo is not one of the titles that thrills her.

When Princess Margaret received the news that the Queen had given birth to Prince Charles and learned his name, she joked, 'I'm Charley's Aunt now!' after the title of Brandon Thomas's famous farce. A month after his birth Princess Margaret became one of his godparents, and it is for the Queen's eldest children that the Princess now feels a particular fondness. In the latter years of King George VI's life, Elizabeth, as his heir, began to undertake more and more duties which kept her away from her baby son and daughter. In the Autumn of 1951, Elizabeth had to pay a state visit to Canada and America. Away for thirty-five days, she and Prince Philip had to miss Prince Charles's third birthday, and, as the King was still recovering from his lung operation, it was Princess Margaret who made the day special for the young boy and organised a birthday tea at Buckingham Palace. Equally, when Lilibet as Queen embarked on a three-month Commonwealth tour in 1953, leaving Prince Charles and Princess Anne in the care of the Queen Mother, Princess Margaret grew particularly close to the two children, reading them stories, playing games, taking them for walks and building up a lasting bond. Prince Charles has often spoken of a special fondness for his Auntie Margo.

What binds Princess Margaret to these two particular members of the family is their shared sense of frustration arising from the uniquely strange position they are in. Prince Charles may be heir apparent, but he still plays second fiddle to the Queen. He waits in the wings as a future King, not wanting the mantle of responsibility, yet in a kind of limbo until it is his. There is no role laid out for him. 'His job is Prince of Wales,' the Queen Mother once said when critics declared him jobless, but there are no hard and fast rules as to what a Prince of Wales should actually do. In the late 1980s Prince Charles threw himself successfully into a number of projects about which he felt strongly – modern architecture, the decline in standards of spoken English, the wilful destruction of the environment – and in so doing has become a champion of causes that will possibly lead to a better, cleaner country over which to rule. Until this time the Prince had suffered anguish as a result of his birthright, and it was his aunt who could provide comfort. The pressure equally had been on the Prince to find a suitable bride, and no one more than Princess Margaret knew the stresses of royal marriage – how falling in love was not sufficient, it meant falling in love with someone right in the eyes of the world, and how ultimately the pressure of being royal can be so great that it can destroy love altogether. Prince Charles was particularly saddened by the collapse of Princess Margaret's marriage and has a determination to make his own succeed.

Princess Margaret is perhaps even closer in spirit to Princess Anne, both born almost exactly twenty years apart (21 August 1930, and 15 August 1950 respectively), both suffering from the second-born syndrome. In Anne, the Princess saw a mirror image of herself, for just as the main interest had been in Lilibet as heir to the throne when she was a child, so she saw Prince Charles overshadowing his sister. In each case it was no fault of the child. Princess Margaret saw Anne rebel in much the same way as she had done when young, but the latter had advantages that had been denied Margaret Rose. Princess Anne and Prince Charles both attended school with other children, whereas Princess Margaret had studied almost solely under Marion Crawford throughout her education. At first Anne was taught by a Scottish governess, Miss Catherine Peebles. With Anne's love of nicknames, she instantly became 'Mispy', derived from the abbreviation 'Miss P.'. Only too well aware of the demands in the Buckingham Palace schoolroom, Princess Margaret encouraged the Queen to reform the Palace Brownie Pack to increase Anne's social circle and broaden her activities. So the 'B'hams', as the pack was known, became reestablished and consisted of girls from Holy Trinity in Knightsbridge and the younger daughters of senior Household staff.

Fully appreciating Anne's position, Princess Margaret knew that the Brownies was the ideal organisation for an intelligent and energetic girl, providing discipline and character-building activities, and this strengthened the bond between aunt and niece. When Princess Margaret married Antony Armstrong-Jones, she enlisted Anne as chief bridesmaid and went out of her way to show the ten-year-old that her wedding was not the end of their relationship. Soon Tony was being encouraged to teach Princess Anne about photography, and the subject of her first photographs in 1960 was her new-born brother, Prince Andrew. Princess Margaret felt a sense of relief when Andrew was born, for it gave Princess Anne the ally that she had never had herself. Anne was no longer pushed out by Prince Charles; she was taken to see her new baby brother within an hour of his birth, and when the Queen had to tour India and Pakistan a few months later, it was Princess Anne who became a substitute mother, and, with Margaret's and Tony's inspiration, took frequent photographs of baby Andrew to send the Queen, keeping her informed of his progress. Had Princess Margaret been granted a brother when young she would not have felt such a loss when Lilibet began royal duties and war work, leaving her alone with Crawfie.

In a strange parallel, Princess Anne married a commoner like Princess Margaret, but resisted the offer of a title for Mark Phillips in the knowledge that it may have done more harm to Tony than good. Like Margaret, Anne had a son born in November, followed by a daughter born in May. Both had marriages that lasted sixteen years, ending in legal separation and eventually divorce. Even as Princess Margaret's name was linked for so long with equerry Peter Townsend, so Princess Anne's became linked with equerry Commander Timothy Lawrence. Townsend and Lawrence are by coincidence remarkably similar in looks, build and colouring. Both Princesses suffered from false press reports and had a 'black sheep' image built up for them to contrast with that of the heir, had rumours of marriage breakdown and 'imminent divorce' ten years before it happened, were attacked for their choice of clothes, their independent streak and failure to play up to the camera. Both were 'fairytale Princesses' at the time of their marriages, an image which quickly tarnished, and both have mellowed with the passing of the years, resulting finally in a more favourable public persona. Both, as women, continue to be pushed further down the line of succession.

Princess Margaret will always be closest to Prince Charles and Princess Anne because of the early bond that existed between them. She was married and setting up home by the time Prince Andrew (now Duke of York) was three months old, and had a child of her own and was seven months pregnant with her next by the time Prince Edward was born, so did not have the time to devote to her young nephews. Nevertheless, she shares an almost wicked sense of humour with Prince Andrew; both were great practical jokers when young. She has great admiration, too, for Prince Edward, not simply because he is pursuing a theatrical career, which interests her, but because he had the courage of his convictions to fight against royal expectations and resigned from the Royal Marines when the going became too tough. The Queen's sons spent time in the Forces because they were the Queen's sons, and for no other reason. The young Prince Charles had a daredevil image built up for him and spent time in all three branches of the Forces, but given the choice, his sensitive and peace-loving character would have turned him against the idea. Looking back, he does not regret his experiences, but possibly regrets not ever having the option to refuse. It took courage, therefore, when early in 1987 Prince Edward decided to quit the Royal Marines after only four months training. The decision was harder because his father was honorary Captain General of the Royal Marines, and he knew that he would be branded for ever by the media, but he took the step and has not regretted it. It broke new ground for a member of the Royal Family, but he had two enthusiastic supporters in Princess Anne and Princess Margaret.

Now, at the time of writing, three of the Queen's children have followed Priness Margaret's example by marrying non-royals. Even though the Princess of Wales received the title Lady when she was fourteen, at the time of her father's inheritance, she was still officially a commoner when she married Prince Charles. Considering that Princess Margaret married a commoner herself and understands the difficulties, it is strange that there is a very definite coolness between her and the new additions. It is not open hostility; perhaps because of the generation gap, her conversations with Diana and Sarah were for a long time merely polite and consisted of social pleasantries. In many ways the girls felt intimidated by her, not just by the air of confidence that she now exudes, the manner in which she seemed to stare at them piercingly as if weighing them up, but as much by what she represents. When Diana married into the family Princess Margaret was fifty, which meant she had half a century's experience of being a senior Princess. Now, here was a girl, still not yet twenty-one, who had come from obscurity not only to gain the title Princess but in doing so to be immediately ranked *above* Princess Margaret. To cap it all, she would one day inherit the title of Queen, a title which had been borne by Princess Margaret's ancestors, her beloved grandmother, mother and sister. That was difficult for Princess Margaret to accept.

In 1986, Sarah Ferguson bounced into the Royal Family, and by her marriage was ranked above Princess Margaret, and was created a Duchess, while Margaret, as the wife of an Earl, was but a Countess. Princess Margaret has been less than impressed by Sarah, and the two have very little in common. Sarah's sense of humour is too unsubtle for Princess Margaret, who appreciates acid wit and sharp repartee. Those close to her suggest that perhaps she feels there has been a lowering of royal dignity and that she regrets the fact that too much 'daylight' has been let in upon the magic. Certainly she has been known to criticise the accents of Diana and Sarah, which have been described by others as 'BBC Newsreader' rather than 'Queen's English'. When Princess Margaret first saw the play *Crown Matrimonial* by Royce Ryton, in which actors portray the events leading to the Abdication of Edward VIII, she attacked those cast as members of the Royal Family because the accent was wrong. 'We do not speak like that,' she said. Diana's and Sarah's relatively low rating in the eyes of Princess Margaret was proved by her absence at the christenings of Prince William, Prince Harry and Princess Beatrice. 'I don't think it is essential to be at the christening of your nephew's children,' a member of the Princess's staff said in her defence, anxious to point out that it was not a deliberate snub on her part. Not wanting to be seen as hypocritical by attending for the sake of appearances, the Princess stayed away. Conscious that she would only be swelling the already large ranks of royals, with no special purpose, she felt that her family was well represented with Lady Sarah Armstrong-Jones a godmother to Prince Harry, and Viscount Linley a godfather to Princess Beatrice. Princess Margaret's sense of duty will prompt her to attend any number of functions for what she considers to be worthwhile causes, but she is not prepared to put on a show simply to satisfy the whims of her family.

With many members of her own family, Princess Margaret feels that there is a barrier because they have so little in common. Although the Princess attends some 'horsey' events because of the social opportunities they provide, she does not share her sister's or her niece's passion for equine sports. The other great love of royalty is dogs, but whereas the Queen, Queen Mother and Princess Anne all have corgis, the Prince of Wales has a Jack Russell terrier and once had one of his mother's second favourite breed, a labrador, Princess Margaret is dogless. Certainly this is not because she dislikes dogs. In her childhood she enjoyed playing with her parents' corgis, and grew up to own a King Charles spaniel called Rowley and later, Sealyhams Johnny and Pipkin. One of her little known patronages is Honorary Member of the Sealyham Terrier Association. The reason for not having a dog today is that her working and social diaries are so full that any animal resident at Kensington Palace would rarely see its mistress and would be an added burden on her staff. Any visit to Clarence House or Buckingham Palace offers ample opportunity to be with dogs if she so wishes.

Princess Margaret has never shared her family's love of sport. Her sister rides every day, but the Princess is seldom seen on a horse now. She will ride occasionally at Balmoral. She has never skied, unlike the Waleses and the Yorks, although she did water-ski for a time to get her figure back in shape after her two pregnancies; whereas the younger members of the family escape to the snowclad mountains for relaxation, Princess Margaret would much rather head for the sun. Once beside the warm sea, the Princess does share one sport with Diana – swimming. She frequently swims when holidaying on Mustique, slowly but for long distances, it is said. Like the Princess Royal, she has raced a greyhound. Called Spike, the dog was raced to raise money for the Sunshine Homes for the Blind, but he was not a great success. Princess Margaret does not share her family's love of shooting. In the past she has organised a day's shoot in Windsor Great Park for friends, but again it has been for the social event much more than the sport.

With the Prince and Princess of Wales there is always one major topic of conversation that Princess Margaret indulges in – opera and ballet, which all three enjoy. In September 1989 the Princess officially handed over the role of Patron of the English National Ballet to Diana. Earlier she relinquished the reins of the Dr Barnardo's Presidency also. Both were associations with which Princess Margaret had been linked for several decades, but she felt that Diana's image might help both in the long run. Because she shared so little common ground with Diana, listened to different music and took less interest in fashion, the passing over of pat-ronages was a deliberate attempt to provide some mutual areas of concern. She may not relish the idea of Diana stepping into Lilibet's shoes and eventually taking over the running of Buckingham Palace and the royal homes that she has loved throughout her sixty years, but one thing life has taught Princess Margaret is acceptance. She and the future Queen will never be bosom buddies, but the Princess has learned to bow to the inevitable.

Of all members of the family, apart from her own children, Princess Margaret is naturally closest to the Queen and the Queen Mother. The three speak on the telephone almost every day if they cannot actually meet, and to see them together is to watch three spirits in total harmony. They have an art of all talking at the same time, and yet each is understood.

On 20 November 1990, Prince Philip and the Queen celebrate forty-three years of marriage, yet he still feels an outsider when his wife, sister and mother-in-law are together in a clique. Princess Margaret's relationship with him over the years has been mixed. When he and Lilibet were courting he tended to treat Princess Margaret as if she were a troublesome child, and would tease her mercilessly, once pinning a sign saying 'Maggie's Playroom' on her door. His attitude towards Peter Townsend was said to have been hostile, and he was not a great fan of Antony Armstrong-Jones either. The men who have been romantically involved with the Princess have always been sensitive and artistic, in many ways the antithesis of Prince Philip. Yes, he himself paints, he designs, but his approach is blunt, his naval humour still in evidence, his enjoyment of the camaraderie is obvious at reunion dinners. When in good humour, he and Princess Margaret can poke gentle fun at each other, but when angered both speak their minds without pulling any punches.

Princess Margaret's relationship with her mother has been less turbulent than with other members of the family. She has been a stabilizing force throughout the Princess's stormy life, never judging or criticizing but seemingly accepting all with a resolute approach. When she first heard of Princess Margaret's love for Peter Townsend she closed her eyes to it, hoping that if she blotted it from her mind it would go away. Still grieving for her husband, she could not cope with any hint of scandal, but eventually she accepted it as a fact of life and although she did not encourage them, she certainly gave the couple ample opportunity to spend time together. Her only concern was her daughter's happiness. When Peter was banished, the Queen Mother shared in her daughter's sorrow. She was to share it again when Margaret and Tony decided to separate, for the Queen Mother had looked upon Lord Snowdon as a son. A sign that Princess Margaret and the Queen Mother share the same sense of acceptance is shown in the fact that Lord Snowdon, once the initial pain of separation had ended, continued to be a close friend to them both. One of Princess Margaret's regrets was that she had not handled the Townsend situation better and therefore lost Peter as a friend. More mature when she split up from Tony, she knew that she still liked him, it was simply that their relationship did not work. Two days before the Queen Mother's eighty-ninth birthday, Princess Margaret, Lord Snowdon and their children took her for a surprise lunch at Viscount Linley's riverside restaurant, *Deals*. Anyone who did not know them, watching Margaret and Tony chatting animatedly and laughing over lunch in 1989, would assume that they were man and wife. Impossible to believe that they had separated thirteen years earlier. As the Queen Mother watched in the convivial atmosphere, she must have been astute enough to realise that what makes Princess Margaret's friendship with Tony work so well today is that the pressure of earlier years has gone. Unlike Captain Mark Phillips who has been saddled with a sad and lonely image as Princess Anne's ex-husband, Tony has managed to retain his own identity. He has an extremely successful career and is highly respected. His friendship with the Royal Family continues, too, because in thirteen years he has never once spoken ill of Princess Margaret. After sixteen years of marriage he had within his power the ability to damage her reputation irredeemably, but he has never spoken out of turn. For Viscount Linley and Lady Sarah Armstrong-Jones it must be pleasing that such family outings can take place without animosity. Just as Princess Margaret has commanded the loyalty of her friends, retaining them for life, so she has managed to remain on good terms with both Tony and his new wife, and Roddy Llewelyn and his wife.

It is from the Queen Mother that Princess Margaret has inherited her sense of humour. On an engagement one afternoon the Queen Mother asked a small boy where he lived.

'Round the back of 'Arding and 'Obbs,' came the boy's quick response, 'Where do you live?'

'Round the back of Harrods,' quipped the Queen Mother. Where the Queen Mother and Princess Margaret differ is in their attitude towards public appearances. For the Queen Mother it has been an acting role; her clothes are her props, and almost like a caricature of herself, she has now settled for one image – the matching coat and dress, the upturned brim of her hat covered with netting – even on her private birthday lunch at *Deals* she looked exactly as if she were about to open a new hospital wing or launch a ship. She has the ability to charm everyone she meets with a sugary sweet smile in her fluffy, grandmotherly style. 'Grannie Glamis', as they call her in Scotland, maintains the public poise throughout. When her helicopter developed a fault and was forced to land, she simply climbed out and said, 'Wretched thing,' with a smile, as if it were a broken handbag clasp. It is surprising, therefore, that in private she can be formidable, her standards high, her wit occasionally caustic.

Compare this to Princess Margaret who has never gone out of her way to appear sugary sweet. Unlike her mother she will not step from her car, stand and turn so that every photographer gets a good picture. Like the Queen and the Princess Royal she gets instantly down to business. She would never adopt a predictable style of dress, enjoying her femininity and the opportunity to surprise. Because of this, she presents a formidable public image, which belies her softness and compassion in private – a total reversal of her mother's persona.

Both ladies share strength of character. The Queen Mother learned how to fire a pistol accurately during the war, 'so that I shall not go down like all the others', and, when approached unexpectedly by a Zulu chief in South Africa, began beating him off with an umbrella, assuming that it was an attack. The hapless man had in fact only tried to give Princess Elizabeth a ten-shilling note as a twenty-first birthday gift. 'It was the most embarrassing moment of my life,' the Queen Mother later revealed. It is easy to imagine Princess Margaret taking similar courses of action, sharing the resolution of the Queen Mother, glad that Buckingham Palace was bombed during the war so that she could 'look the East End in the face', listening to *Mrs Dale's Diary* on the radio as the 'only way to find out what goes on in a middle class family', never listening to the National Anthem on radio or television 'unless one is actually there it is like hearing the Lord's Prayer while playing Canasta'.

The great bond between the two is apparent also in that

when Princess Margaret has a weekend free, she likes nothing better than to spend the time at Royal Lodge with her mother. Perhaps it is as much for the sense of security, for being able to escape from London to the home filled with happy childhood memories that Princess Margaret so enjoys. Whatever troubles there have been in her life, Royal Lodge has stood there like a refuge, its surroundings relatively unchanged. When Princess Margaret was twenty, the artist John Gunn painted a domestic scene of the Royal Family in a picture called *Conversation Piece*. It depicts King George VI, the then Queen Elizabeth and Princess Elizabeth seated at the tea table, with Princess Margaret standing. If you study the room at Royal Lodge, painted in accurate detail by Gunn, and then look at the same room today, forty years on, little has changed. The carpets, paintings, upholstery are still the same. The mantlepiece is still adorned with the same clock and china, with two classically ornate candelabra standing at either end. Flanking the fireplace are firescreens embroidered with the royal arms and the motto 'Honi Soit Qui Mal Y Pense', showing even though this is a private residence it is also a *royal* home. The same glass chandeliers hang from the ceiling, sparkling as they did in Princess Margaret's childhood. An artist visiting Royal Lodge for the first time today could recreate the scene John Gunn saw in 1950; only the players would now be changed.

Under the Queen Mother's influence, which the Queen and Princess Margaret have never disputed, Royal Lodge remains very much as it looked in King George VI's time. When Royal Lodge is redecorated, it is in the colours chosen by the King and Queen in 1931; if upholstery becomes worn it is repaired or replaced in an identical pattern, and the King's desk remains in its original position as if waiting for him to return. It is believed that Royal Lodge will one day be inherited by Princess Margaret, the only member of the Family without a country retreat. For nostalgic reasons, any changes she makes will be small. Princess Margaret's inner conflict is soothed by the reassurance and continuity provided by her family and their homes.

While Princess Margaret needs and enjoys the familiarity that her family's homes provide, in her own life she has not been able to achieve the same stability. Although much of her Kensington Palace apartment looks very much as it did a decade ago, when her marriage failed she was left with rooms in Lord Snowdon's style that were of no use to her, and she had to change them. For example, Tony's study became Princess Margaret's library, now housing her large collection of books.

Princess Margaret fits in with some of the Family's routines, but part of her is drawn closer to her friends and warm countries, which prevent her from complying totally with their lifestyle. Although deeply religious, she sometimes does not join her family at church on a Sunday, because they have the ability to get up early in the morning and appear fresh as a daisy, while she would be happier with evening worship. Where possible, Princess Margaret tries to fit into family routines, but obviously likes variety. The Queen Mother always celebrates her birthday at Clarence House, making a public appearance at an appointed time; the Queen, apart from her sixtieth birthday celebrations, remains quietly at Windsor Castle on 21 April; but Princess Margaret celebrates her birthday in different parts of the country; she even spent her fifty-eighth birthday abroad with friends, completely away from the family.

Failure to follow the rigid royal timetable is consistent with Princess Margaret's character. She has achieved a balance; fitting in with the family for important events, but retaining her independence enough to decline invitations if a more exciting proposition comes along. Making purely duty visits is not her style. She missed the christening of Prince William, yet agreed to attend the baptism of the baby of the Earl and Countess Alexander of Tunis in the same year. It is a sign of the affection that close friends have for the Princess that the Earl and Countess decided to call their daughter Rose Margaret, after Princess Margaret Rose. The Princess agreed to be a godmother, but had to miss the ceremony due to severe gastric flu on the day. Godmother Margaret takes a great interest in her young namesake, as if she were an extension of her own family, just as she is concerned about the welfare of the late Judy Montagu's daughter. Although the children of friends look upon the Princess as 'exciting and fun', young members of the Royal Family are just a little in awe of 'Auntie Margo'. The older members of the family liken the Princess to her maternal grandmother – Cecilia, Lady Glamis, later Countess of Strathmore – who was a very direct woman. She loved music; reputedly she took her young daughter, Lady Elizabeth, to the Music Halls to see Marie Lloyd and Vesta Tilley. She had a very down-to-earth approach to royalty, detesting snobbery and society hostesses who delighted in entertaining members of the Royal Family, saying, 'some people, dear, have to be fed royalty like sea-lions with fish'. Her simple creed was Christianity strengthened by paternalism, and at her funeral in 1938 the then Archbishop of Canterbury, Cosmo Lang, said that she had brought up her family by 'simple trust and love'. Although Princess Margaret had not reached her eighth birthday when Grannie Strathmore died, it is her creed that she has subconsciously adopted. Of family and friends, trust and love are all that Princess Margaret demands.

In the final decade of the twentieth century, subtle changes are creeping into Princess Margaret's family. There is now a certain lack of formality in private, which can only be for the better. At the very heart of this change is our future Queen Consort, Diana, who does not enjoy the cloistered atmosphere at Kensington Palace, nor the fact that members of the Royal Family can live side by side yet not visit without formal invitation. When Princess Margaret had her lung operation in 1985 she made it known that she did not want visitors until she was feeling better, but the Princess of Wales ignored this edict and called unannounced, taking flowers and offering to undertake any engagements that Princess Margaret might have to cancel. Rather than being angry, Princess Margaret was touched that this young girl had displayed such consideration. Diana went on to stand in for the Princess on an engagement in Wales, and when Margaret had recovered she invited Charles and Diana to dinner.

Following suit, Princess Margaret's nearest neighbours, Richard and Birgitte, the Duke and Duchess of Gloucester, began to invite her to travel with them when attending family functions and State Banquets so that the Princess would not have to travel alone. It is an informality that Princess Margaret has shared only with close friends until now, coming from a family where position and protocol is paramount. When the Princess of Wales returned home from hospital with Prince Harry, Princess Margaret encouraged her staff to wave towels from the widows like flags; when Prince Philip came with the Queen to dinner at Kensington Palace on his birthday, the Princess lined her staff up in the entrance hall to sing a sheepish chorus of 'Happy Birthday'; on another occasion, the staff were asked by the Princess to applaud the actress Elizabeth Taylor when she came to dine at Kensington Palace so that she would 'feel important'. Always torn between the dignity of her role as a King's daughter, and the natural desires to let her hair down and have fun, Princess Margaret enjoys the fact that her family are falling into line with the twentieth century, just as long as standards are not allowed to slip too far.

In 1989, on a visit to Malaysia, shortly after Princess Alexandra's daughter Marina had caused a public scandal by giving an interview to a newspaper claiming that she was estranged from her parents because she was expecting her boyfriend's baby, the Queen made very pointed references to the Commonwealth being like a family with its wayward children as well as its wise uncles. In her youth, Princess Margaret had the image of the wayward child, causing the scandals, kicking back at convention. Today her family have overtaken her with their behaviour. Standards have been amended. From being the 'black sheep' of the family, Princess Margaret has emerged as the wise aunt.

CHAPTER SEVEN

Yours and Mine

Passengers on board the British Airways flight BA255 held their breath as a loud bang came from the front of the plane and the cabin lit up in a brilliant flash of light. Although the aircraft was severely jolted by a bolt of lightning which left a gaping hole in the plane's nose, Princess Margaret and Viscount Linley, on their way to Mustique, remained completely unruffled by the experience. 'They showed typical sang-froid,' said a fellow passenger, and although their 1990 holiday was delayed for 18 hours while repairs were carried out, the Princess and her son were accommodated in a hotel near Manchester Airport along with more than 300 other passengers and neither received nor requested preferential treatment. For this mother and son it was just another unexpected setback, one more adventure to recount.

Princess Margaret's children have had much to contend with in their comparatively short lives. 'My children are not royal; they just happen to have an aunt who is the Queen,' Princess Margaret has said matter-of-factly, but even she cannot deny that these 'non-royal' children have been greatly influenced by their royal relatives. Princess Margaret, like her niece the Princess Royal, is not particularly maternal, yet both have proved to be particularly successful mothers. Peter and Zara Phillips, Viscount Linley and Lady Sarah Armstrong-Jones seem to be developing into the most mature and best adjusted children in the Royal Family. From an early age, Princess Margaret's children have behaved with unexpected dignity, yet have given the appearance of continual contentment.

As a small child, Princess Margaret had tea one Christmas

117

at Glamis Castle with the playwright J.M. Barrie, the author of *Peter Pan*. Pointing to a cracker Barrie asked if it was hers. 'It's yours *and* mine,' she said with great maturity. So delighted was Barrie that he later used the line in his play *The Boy David*, and gave the Princess one penny each time it was performed. It is with the same straightforward approach that Princess Margaret brought up her own boy David. Even today, when you see her with children, she has a very direct approach and talks to them as adults rather than down to them as children.

Princess Margaret gave birth to her first baby at Clarence House on 3 November, 1961. As Tony had accepted the title of Lord Snowdon a month earlier, their son instantly became Viscount Linley of Nymans. Although one reason for Tony's peerage was to ensure that Princess Margaret's son would not be a 'commoner', the title has become a millstone around his neck. 'Titles inhibit people and set me apart,' he says today, and in adulthood prefers to be known simply as David Linley. Though he strives to be ordinary, he will one day inherit the title Earl of Snowdon, whether he likes it or not.

At the time of David's birth, the marriage of Princess Margaret and the newly created Earl was at its happiest, without the arguments and petty squabbles that were later to develop. When her children were young, Princess Margaret went against convention and tried to spend as much time with them as possible rather than leaving them completely in the control of a nanny. When you look back at her engagement diary it is clear that she kept their birthdays free. For example, when she and Lord Snowdon undertook an official visit to the United States of America and Bermuda in 1965, it was no coincidence that they flew from London Airport on the 4 November, the day after David's birthday.

David's early life was spent in the nursery at Kensington Palace with Nanny Sumner, before he began lessons in the schoolroom at Buckingham Palace, in the same room where Princess Margaret had studied until the outbreak of war. Here he studied under Miss Peebles with Prince Andrew. Although they have remained friends, and both progressed to the London school, Gibbs, even as boys it was clear that two highly different personalities were developing. Prince Andrew, like his father, was very keen on sport, enjoyed playing rugby and football. Eventually he went into the Services, enjoying life in the Navy. David Linley hated sport and, as a pacifist, refused to go into the Services. From both his parents he had inherited a creative flair which was obvious from very early on.

David was not a great academic, but when he went to Ashdown Preparatory School in Sussex he excelled in music and enjoyed playing the piano, like Princess Margaret, and made a first attempt at carpentry, encouraged by his equally practical father. One Christmas Princess Margaret received a wooden bird-box which David had made himself. This was a foretaste of things to come, for today, when Princess Margaet dines with the Prince and Princess of Wales, it is at a table made by her son and given to Charles and Diana as a wedding gift.

When the Snowdon marriage began to crack, David had begun to board at Bedales co-educational school in Hampshire and so was away from the tensions at home. Originally Lord Snowdon wanted his son to follow in his footsteps, and study at Eton, followed by Jesus College, Cambridge, but David refused to go, the academic demands being too great. Like Princess Margaret, David was already failing to match up to the conventional image, and rebelled against being royal. Fortunately, at Bedales David's creativity was nurtured and he began to take a particular interest in furniture-making. As someone interested in well-crafted furniture, David Linley was born into the perfect family. He had in his Aunt Lilibet's homes the finest examples of Sheraton, Heppelwhite and Chippendale designs. In his father's workshop he was able to create simple pieces of his own, and at school he shared this interest with a friend Matthew Rice. Determined that her son should not be restricted in his life by royal pressures, Princess Margaret has always given David the freedom to follow his own inclinations and whatever career he had chosen, he could count on his mother's support.

After Bedales, David decided to enter for a two-year course in cabinet-making at the John Makepeace School for Craftsmen in Wood at Parnham in Dorset. First he had to prove his talent; there was no question of his being able to study a very practical course simply because he was Princess Margaret's son if he lacked the necessary skills. He was accepted and emerged two years later with his own rough edges refined. At the end of the course, Princess Margaret went to see some of her son's work on display and was amused, but not surprised, that the items he had made included a toilet-roll holder and a towel rail. The towel rail that she still uses in her own bathroom had been made by Lord Snowdon.

The latter years of David's study had been dominated by his parent's divorce and it was noticed that he spent some of his free time in the workshops at Buckingham Palace where the Queen's furniture is repaired and re-upholstered. He found that the physical activities used to create something out of wood, sawing, planing, chiselling, sanding, helped to release tension. On a piece of wood he could creatively release pent-up aggression.

Within days of leaving the John Makepeace School, David set up his own woodworking business in a converted bakery in Dorking with his first partner, Charles Wheeler-Carmichael. Single-mindedly, he was intent on pursuing a career of his own and wanted to make his money through his own endeavours rather than by inheritance. His entrepreneurial spirit is strong. He knows full well that being Princess Margaret's son has its advantages, giving him first-class publicity and in some cases gaining him customers simply because, and only because, he is the Queen's nephew. He is, however, sensible enough to realise that unless the standard of his work is high, the business will collapse. People may be prepared to pay more for David Linley products, (one of his tables cost an American buyer £55,000), but ultimately, if his workmanship is shoddy, his reputation will suffer.

In July 1984 it was necessary for him to move to larger premises, this time a Victorian building in Betchworth, Surrey, called The White House. Princess Margaret, with tongue firmly in cheek, performed a mock opening ceremony by cutting a silver ribbon across the door with an enormous saw.

Throughout his career Princess Margaret has always been there to support him, but the facts clearly prove that David Linley's craftsmanship have won him more orders than royal patronage, which has only been the icing on the cake. In September 1982 the Princess went to Regent's Park, to the former New Zealand High Commission residence, to see a woodwork exhibition which included some Linley pieces, a white sycamore box and one of his rainbow screens. The box sold for £2,500 and orders poured in for the screens. Five months later, Princess Margaret again went to another exhibition at the Park Lane Hotel, but it was through David's products, not her presence, that an order came in for fourteen tables from the Theatre Royal in Bath, plus numerous orders from America.

In 1985 a shop opened at Number One New King's Road in Chelsea, bearing the trade name David Linley Furniture Ltd. Having built up a reputation, David felt confident enough to set up a new business with his Bedales schoolfriend Matthew Rice, with Dr Miriam Stoppard as Marketing Director. In October of that year, Princess Margaret, vibrantly dressed in red and gold, went along to the shop launching party at Christies with seven other members of the family. As always, the Princess put on her glasses and inspected David's furniture thoroughly. Since he and Matthew had holidayed in Venice, much of their work had a Venetian influence. They were selling intricate marquetry screens for £7,500, mirrors for £5,000 and at the opposite end of the spectrum, stationery items, letter racks and pen holders, for under £10. Many smaller pieces resembled classical buildings, each having an antiqued appearance in line with the vogue for nostalgia.

That same year David moved out of Kensington Palace after buying a £200,000 apartment of his own, once part of a women's prison, from the actor John Standing. Princess Margaret had to accept that her son had finally grown up and flown the nest.

In 1988 Princess Margaret saw David's career develop still further. When in the spring he launched a new range of china and glass at the prestigious Mappin and Webb store in London's Regent Street, he was again influenced by the Princess, who uses a china tea set which she designed herself. It is cobalt blue porcelain with a white feather design (a joke on cowardice?). The teapot has a knob on the lid shaped like a coronet and each piece bears her personal monogram – the letter 'M' beneath a coronet, which also appears on her personal stationery. David and Matthew Rice also launched a range of notepaper under the name 'Rice Paper'.

Also in 1988, David went into partnership with Lord Patrick Lichfield, his photographer cousin, and opened the Chelsea restaurant Deals. The man responsible for the cooking in the restaurant is Eddie Lim, which is how the name developed. *D*avid *E*ddie *A*nd *L*ichfield*S*. The restaurant has high-backed chairs that form screens, enabling diners to eat in relative privacy if they wish. With typical business sense, David invited 500 taxi drivers to the opening so that they would all know where to drive their passengers. He jokes that he wants to open a chain of restaurants throughout Britain. Already he is floating his furniture company on the stock market and looks set to become the first member of the Royal Family to become a millionaire through his own work.

Princess Margaret is extremely proud of her son's success. Although she is herself artistic, David has also in his ancestry not only Linley Sambourne after whom he was named, but also the famed singer Elizabeth Linley, lover of the playwright Richard Brinsley Sheridan, with whom she eloped. Elizabeth posed as St Cecilia for the artist Sir Joshua Reynolds, so is now immortalised in oils. From the Princesss, David has also inherited a love of parties. In 1984 he offered his patronage to charity for the first time by organising a Raj Ball at the London Lyceum which eventually raised £35,000 for OXFAM. He sat on the committee with Rosie Clayton (daughter of Lady Mary Clayton, who lives at Kensington Palace) and Susannah Constantine, with whom his name has been romantically linked since 1983. David sold tickets to his many friends and younger members of the family. Even his sister, Lady Sarah, had to pay £25 for the ticket, as did Prince Edward and Lady Helen Windsor. He persuaded Tom McPhillips, an artist friend, to paint a large backdrop of the Taj Mahal, but he built large cages himself to house white doves and on the night joined the throng dressed as an Indian Prince. Princess Margaret took a great interest in the affair and lent her son a brooch to wear on the high collar of his costume.

David Linley has inherited many of his mother's characteristics. He may resemble his father, Lord Snowdon, physically, but when photographed beside Princess Margaret there is no question as to his parentage. He has his parents' small stature and his blue eyes can be as icy as his mother's when anyone becomes too familiar; despite a craving to be non-royal, he demands that Kensington Palace staff refer to him as Sir, just as Princess Margaret requires respect. Holidaying on Mustique in the summer of 1989 he was seen constantly driving around the island in his open-topped jeep, wearing Bermuda shorts patterned with frogs, but whether in the company of Elton John's manager, John Reid, or dancing at 'Basil's' bar, his face bore a permanent scowl. Reminiscent of Princess Margaret's 'acid drop' expression, if it is to make him unapproachable to outsiders, it certainly works.

In total contrast is Princess Margaret's daughter, Lady Sarah

Armstrong-Jones, whose large smile seems to be her permanent expression. Although said to be an adored 'Daddy's Girl', Lady Sarah seems to have emerged relatively unscathed from her parents' divorce. Divorce still remains an ugly word in her family, however, and when she became romantically involved with the chocolate heir, Cosmo Fry, she ended the relationship because he had been divorced. She knew that if they ever became engaged they would instantly be compared to her mother and Peter Townsend, and ill feeling might arise if she could marry a divorced man when her mother could not. It would also open up the age-old question: as Lady Sarah is currently 13th in line to the throne, she would be subject to the 1772 Royal Marriages Act, which had dogged Princess Margaret's happiness.

Like her brother Viscount Linley, Sarah has inherited her mother's and father's artistic streak. Born at Kensington Palace on 1 May 1964, she began her education in the now familiar pattern, in the Buckingham Palace Schoolroom with Prince Edward and James Ogilvy. From there she went to Frances Holland School, a day school in London, before following her brother to Bedales. She too was artistic rather than academic, and Bedales encouraged her talents. When she left with one 'A' level in art she went immediately to Camberwell Art School. On completion, she took a year away from conventional study and developed her own form of education. She joined her father in India, Lord Snowdon having been commissioned to take the still photographs on the set of David Lean's film *A Passage to India*; she acted as photographic assistant and unpaid wardrobe assistant. On returning to Britain, she took a course in stained glass in Cambridge; she undertook a make-up course with Mandy James, learning tricks of the modelling trade, and studied wood-gilding with Lord Snowdon's cousin, Thomas Messel.

When her year's sabbatical had ended, she enrolled for a two-year course in textile and fabric design at Middlesex Polytechnic for a BA degree, then applied for, but failed to get, a place at the Royal College of Art. In 1988 she began a three-year postgraduate class at the Royal Academy Art School which she will complete in 1991.

What is immediately apparent is that both Princess Margaret's children appear to have boundless energy and a desire to learn. This is something that Princess Margaret instilled into them at an early age. Queen Mary had taught her always to ask questions – there is no better brief for someone undertaking royal duty – and Princess Margaret told her children to do the same. Even when not studying, Sarah has worked part-time in a small film studio in Rotherhithe, where she met one of her former boyfriends, Piers Lea. It cannot have escaped Princess Margaret's notice that the location of Sarah's meetings was an area of London so familiar to herself. Sarah's name has not been linked with as many future husbands as the Princess, perhaps because she has the great advantage of being able to travel on the buses and undergrounds dressed in typical student clothes and totally unrecognised. Serious boyfriends have been few, apart from Cosmo Fry and Piers Lea, there has been Gerard Faggionato, an Italian art gallery assistant, and currently Daniel Chatto. Daniel is the son of theatrical agent Ros Chatto and impresario Robin Fox, and is himself an actor, appearing notably in the highly acclaimd film of Charles Dickens' *Little Dorrit*. Many think that the couple, who have known each other since 1982, will eventually marry. Certainly neither Sarah nor David is in any hurry to marry, determined not to follow in their parents' footsteps.

By venturing into the worlds of carpentry and art, Princess Margaret's children are getting deliberately as far away from a royal lifestyle as possible. It is possible that Prince Edward has followed suit by entering the theatrical profession. These are all areas that anyone, from any class, can make a stab at; the only requirements in each case are talent and an aptitude for hard work. Neither David nor Sarah could hope to succeed in their professions if they lacked essential skills. No amount of string pulling from members of the Royal Family can create a carpenter or an artist.

When David moved away from the security restrictions at Kensington Palace and opted for the independence of his own home, it was not long before Sarah wanted to move out also. Never one to hold her offspring back, Princess Margaret had set up a trust fund for her children which enabled Sarah to buy a house. She rents out the basement to a singing student, Dominic Best, and shares the top two floors with an old schoolfriend from Bedales, Katherine Blisher. When Sarah submitted work to the Royal Academy's Summer Exhibition, she did so anonymously so that it would be included and judged on its artistic merits alone rather than because of her name. Despite Sarah's constant attempts at anonymity, she still confessed that boys were intimidated by her royal connections.

Staying deliberately out of the limelight has not prevented the carefree Sarah from finding herself the subject of press fairy stories. In the autumn of 1989 one Sunday newspaper reported that Sarah had deliberately boycotted the wedding of actress Emma Hardy (daughter of actor Robert Hardy) to merchant banker Hamish Bullough, on the grounds that he was an old boyfriend. Sarah had never been linked with Bullough and stayed away from the wedding for one very good reason. She was not sent an invitation.

The childhood of Princess Margaret's children was anything but normal, no matter how hard she strove to keep them out of the public eye. There were times when Princess Margaret may have overcompensated her children for the disruption caused by her marital problems, for example, by overindulging Viscount Linley in his passion for cars. Close friends suggested that he had a confidence problem and that the vehicles helped provide a macho image – shades of Princess Margaret herself, who lacked self-confidence when young while managing to give the appearance of being in control. Although Viscount Linley used to be spotted riding to work on a sporty red and yellow pushbike, by the age of twenty-five he owned a Mercedes SL, a Ford Escort XR3i Cabriolet, an Aston Martin DB5 that had once belonged to Peter Sellers, and a large BMW motorcycle, and by the end of that year had received a six-month ban from driving after a collection of motoring offences. In February 1982 he was fined not only for driving at 98 mph on the M1 but also for failing to produce a licence. The following April he was fined after driving through red traffic lights. A year later he had his licence endorsed for allowing a friend to drive his BMW motorcycle without insurance. In August 1987 he was stopped on the A1 in Hertfordshire for speeding at 100 mph, and again five days later for travelling at 98 mph on the M4 near Heathrow Airport. In August 1989 he crashed his Aston Martin into a Porsche within yards of Kensington Palace, damaging both cars. He travelled on his BMW motorcycle to the police station to report the incident and while inside, a motorist knocked the cycle over while trying to park. In private, he once sent his girlfriend, Susannah Constantine, flying as she perched on the bonnet of his car and he put his foot on the accelerator. He received a warning from the police for riding his motorcycle too fast along the exclusive road that runs along the back of Kensington Palace, and received complaints from residents when he returned home at night playing music on his car stereo too loudly. It would seem that he flaunts his position, as if being the son of Princess Margaret places him above the law. It is taking a long time for him to learn that it does not. Princess Margaret has allowed her children to have the independence when young that she was never free to enjoy herself and as a result has not interfered. While David and Sarah have ben allowed to enjoy the fruits of their own success, so too they must pick up the pieces when they make mistakes.

Lady Sarah Armstrong-Jones and Viscount Linley have deliberately opted not to receive a Civil List income and do not therefore have official duties. They are seen in public only at major family events, where they play a supporting role. One notable exception came in May 1987 when they chose to accompany Princess Margaret on an official visit to China and Hong Kong. It was a real family affair, with an official portrait of the Princess taken to mark the visit by Lord Snowdon. For the portrait, Princess Margaret chose to wear the Poltimore tiara that she had worn on their wedding day. It was said that the reason for the children's rare inclusion on this visit was that it was a birthday treat for Sarah, but many felt that the Princess and Lord Snowdon still try to compensate for the unhappiness that their divorce must have caused. The official picture Tony took of all three, as opposed to Princess Margaret's solo portrait, included a large globe, symbolic of their journey; it echoes the very first royal photograph he took more than thirty years before, when he photographed Prince Charles and Princess Anne in 1956.

The Queen's visit to China a year earlier, from which she had returned with enthusiasm, spurred the Armstrong-Jones family to see that exciting country. Princess Margaret requested that pageantry and protocol be kept to the minimum so that the official visit became a relaxed family holiday despite her full programme. The fun of the preparation, the choosing of their wardrobes, the laughter on the flight, the constant taking of family photographs and the purchase of mementoes, turned the trip to China into one of the happiest and most relaxed of all royal visits. They do all holiday on Mustique, but there Princess Margaret is surrounded by friends, David and Sarah take along companions, and it becomes a houseparty. In China, despite the necessary formalities, this was not *Princess* Margaret, *Lady* Sarah Armstrong-Jones and *Viscount* Linley but instead merely a mother with her two children.

Princess Margaret's approach to bringing up her children may have been seen as unconventional in its time. The Queen seemed progressive when she sent Prince Charles and Princess Anne to exclusive boarding schools, but Princess Margaert quickly took her children away from the Palace schoolroom and placed them in local day schools, which prevented them from feeling set apart from other children. When Sarah and David eventually went to boarding school, the Princess visited as a parent, going to prize-givings and sports day, watching pantomimes and nativity plays; the only concession she made was in once agreeing to draw raffle tickets. In private she took the children to the Ideal Home Exhibition, visited galleries and concerts, theatres and cinemas. These were adventures she had herself experienced in the company of Crawfie while her parents placed duty first. Princess Margaret was determined from the outset that she was going to share in her own children's development rather than place them in the hands of a governess, to be kept in the nursery and brought out for just a few hours a day.

Today Princess Margaret and Lord Snowdon still enjoy their children and have never stopped being mother and father, never vying for affection or creating difficulties over access. Sarah and David accepted their parents' separation as a fact of life and they are none the worse of the split. They have gained in having two contented parents apart, rather than two feuding parents under the same roof.

When the Princess sees the sometimes uncontrollable antics of Princes William and Harry, hears criticism of Prince Edward for not pulling his weight, knows of the heartache Marina Ogilvy has caused her mother and father, then looks at her own two children carving out successful lives in their own right, she must feel that her abilities as a mother are now beyond reproach.

CHAPTER EIGHT

Life in a Goldfish Bowl

'Some people imagine that I lie on a sofa all day waiting for the evening to come and the next party to begin,' Princess Margaret once said. When I began studying the Princess's working life someone said to me, 'It must be difficult. She's not done anything for the last twenty years.' This assumption is common, unfounded and sad; in fact her engagements over the last two decades total in excess of 3000. Yet how many are reported by anyone other than the local media in the area that she visits? Considering the coverage that the Princess of Wales and Duchess of York receive, it must be extremely frustrating not only for Princess Margaret, but for her equally hard-working staff.

As a working member of the Royal Family, in 1987 for example, Princess Margaret made 95 official visits, attended 25 receptions and dinners, undertook 9 investitures and audiences, attended 129 engagements in the United Kingdom and spent 17 full days of engagements in official overseas tours. In a study compiled by *London Illustrated* magazine between 1 May 1988 and 30 April 1989, it is revealed that the Princess undertook 155 engagements, comprising 55 opening ceremonies, 31 charity shows and galas, 7 lunches and 3 official receptions, 11 banquets and dinners, 8 Privy Council meetings, 4 audiences and spent 16 days overseas on official tours during which time she undertook 36 engagements. Not bad for someone who lies on a couch all day and does nothing. She came ahead of the Queen Mother (105 engagements), the Duke and Duchess of York (15 and 109 respectively) and Prince Edward (92).

Princess Margaret's working style is individual and at times unconventional. She will not flatter her hosts, for example, refusing to eat with chopsticks when she visited China, even though the Queen and the Duke of Edinburgh had done so a year earlier. Yet she shows unexpected compassion to those in need. Events in China dominated the news in mid-1989, and when the Princess attended a performance of *Carmen* at Earl's Court on 7 June, the title role was sung by the Chinese soprano Ning Liang. When she was introduced to the Princess after the show, the conversation centred around her relatives in the strife-torn capital, Beijing. 'I'll say a special prayer tonight for you and your family,' said the Princess as she departed. Her concern had been genuine and her interest deep-seated, after her visit to China in 1987 with Viscount Linley and Lady Sarah Armstrong-Jones. The country, like so many that she has visited (see Appendix III), has made a great impact and she has an album full of her own photographs.

More than forty years have now passed since Princess Margaret began her official royal career. This has inevitably led to the development of her own style. She has no time for officials or sycophants, and shuns events such as Buckingham Palace Garden Parties which simply involve making small talk, yet she has a vast knowledge of the fifty organisations of which she is Patron, and will often arrange tea parties at Kensington Palace for the Girl Guide movement, for example, where she feels a much closer involvement.

Her method of coping with imperious officialdom is often to send it up. Faced with a long line-up of people to meet, she was introduced to a man who had announced:

'I'm in textiles, and I sit on the Bench.'

'You sit on the Bench in textiles,' said Princess Margaret coolly. 'How interesting, but uncomfortable.' She walked on to the next person. Whereas the Queen has the art of making everyone she meets feel as if she has the greatest interest in all that they have to say, her sister is interested in worthwhile causes and people who really have something to say. She gives endlessly of her time to the Sunshine Homes and Schools for Blind Children, an organisation with which she has been involved for four decades, because she feels that her work is beneficial. However if she gets the idea that her presence at a function is gratuitous then her patience snaps. After one particular engagement the organisers had arranged a small private party for the Princess and her entourage, and pre- suming that the Princess would appreciate something 'out of the ordinary' they set up a buffet in the cellar and lit it with candles. 'What on earth are we doing in this dump?' Margaret asked, and the buffet had to be moved. Her lack of tolerance and no-nonsense approach have inevitably led to criticism, sometimes justifiable, but the Princess becomes irritated when taken for granted, or treated like her media image rather than her true self. She has arrived at receptions to find that large bottles of gin will be provided for her use, even though she does not drink alcohol.

Anyone who has closely watched Princess Margaret and the Princess Royal at work will be aware of a striking similarity. They are both curious for knowledge and ask blunt questions which invariably take people off guard. Both do their homework beforehand, which can lead to disconcerting questions for the ill-prepared. When Princess Margaret talks about one of the charities with which she is involved she will continually say what 'we' have achieved or 'our helpline' rather than what 'they' have done or 'the NSPCC helpline', because she is inextricably involved in their work. She is not a figurehead but part of a team. When attending special Girl Guide functions she will wear a full uniform to prove that she is not simply there as Princess Margaret but as President of the Girl Guides. Her patronages are fewer in number than those taken on by some members of the Royal Family, but the Princess has always deliberately kept them to a manageable number to enable her to have a greater degree of involvement. At the start of her working life invitations requesting her patronage poured in to Buckingham Palace by the thousand, but she carefully selected only those in which she had a particular personal interest and to which she could provide practical help. Much of her work involves fund-raising and meeting charity workers and it would be extremely difficult to do this successfully if she lacked enthusiasm for the cause.

To take an obvious example, her involvement with the Girl Guides Association has lasted more than fifty years. It was on 13 December 1937 that she enrolled as a Brownie and she feels that her early love of Guiding as a Brownie, Guide, Ranger and Sea Ranger held her in good stead, not only for her role as President, but through the challenges of life. She says that she was 'brought up to know that one shouldn't do things only for oneself, but for other people too'. Throughout the year Princess Margaret takes a very active role. She takes the Chair at Council Meetings, attends

Officially engaged. Princess Margaret and Antony Armstrong-Jones at Royal Lodge on the day their engagement was announced. (Hulton)

Above: Princess Margaret in pensive mood on her wedding day. (Camera Press)

Below: The bride and groom wave to the crowds from the balcony of Buckingham Palace, 6 May, 1960. (Popperfoto)

Left: The Snowdon family at play in their garden at Kensington Palace, October 1965. (Camera Press)

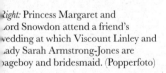

Right: Princess Margaret and Lord Snowdon attend a friend's wedding at which Viscount Linley and Lady Sarah Armstrong-Jones are pageboy and bridesmaid. (Popperfoto)

Before embarking on an official visit to China and Hong Kong in 1987 Princess Margaret posed for Lord Snowdon with her children, Viscount Linley and Lady Sarah Armstrong-Jones, for this relaxed official portrait. (Camera Press)

A formal portrait of Princess Margaret wearing the Poltimore tiara which she purchased herself. (Camera Press)

Above: In November 1989 as President of ICAN Princess Margaret visited Pilgrims' School, Seaford, which she helped found. With the Princess are (left to right) actress Nanette Newman, Dr L. Scott (Chairman), a student, Dr K. McGhee (the school's G.P.) and Miss R. Scott. (ICAN)

Below left: For more than half a century Princess Margaret has been actively involved in the Girl Guides Association and attends many functions each year as their President. (Popperfoto)

Below right: Having reached the milestone of her sixtieth birthday Princess Margaret proves that she has not lost any of her earlier glamour. (Rex Features)

Above left: Defying medical opinion, Princess Margaret still continues to smoke despite one serious cancer scare. (Syndication International)

Above right: Holding court on Mustique. Princess Margaret's houseparty includes (from left) Dominic Elliott, Colin Tennant, Basil Charles, Nicholas Courtenay and Lady Anne Tennant. Behind the camera is her cousin Patrick Lichfield. (Camera Press)

Below: Within days of Lord Snowdon's remarriage in December 1978 Princess Margaret appeared publicly with Roddy Llewellyn to see a performance of *Under the Greenwood Tree* at London's Vaudeville Theatre. Her children seem very ill at ease. (Camera Press)

Past and present. Princess Margaret stands in the entrance hall of her Kensington Palace apartment beneath the Annigoni portrait, painted when she was twenty-six. (Photographers International)

rallies, conferences, adventure days and festivals, visits camps, launches dinghies, opens new buildings, and each year since 1986 has given, on average, two receptions for recipients of the Queen's Guide Brooch in her apartment at Kensington Palace. Following the formal presentations, those present are entertained to afternoon tea and the Princess makes a point of talking to every person present. 'We know Her Royal Highness loves meeting and talking with the girls and we always ask that this is taken into account when her programme is being planned,' says Dr June Paterson-Brown, the Chief Commissioner, who knows from experience now that when the minute-by-minute schedule is drawn up for a royal visit, sufficient time must be included to allow the Princess to chat.

The year 1990 marks the eightieth anniversary of the founding of the Girl Guides Association. A new uniform has been introduced, with suggested designs submitted to the Princess, and she took a great interest in viewing the first samples, well remembering her first uniform fifty years ago. Because of her long involvement, she took an active part in the 80th anniversary celebrations and no doubt looked back over some of the highlights in her life:

1937 Enrolled as a Brownie, 1st Buckingham Palace Brownie Pack. Gained her Swimmer Badge.

1942 Enrolled as a Guide, 1st Buckingham Palace Company at Windsor. Gained 2nd Class Badge.

1943 Elected Patrol Leader of the Bullfinches.

1944 Gained 1st Class Badge.
Also went to camp 1943, 1944 and 1945

1945 Gained Little House Emblem and All-Round Cords.
Gained following Interest Badges:
    Artist
    Athlete
    Child Nurse
    Cook
    Emergency Helper
    Home Maker
    Horsewoman
    Hostess
    Interpreter
    Laundress

Needlewoman
Pioneer

1946   Enrolled as a Sea Ranger in SRS *Duke of York*.
Spent four days aboard the training ship *MTB 630* at Dartmouth.

1947   Took the salute in the Mall at the Scout and Guide International Folk Dance Festival.

1949   Became Commodore of the Sea Ranger Section.

1950   Attended the camp fire ceremony at Oxford in connection with the 13th World Conference of the Girl Guides and Girl Scouts.

1953   Became Chief Ranger of the British Commonwealth and Empire.

1960   Guest of Honour at Gala Night of the Wembley Pageant to celebrate Golden Jubilee Year.

1965   BECAME PRESIDENT OF THE GIRL GUIDES ASSOCIATION.

1968   Attended launch of new Eight Point Programme.
Presented with Silver Fish for service to the Movement.

1970   Diamond Jubilee Year. Attended camps in Cheshire and Scotland.
Wrote for the first issue of magazine *Today's Guide*.

1975   Opened 22nd World Conference of Girl Guides and Girl Scouts.

1977   Attended film première in aid of G.G.A. Training Centres.

1981   Attended the Service of Dedication of a joint memorial to Robert and Olave Baden-Powell.

1983   Attended the press launch to mark the introduction of the Baden-Powell Trefoil and Queen's Guide Brooch.

1985   Launched 'Guide Week' – highlight of the 75th Anniversary celebrations.

1986   Presented the first 50 Queen's Guides with their brooches at Kensington Palace.
Became a founder member of the Olave Baden-Powell Society.

This brief catalogue skims only the surface of Princess Margaret's involvement, but it emphasises her qualifications as President and her true seniority which has given her more experience than any Girl Guide or Guide Leader today. She understands every aspect of the movement from finances to executive policy and is quick to point out anything that seems amiss.

Each year Princess Margaret will travel all over Britain to attend Guide functions, but despite her personal enjoyment of the visits each has to be planned like a military manoeuvre beforehand. In line with every other working engagement, it begins with a simple invitation addressed to her Private Secretary, the Lord Napier and Ettrick. He will sort the many invitations received into piles of 'maybes' and 'definites', with occasional 'nevers', before presenting them to the Princess. Contrary to popular belief, there has never been any shortage of invitations to Princess Margaret and there has never been any question of other members of the Royal Family passing engagements on, to give her something to do.

Tentative planning of the engagement diary always begins some six months in advance, although invitations arrive every week. It is easier to fix dates together in concentrated sessions, and enables the Princess to plan a series of engagements in an area of the country. If they were accepted at random she could find herself in Scotland one day, Devon the next, and back to Scotland the day after. For that reason alone, all the Scottish invitations will be grouped so that a programme can be fitted neatly together. At the end of November 1989, for example, Princess Margaret undertook a series of engagements in the North of England in ten days, visiting Newcastle-upon-Tyne to open a new shopping centre (17th); as Grand President of the St John Ambulance Association and Brigade, she accepted the Freedom of the City of Newcastle-upon-Tyne (18th), went to Berwick-upon-Tweed (20th), opened the NSPCC's Derbyshire Child Protection Team's Unit in Ripley (24th), met workers and sponsors of the NSPCC and attended a lunch in Derby and after lunch visited the restored Market Hall (27th). In the same month the Princess had received press criticism because she had not been present with other members of the Royal Family at the Cenotaph in London on Remembrance Sunday. Why, it was asked, does Princess Margaret not feel it necessary to pay tribute to those who gave their lives for their country? So angered was Lord Napier that he wrote to the Press to explain that the Princess had been present at the Remembrance Day Service in Lichfield Cathedral in Staffordshire. On Friday 10th she had visited the

University of Keele in Staffordshire and later a factory, and had remained in the county over the weekend to fulfil duties in Hanley, Stafford, and Stoke-on-Trent on Monday 13th. Conscious that many members of her family would be present at the London Remembrance Services and her presence would only swell the ranks, she had felt that her presence at Lichfield Cathedral would be of greater benefit. Had Lord Napier not felt compelled to write to the newspapers, all would have assumed that Princess Margaret had simply had the weekend off.

In the Press's defence, however, both Clarence House (whose press office releases details of Princess Margaret's public duties) and Kensington Palace (where engagements are organised) are extremely difficult about giving out information regarding the Princess's public life. For several years I have regularly broadcast for the BBC, giving details of when, where and how the Royal Family can be seen, and discussing some of their more interesting engagements. While the Queen's staff at Buckingham Palace are extremely efficient at giving me information, as are the staff of the Duke and Duchess of Kent, and Princess Alexandra, often great secrecy will surround Princess Margaret's work. Popular magazines such as *Royalty* and *Majesty* always publish a monthly engagement diary, but often Princess Margaret's is missing. As a result, she is the one who suffers through public ignorance. Even her engagement diary of November 1989 did not state that she would be at Lichfield Cathedral on Remembrance Sunday. Her presence there may have been through personal choice rather than official invitation, but it is little wonder that misunderstandings arise.

The problem with Princess Margaret's staff is that they are intensely loyal, but this results in their being too protective towards her. The author James Pope-Hennessy, respected biographer of Queen Mary, wrote: 'It is *courtiers* who make royalty frightened and frightening. Taken neat . . . they are perfectly all right. This does not mean that they are as others, but you can get on to plain terms with the species.'

Lord Napier has become so used to fielding newspapers and magazine reporters intrigued by Princess Margaret's life, that on occasions public information is withheld also.

The task of planning the royal diary was described by biographer Harold Nicolson as 'a nightmare' and Lord Napier would undoubtedly agree, for once Princess Margaret has accepted an invitation it is he who must plan a minute-by-minute itinerary, arrange for the necessary travel to be made available, which means if necessary booking a helicopter of the Queen's Flight (which the Princess must pay for) or ordering the royal train (now only a special carriage attached to a British Rail passenger train). Princess Margaret's main consideration will be to give priority to the charities she patronises. She will take into account those that she has visited in recent months, which perhaps do not warrant a return visit quite so soon. There may be an event which she considers might be 'exciting' and requires to be looked into further. Centenaries and anniversaries are always borne in mind, as these are not events that can be postponed until another year. The main credentials are date, location and justification.

Once Princess Margaret has agreed, it is then usually Lord Napier's role to undertake a recce to the place in question to make arrangements. This even necessitated a visit to China in 1987 *before* the Princess, to put plans into operation. The planning of official duties and foreign tours involves far more than simply filling in blank spaces in the diary. Each detail is planned, down to measuring every step the Princess will take. Up to twelve weeks' preparation can go into a two-hour visit, with itinerary after itinerary drawn up. Lists of people that the Princess will meet are compiled and vetted. Lord Napier will deal with the more mundane details, such as cloakroom facilities, and on the final itinerary you will see the words 'Retiring room has been set aside for use by Her Royal Highness'. If Princess Margaret is to eat, there has to be a rehearsal beforehand with the complete meal cooked and presented to make sure that it fits exact requirements. Lord Napier will not give out a list of the Princess's likes and dislikes, but will instead ask to see a menu which can be amended accordingly. Princess Margaret is a great lover of soup at home, but seldom eats it in public as it can be filling and might lead to more visits to the 'retiring room' than necessary. She dislikes fruit with meat, such as lamb with apricots or duck with orange, and prefers plain, simply cooked food that is British. Scotch beef followed by English raspberries or strawberries, perhaps with an asparagus or Scotch salmon starter would be met with approval.

For a two-hour visit to Quedgeley in Gloucestershire, for example, Lord Napier had to arrange for a helicopter to take the Princess to RAF 7MU Quedgeley, plus a royal car to take the

Princess on the five-minute journey to the Scout and Guide Headquarters that she was to open (22 June 1988). It had to be decided
who would meet her. The County Commissioner for Scouts? The
Chief Commissioner for Guides? Eventually it was settled that the
Lord Lieutenant of Gloucestershire should welcome the Princess
off the helicopter. A list was drawn up of who she should meet,
starting with dignitaries from the local Council, followed by the
senior members of the Scout and Guide movement. As the Princess
was to tour an exhibition, the Commissioner for the Guides and the
Group Scout Leader had to escort Lord Napier around the displays
to work out the exact timings. This was to be followed by a short
ceremony at which the Princess would unveil a commemorative
plaque.

Lord Napier issued special instructions regarding the plaque
that Princess Margaret would unveil:

> The Plaque will measure 24" x 18" and will be made of wood,
> with the following inscription painted thereon:
> 'Her Royal Highness, The Princess Margaret, Countess
> of Snowdon, opened these Headquarters on the 22nd June
> 1988'.

It was decided where the Visitors' book would be and when
the Princess would sign. It was agreed that a marquee should be
made available with light refreshments, if required, and to act as
a retiring room. Again specific instructions were issued:

> The Marquee will be erected by the Scouts as part of their
> contribution to the event . . . The retiring period will pro-
> vide time to 'muster the troops' outside, ready for HRH's
> departure.

A large umbrella was to be provided by the Scouts and Guides and
made 'available in case of inclement weather', and it was decided
that Princess Margaret would be presented with a posy of flowers
(in season and un-wired) by nine-year-old Brownie Erica Smith, at
the very end of the visit, so that Princess Margaret would be able
to attend to her duties throughout the afternoon without being
burdened by flowers. For her arrival and departure it was arranged
that a Guard of Honour would be formed:

The composition of the Guards of Honour will be a mixture of Beavers, Brownies, Cubs, Guides, Scouts and Young Leaders. This is to ensure that the maximum number of children will be afforded the opportunity of actually seeing HRH.

Similarly detailed arrangements have been made for every one of Princess Margaret's engagements. On the day before the event, such as for the opening of the Scout and Guide Headquarters, she will study a sheet of background information supplied to her by Lord Napier.

This brief will offer sufficient details for the Princess not only to understand what she is about to visit but also to plan the questions she will want to ask.

From Lord Napier's and the organisers' groundwork, a final detailed itinerary will be drawn up and it will be photographically reduced to fit inside Princess Margaret's handbag. It will contain an elaborate account of the afternoon's proceedings, listing precisely what she will see and who she will meet.

On 10 May 1989, Princess Margaret was Guest of Honour at a Charity Luncheon held at the Mansion House in London. With the Lord Mayor, Sir Christopher Collett, the Princess joined the 180 guests to launch the Silver Jubilee Appeal of The Migraine Trust, hoping to raise £500,000 towards research. The Migraine Trust was set up in 1965 to raise funds for research into this debilitating condition which affects some ten million people in Britain alone. The most famous sufferer was Princess Margaret, who used to be troubled with severe migraines for many years but, with the help of the Trust, now knows how to avoid them. Today she no longer suffers. As with the Girl Guides Association, the Princess therefore had a very personal interest in the work of the Trust, which she continues to support as Patron. In May 1973 she opened the Princess Margaret Migraine Clinic in London, the first of its kind in the world to observe and treat sufferers in acute attack; it is now run in association with the Charing Cross Hospital.

Migraine has been defined as 'the worst form of headache imaginable'; often it is preceded by distorted vision and vomiting. For some it strikes only a few times in their whole life, others suffer weekly. Those who suffer often receive little sympathy. Common causes of migraine are 'stress, worry, tension and anxiety in private and business life'. These are the words of the Trust, but who more than Princess Margaret has experienced stresses and anxiety in private and public life? The Migraine Trust produce a 'Trigger Check List' of the most likely causes, which apart from tension, include alcohol (Princess Margaret used to drink heavily), late rising, especially at weekends or holidays (when not working the Princess hates getting up early), irregular meals (royal duty means that there can never be a routine), bright sunlight and changes of climate (Princess Margaret has frequently travelled from the cold of the English winter to the heat of Mustique), travel (which is a basic requirement for all members of the Royal Family), missing meals and slimming (the Princess constantly watches her weight), plus, in individual people, certain foods such as chocolate, citrus fruits, dairy products, pork, fatty foods, even ice cream can bring on an attack. In others it can be hot baths, bright lights, the menopause, loud noises, even sexual intercourse. Princess Margaret has now established what her personal triggers are and knows how to avoid the problem, but her own suffering in the past has made her a firm believer in the Trust's work. She is anxious that people should make known their problem if they get migraines so that the severity can be recognised and understood. The Trust say that men in particular are frightened to reveal that they suffer, fearing they will be considered to be unstable and might be judged unsuitable for promotion in their work. In its varied forms migraine affects one in ten members of the population, and the Princess is delighted that the Trust and the Princess Margaret Migraine Clinic have helped promote a greater understanding and awareness of the condition. By the summer of 1989 Princess Margaret was already involved in the plans for the biennial symposium to be held over four days in September 1990 at Kensington Town Hall, just a few minutes' drive from her home, and had even then been told of the search for an even larger venue for what will be the 9th international symposium in 1992.

Once again, the Princess's involvement is total, her commitment greater because of personal experience, her fund-raising efforts inexhaustible in the knowledge that the Migraine Trust, which has funded more than sixty projects, is entirely dependent upon donations to survive. Although Princess Margaret's efforts have been successful in their way, her causes seldom receive the publicity given to the Princess Royal and the Save the Children Fund, or the Princess of Wales and Dr Barnado's, leaving much of her work unrecognised. A holiday on Mustique is more newsworthy, it would sometimes seem, than helping the millions of lives blighted by migraine in the United Kingdom alone.

One aspect of her work that Princess Margaret enjoys is witnessing the progress made by the organisations that she patronises, and knowing that her assistance with fund-raising and the publicity that her involvement provides has helped make the advances possible. In June 1989 Princess Margaret clocked up forty years as President of the Sunshine Homes for the Blind and when she first took on the Presidency, blindness in premature babies was common. A condition known as Retrolental Fibroplasia was the reason, but the cause had yet to be discovered. It took more than a decade's research to discover why some premature babies went blind – too much oxygen when confined in incubators for too long. Now very few babies go blind, and usually it is because of a congenital defect. A major step forward.

The Princess was also President of Barnardo's for forty years before handing it over to the Princess of Wales (see Chapter Seven), but she has gained the greatest acknowledgment for her role as President of the National Society for the Prevention of Cruelty to Children (NSPCC).

'Princess Margaret has been President of the NSPCC since 1953,' Giles Pegram, the Deputy Director, told me. 'She keeps up to date in all developments and is a regular visitor to our Child Protection Teams around the country. Over the years she has attended numerous openings, film premières, gala shows and other fund-raising events. But her interest goes much further. She is passionately interested in the plight of abused and neglected children and is committed to seeing that the NSPCC is geared to provide the best service to help them and their families. Princess Margaret, as President, is a great strength to the NSPCC.'

Her strength in this cause comes from regret. Regret that 106 years after it was founded the NSPCC is still necessary, handling more than 48,000 cases every year, a number that is increasing now that child abuse is discussed more openly and an NSPCC Helpline has been set up. When the charity reached its centenary, naturally Princess Margaret was there to mark the anniversary, but she was keen to point out that it was in no way a celebration. Because she comes from the most stable of backgrounds herself, Princess Margaret fully supports the Society's aims to make children feel safe and secure in their own homes. She also realises only too well how divorce can turn a child's world upside-down. Those scars can be helped to heal, but what shocks the Princess most are the large numbers of cases she comes across of incest, sexual and physical abuse of children, and deliberate cruelty which cause scars that can be permanent. The NSPCC is the only voluntary organisation which works to prevent cruelty and is authorised to bring proceedings in court for children's protection. The Society was set up because, while cruelty to animals was illegal by 1884, there were no such laws to protect children. More than a century later, an estimated 200 children still die each year from neglect or abuse. Thousands more suffer cruelty in their own homes from parents or guardians. Princess Margaret has opened a series of Protection Units throughout Britain which have teams of social workers who can help solve the problems by getting together with the families and children concerned. In the majority of cases children are, as a result, able to stay in their own homes rather than suffer further trauma by being taken into care.

On 8 June 1989 Princess Margaret opened the National Child Protection Training Centre in Leicester. The Princess was greeted by the NSPCC's Chairman, Mr Michael Moore, and its Director, Dr Alan Gilmour, after whom the Centre was to be named. Inside the Princess met senior NSPCC staff and representatives from Leicester University who were collaborating on a course for Social Workers. She also met the builders and architects who had designed the building. After a twenty-minute presentation Princess Margaret unveiled a plaque commemorating the opening of The Gilmour Centre, and received a posy from the daughter of one of the staff. The formalities over, Princess Margaret's real work began. For the next forty-five minutes she toured the building, meeting training staff en route and discussing their work. She met Child Protection Officers and some twenty representatives from the local social services, including the police. All experienced at first hand the Princess's in-depth knowledge of their work, and in turn she gathered new information herself. Already she had opened fifteen Child Protection Teams and was due to open three more before the end of the year, so could talk at length about the work.

Princess Margaret's support brings many benefits. First and foremost, her presence raises hard cash. In June 1987 a gala performance of Massenet's opera *Manon* was held at Covent Garden in London in aid of the NSPCC, and was followed by a ball in the Jubilee Hall. Tickets for the opera and ball cost £750 for one or £1,000 for two, raising considerable sums of money. People were prepared to pay the ticket prices not just because it was for charity but because Princess Margaret was there. Secondly, when the Princess pays an official visit to one of her organisations it not only gives the cause much needed publicity, but is an enormous boost for the morale of the workers. With the NSPCC, for example, this is very necessary. Child Protection Teams provide a 24-hour service and come across harrowing cases of child abuse. They do not know if abuse is on the increase, but the number of cases coming to light certainly is, due to higher public and professional awareness of the problem and a greater willingness to report suspected cases.

The very fact that the NSPCC's work is proving beneficial gives Princess Margaret heart. But her work with them is not all doom and gloom, for much of the fund-raising she does is fun, and in the call of duty she has been hoisted up on a mock cloud on stage at the Royal Opera House, Covent Garden, to lead the singing of 'Hark the Herald Angels Sing' at a Christmas concert. In 1984 she became the first member of the Royal Family to appear in a BBC drama, playing herself, in the long-running radio serial *The Archers* to publicise the NSPCC. That same year she flew secretly and under heavy security to Northern Ireland, attending a reception, and then later a garden party at Hillsborough Castle to raise money for the NSPCC. She managed a visit to Short Brothers Ltd to give them the Queen's Award for Export Achievement, and to take part in a Girl Guide rally at Lorne on the same trip. All in a day's work!

The appeal to Princess Margaret herself is that her work offers continual excitement and stimulation. It is never short of variety, and for someone who is easily bored that is a distinct advantage. One day she can be touring a Sainsbury's supermarket, the next attending a glittering State Banquet for a visiting Head of State. Some members of the Royal Family bemoan the fact that in their working life they meet so many people once, and only once. Princess Margaret's patronages have now spanned so many decades that there is continuity and she can return from time to time to old pastures and see the fruits of her labours. In 1955 she helped found the Pilgrims School in Seaford, Sussex (see Appendix IV) which is run by the Invalid Children's Aid Nationwide (ICAN); she returned twenty-five years later to take part in the school's silver jubilee celebrations in 1980, and in 1989 paid her fourth visit to this unique boarding school for asthmatic children. Originally the school was for boys only, but in 1985 it began to admit girls, necessitating a visit by the Princess to open a girls' wing; then in November 1989 she returned to open an extra wing for girls, the new block also housing a computer room, library and staff room. The new wing was named after the actress Nanette Newman, a supporter of ICAN, who had given royalties from her books to the charity. During the visit, Princess Margaret was welcomed by a message on one of the computer screens, a far cry from her first visit. It must have been with satisfaction that the Princess renewed acquaintance with the school she had founded thirty-five years earlier, knowing that it is still the only one of its kind in Europe to offer pupils with asthma, eczema and related problems round-the-clock medical attention.

Princess Margaret is also lucky that many of her engagements are as much pleasure as work. Every year she makes an official visit to the Daily Mail Ideal Home Exhibition, often accompanied around the exhibits by Viscountess Rothermere, but invariably she will return again for a private visit and will jostle through the crowds unnoticed. On her visit in March 1989 she was delighted to see a walnut dining-table inlaid with ebony, and a sideboard (both with £7,500 price tags) that had been made by David Linley Ltd. 'This is David's, look how beautifully crafted it is,' said the proud mother. In October 1989 the Princess went to a royal gala at the baroque Church of St John's, Smith Square, London, to help raise money for the St John's Organ Restoration Appeal. As she sat listening to Dame Joan Sutherland singing Tosti's *Serenata*, Gounod's *Garde La Couronne des Reines*, and Massenet's *O Si Les Fleurs Avaient Des Yeux*, she could have echoed her late friend Noël Coward, who said that 'Work is much more fun than fun'.

The world may like to believe that Princess Margaret lies on her sofa all day, in the world that she once described as a 'goldfish bowl', waiting for the next party to begin. That may be untrue, but as she now fulfils her official role with ease and panache, it is hard to believe that her life isn't a perpetual ball.

CHAPTER NINE

Off Duty

Once a month, an unexpected ritual takes place in the Garden Room of Princess Margaret's Kensington Palace home. This former guard room, now decorated in salmon pink and sea green, has large purpose-built cabinets in which Princess Margaret's prized collection of sea shells are displayed. She has collected them over the years from Italy, the West Indies, the Virgin Islands, the Seychelles, Australia, Bermuda and, naturally, Mustique – almost every coast that she has ever visited – resulting in what the Natural History Museum in London have classed as the most comprehensive assemblage of shells collected by an individual. Approximately every four weeks, the Princess and her staff face the onerous task of keeping the hundreds of shells clean. The staff remove them from the display, the Princess washes each delicate shell herself and then personally replaces them in their exact position, each specimen carefully labelled.

To Princess Margaret this is not a chore as every shell has its own special memory of a place where she has been happy. The Garden Room opens out on to a veranda looking out onto the largest walled garden in Kensington Palace, where the Princess spends as much time as possible sunbathing, especially in the hot summer of 1989. Here in the heart of London is what she considers to be a little piece of Mustique. Here, in total privacy, she is able to relax, surrounded by roses, two of which were planted to commemorate the birth of her children, and a large magnolia tree planted on the very first weekend she moved into Apartment 1A, almost thirty years ago.

Home for Princess Margaret is a four-storey wing of Kensington

Palace that has 21 rooms, including an elegant drawing-room, din-ing-room, kitchen, library, her own master bedroom, and rooms once occupied by Lord Snowdon, the two children, a nanny and a nursery which now offer guest accommodation. In the basement the staff have their own sitting-room and dining room; here Lord Snowdon once also had a dark-room and an office. On the top attic floor are staff bedrooms, and included in the house are now offices for Princess Margaret's Private Secretary, Lord Napier, and her Personal Secretary, Muriel Murray-Brown. Visitors entering the heavy front door of Sir Christopher Wren's Clock Court, one of three private courtyards in the Palace, find themselves in a large entrance hall with doors leading off to the drawing-room, dining-room and library. They are left in no doubt as to whose house this is. Dominating this hall, paved so effectively with black and white squares of Welsh stone, is the large portrait of Princess Margaret painted by Annigoni in 1957. The painting took six months to complete and required fifteen sittings from the Princess. The result has a dramatic, timeless quality; the Princess seems to be walking through a garden of wild roses at dusk, possibly symbolic of the sharp thorns that she has encountered in life. Annigoni has captured her full sensuous lips, and the penetrating blue eyes seem to watch you from any angle in the hall. In October 1988 Princess Margaret was photographed for a magazine, standing beneath the portrait, her hairstyle identical to that she had worn for her sittings. Despite the passing of thirty-one years the accuracy of the artist's work was striking. In this large hall the items on display reflect her personality. Beneath the portrait, on a marble-topped console table stands an antique mahogany and brass bracket clock, a pair of marble and ormolu urns, yet also a modern glass paperweight and a china plate from HMS *Norfolk*. Whereas the Queen's homes have elaborate floral displays very much in evidence, in Princess Margaret's home you will notice a small vase of dried flowers, a potted geranium, or a single-stemmed amaryllis.

At the heart of the house is Princess Margaret's impressive drawing-room, large enough to accommodate 100 people for a reception, a deliberate mixture of eighteenth-century elegance and homely comfort. The five tall windows looking out over the garden are draped with heavy grey silk curtains which fall from ceiling to floor, impressively swagged and tasselled, yet there are two large comfortable sofas on either side of the fireplace and several armchairs all upholstered in different colours as if brought together from another room, each piled with cushions. Princess Margaret's two favourite colours are blue and coral pink and these provide the themes of her home and her wardrobe. The walls of the drawing-room are wallpapered in rich kingfisher blue, the floor of dark polished wood is adorned with a huge carpet in patterns of blue, gold and peach, a wedding gift from the City of London, designed by Carl Toms.

At one end, a door leads into the library and at the same end of the room is a mahogany cabinet more than 18 feet long, with six arched glass doors which look almost like church windows. The spectacular cabinet displays Princess Margaret's collection of porcelain and curios, and at one time a glass spy-hole through from what was then Tony's study, so that people in the drawing-room could be secretly observed. This gadget enabled Lord Snowdon to make his entrance into the room when he knew that his own guests, journalists or business colleagues had arrived and were waiting for him. The chances are that the spy-hole still exists, disguised behind Princess Margaret's bookshelves. At this end of the room is Princess Margaret's piano, a baby grand, a wedding gift from Tony's mother and stepfather. It was one of their possessions that would obviously offer more enjoyment to the Princess than Lord Snowdon, and so it remained in position after the divorce. Princess Margaret's piano houses a collection of family photographs on the lid. Photographs of her children also dominate her desk at the opposite end of the room, beside two double doors which lead into the dining-room. Two blackamoor statues stand on either side of these doors as if heralding guests' entry in to dinner.

Princess Margaret's desk in the drawing-room, which is used for her personal correspondence as well as official papers, always appears to be cluttered. Besides the practical items of ornate letter openers, magnifying glass, paperweights, gold-colour sellotape dispenser, pens, pencils, rubber stamps and ink pads, plus two pushbutton telephones (one for internal, one for external calls) and a pile of official documents and engagement briefs to read, there are just as many ornaments. Her love of Bristol blue glass is apparent on the desk as throughout the house, but also on the desk will be a dozen rolls of film for the Princess's camera, a clock, wooden crucifixes, a collection of ornate pots and vases, sunglasses, credit cards, a leather framed calendar, and the ever-present ashtray. All items are there to provide subconscious security while the Princess is at work. Once her desk was positioned at right angles to the window, so that when seated the Princess faced the wall. Now it has been turned so that she can look out over the garden, and where her desk once stood is an elaborate three-tiered wooden plant stand which displays dozens of small porcelain boxes and pots. It is characteristic of the Princess that she works in the drawing-room surrounded by her *objets d'art*, not in a practical, purpose-made office. Beside her desk is always a small side-table so that books and papers can overspill. Handbags and shopping bags may be pushed underneath, with no attempt at tidiness. It all adds to the homely atmosphere that the Princess appreciates.

Around the walls are ornate gilded mirrors, adding to the impression of space. On the walls hang paintings by her favourite artists, Edward Seago, John Piper, Bryan Organ, Oliver Messel, and Anthony Fry. There is no central light-fitting in use, but a variety of lamps provide a subdued, romantic glow at night; this not only gives a cosy feel to the large room but is kinder to Princess Margaret's eyes, who, as a former migraine sufferer, dislikes very bright lights.

Privileged guests may see inside the library which contains more than 10,000 books that Princess Margaret has amassed over the years. Here are gifts from authors she has met, the works of Graham Greene, Iris Murdoch and Edith Sitwell; there are many large volumes about art with titles such as *Masterpieces of Painting*, *Great Paintings from the National Gallery of Art*, *Hubert and Jan Van Eyck*; not surprisingly there are many books on travel, Italy, Naples, Versailles. Like many of her rooms, the library has a feeling of space and timelessness, but the most noticeable point about the room is that every single book has been well read. Nothing appears pristine and untouched, none is there only for display.

The room that most guests see is the dining-room. The walls are sand-coloured, to match the Princess's love of the coast, with an oval mahogany table that can seat fourteen guests with ease, and decorated with paintings of Italy and Venice by John Piper. At Princess Margaret's place setting is a glass bell made of her favourite blue glass, and in the shape of a sea-shell. Like the drawing-room, the dining-room looks out over the garden. It is essentially an English room, despite the paintings; the fireplace is decorated with English oak leaves and acorns, and an antique bracket clock ticks soothingly in the background.

When the Snowdons refurbished the apartment in 1961 practically from scratch, they chose a style that was totally in keeping with the original building. They removed very ornate, oppressive ceilings, and made them completely plain so that the coving became easily discernable and the walls became a background to their favourite objects. Plain ugly fireplaces were removed and were replaced with elegant pieces of the appropriate period. Dark, rotting Victorian doors were removed and were replaced by elaborately ornate panelled doors. Where possible, they made the most of existing features, for example by fitting the bath into an alcove. In the bathroom they added Gothic cornices and columns and Lord Snowdon designed a hexagonal towel rail that has a glass top in which to display more sea-shells. Everywhere blue and pink are the predominant colours and shells, the favourite motif, even in the Princess's own bedroom.

Apartment 1A is now so indelibly stamped with Princess Margaret's character that it has become the place where she feels most secure. This is partly why she has never wanted nor needed a country house. Everything she possesses is under one roof, and her house has the advantage of exuding a country-house feel and yet being in the centre of London. She can therefore work there and use it as the centre of her social life. One minute she can be sitting at her cluttered desk, her large half-round half-hexagonal bi-focal glasses firmly in place, and the next she can be enjoying lunch with friends in her dining-room or on the terrace, as if work were a million miles away. Under one roof these two aspects of her life work in unison.

One disadvantage of this lifestyle is that it becomes difficult to be completely off duty. The Queen looks upon Buckingham Palace as being her place of work. She can escape to Windsor in relative privacy but still entertain dignitaries, then she has Sandringham House and Balmoral Castle for total privacy. Sandringham and Balmoral are her own properties and she pays all costs relating to them. Princess Margaret's home is classed as an 'official residence'. It is not her own to sell, and she has to have a household consisting effectively of two ranks, official and domestic staff. Her 'business expenses' are covered by Princess Margaret's Civil List allowance, and her domestic expenses have to be paid for out of her own private funds.

The Civil List income stems back to 1761 when King George III surrendered all the revenue from Crown lands in return for a fixed allowance to cover his duties as monarch. This allowance became known as the Civil List and since 1971 has been increased annually, but always below the rate of inflation. The Crown Estates today include shops, offices, residential and industrial properties throughout Britain, large areas of forest, rents from offices in the City of London and from offices and shops in plum areas such as Regent Street, Oxford Street, Trafalgar Square, the Strand, Whitehall, Victoria and Regent's Park. This gives an annual revenue in excess of £40 million which goes to the Treasury. In 1989 the Treasury paid the Royal Family £6 million pounds as a Civil List allowance and therefore kept over £30 million pounds from the Crown Properties. In essence the Royal Family are paid out of their own money.

Of Princess Margaret's Civil List income, more than 70% goes in wages to her ten staff and the cost of administration. The remainder pays for the cost of official entertaining, heating, lighting, resident staff's community charges, and travel. On her Civil List income Princess Margaret does not pay income tax, but she is not exempt from Customs and Excise duties and pays VAT on her purchases. The staff themselves pay tax, so are returning a large percentage of Princess Margaret's allowance to the Treasury. Princess Margaret's need for an accountant stems from the complicated reconciliation between her private and public expenditure.

One area in which the Princess differs from many members of the Royal Family is in her clothes. There is little money in the Civil List allowance to provide official clothes for public duty, which results in Princess Margaret's paying for all her clothes out of her own money. This means, in simple terms, that her public and off-duty clothes are the same.

Unlike the Princess of Wales, who gains obvious enjoyment out of buying clothes, adding to her wardrobe is not one of Princess Margaret's favourite hobbies and she has likened it to visiting the dentist. It happens twice a year. Because she has to have a wardrobe that will cater for all occasions, certain restrictions are imposed. Dresses have to be functional rather than fun; nothing too tight as she has to be able to get in and out of cars elegantly; nothing too short as she frequently has to go up steps. Sleeves must have enough room to allow the arm to be raised in a royal wave. Midriffs cannot be too tight in case they prevent her from bending over to talk to people in wheelchairs, or patients in hospital or to receive bouquets from children. Materials must not be too flimsy so that they are transparent with the light behind them, and skirts must not blow in the wind – hems have to be thick or weighted with tiny lead beads. Fabrics that crease are out, too, as the Princess must look crisply smart, and an important consideration is how the whole outfit will look in photographs, for this is often how the Princess will be remembered. Those who see her at a function or on a walkabout often do so for a fleeting moment only, and it is her photographic image that they later study. For this reason, when clothes are designed for the Princess she insists always that they look as good from the back as they do at the front. She tends to choose either a bold pattern in dark colours that will not prove too garish in photographs, or totally plain materials in bright colours which will make her stand out. Occasionally her bright lipsticks have been criticised, but she knows that it is essential to consider how she will look in black and white photographs.

Because clothes have to last, the Princess cannot be an absolute follower of fashion, knowing that the clothes will date too quickly. In her youth she was a leader of fashion, but she quickly learned that if she wore something instantly striking, she was unable to wear the garment again as it would be immediately recognised. It is a lesson that the Princess of Wales understands and fashion experts notice that she now wears the same outfits time and again, and has many remodelled to give them a new look. Now in her sixties, Princess Margaret also has to make a concession to the years and says that she does not wish to look like 'mutton dressed as lamb'. In her youth, Princess Margaret enjoyed the attention that her wardrobe received from the press; there was a thrill that people her own age were adopting her image, but it turned sour when the press began to attack her clothes and criticised her style. From then onwards she adopted clothes that she felt suited her and were comfortable rather than pandering to the fashionable set.

One item for which the Princess has constantly been attacked is her choice of footwear. She is ever conscious of her five-feet two-inch height, so most of her shoes have a three-and-half inch heel with a slight platform on the sole to give her a 'lift'. She feels most comfortable in shoes with open-toes and ankle-straps, but has been accused of being locked in a 1940s timewarp. Most of the Princess's shoes are made by Rayne in London's Bond Street, who hold a royal warrant as shoemakers to the Queen and the Queen Mother. By coincidence, the present Bond Street shop was designed by Lord Snowdon's uncle, Oliver Messel, in 1959. In 1987 the firm was taken over by David and Rosie Graham, who updated the classic image of the company and gained the Princess of Wales as a customer, but Princess Margaret has remained with her favourite 'peep-toed' style. At their factory in North London, Rayne have a plastic cast of Princess Margaret's foot which enables them to make any style or design without the need for her to visit. Each shoe is handmade and can go through more than 150 different stages before it is ready for the royal foot. Rayne also make handbags to match each pair of shoes.

Princess Margaret's clothes have made concessions to fashion in recent years, unlike her sister's classic, unadventurous suits, and she does not stick with one tried and trusted designer. Today she wears clothes by the French designer Roger Brines, also Sally Crewe, Caroline Charles – who also designs clothes for the Princess of Wales – and even Carl Toms, who designed her drawing-room carpet at Kensington Palace! As a night person, Princess Margaret enjoys selecting evening wear, and has remained faithful to long evening dresses for their elegance even if they are temporarily out of fashion. Embroidered brocades, rich silks and satins are favoured. Occasionally she will bring back lengths of material from overseas tours, and invariably she will have drawn possible designs herself even before she has shown it to her dressmaker. She pays great attention to every detail of her outfits, including choice of jewellery, make-up and hair.

For several years Princess Margaret's hair has been styled by Josef in London's Berkeley Street. Although Josef will visit Kensington Palace, the Princess enjoys going to the salon herself, as an outing into the 'real world'. She always has her hair washed, cut and styled in a private room, however, and remains out of sight from the other clients. Her hair is fine and fly-away, needing constant attention, especially when short. In recent years she has decided to grow it long to provide a fuller look and a wider variety of styles for evening wear. Being Princess Margaret's hairdresser requires dedication, for it means not only washing and styling her hair regularly when she is in Britain, but also accompanying her on trips abroad. Josef has travelled all over the world with the Princess and is prepared for any eventuality, which includes taking equipment that is the correct voltage for the country to be visited. By providing such a personal service, he has become part confidant, part friend to the Princess, and his loyalty is paramount. As with all who work for her, maintaining her trust is essential.

Princess Margaret is an intensely private person off duty, and is horrified when areas of her personal life are sensationalised out of all proportion. As a teenager she could cope with fanciful gossip about her private life which was often so wide of the mark as to be unimportant, but the worst moment came, very early in her marriage, when her first butler, Thomas Cronin, sold his revelations to the *People* in September 1960. Cronin had worked for an American ambassador, John Hay Whitney, before being employed by the Snowdons, and had ideas that life with the Royal Family would be far grander than it actually turned out to be in the cramped Apartment 10. Princess Margaret had been used to having staff throughout her life, but this was her first taste as employer. Those who visited the newly married couple felt intimidated by Cronin, who seemed grander than 'Mr and Mrs Jones', and the butler took umbrage when Tony began to check up on his work. In the liberated sixties, the Armstrong-Joneses were the liveliest and least inhibited members of the family and lacked the decorum that Thomas Cronin expected. He departed after only a few weeks; Kensington Palace said he was 'dismissed', Cronin insisted he had resigned. Whatever the reasons, Thomas Cronin had not signed the Official Secrets Act and so sold his story. 'For the sake of the Royal Family, I must speak,' he declared, 'I was mortified by the strange standards imposed upon me.' From then onwards the Princess took staff only on personal recommendation.

Once the divorce from Tony was made absolute, and even before, it was inevitable that rumours of romantic attachments would once again surround her. Princess Margaret's friendship with Roddy Llewellyn turned her, almost overnight, into a scarlet woman. The scandal caused by her love for Peter Townsend, sixteen years older than the Princess, was almost matched, this time because Roddy was sixteen years younger.

To the Princess, it seemed as if she could do no right in her choice of men. She had been forbidden to marry someone older, her marriage to a man of her own age had failed, now eyes were raised to Heaven in disapproval when she dallied with someone younger. Her friendship with Roddy Llewellyn began in September 1973 while she was staying with Colin Tennant and his wife at their Scottish estate at Innerleithen. It was not the sordid 'blind date' that one newspaper suggested, but instead their first encounter came at the Café Royal in Edinburgh where Colin Tennant had organised a special luncheon at which Roddy was one of the guests. Also there were both of Princess Margaret's children. Roddy was present for no other reason than that he was a friend of the Tennants. Although by 1973 Princess Margaret knew that her marriage had ended in all but name, she was not searching for a relationship. Her first words to Roddy were, supposedly, 'Explain yourself' – a disconcerting request from anyone. How could Roddy be expected to reveal twenty-five years of his life, experiences and personality in a short answer? The fact that he was not thrown off balance by Princess Margaret's deliberately provocative approach met with her approval.

Like Peter and Tony before him, Roddy gave off the same sensitive, slightly effeminate air. He shared their boyish good looks. He wore one silver earring long before it became an acceptable male accessory in the 1980s. Lord Snowdon had similarly worn outfits that shocked – brightly coloured socks, extravagant velvet and moiré silk evening jackets, casual wear with an ostentatious number of zips, and when, for the Investiture of the Prince of Wales, he designed for himself a one-piece zip-front bottle-green uniform, finished off with a corded belt complete with tassels, he was described as 'Buttons', 'one of Robin Hood's Merry Men', and 'a bell-hop at a wedding'. Like Tony, Roddy Llewellyn came from the bohemian world that Princess Margaret so enjoyed. He showed respect for her position, yet was not the least bit intimidated. They shared the same sense of humour, enjoyed playing the same songs on the piano; there was an immediate rapport between the two.

Roddy Llewellyn was the son of Sir Henry Llewellyn and brother of the nightclub host and former playboy, Dai Llewellyn, who was already dominating the gossip columns. In Roddy, Princess Margaret saw the gypsy spirit which she envied. After leaving school he had travelled abroad, with no specific aim, working where he could, touring France, visiting South Africa (a country which holds so many idyllic memories for the Princess), through Rhodesia, Uganda and Kenya. Unlike Tony, Roddy was happy to lie on a sun-drenched beach and do nothing – Princess Margaret's idea of Heaven. Eventually Roddy settled for a permanent career as a landscape gardener and graduated from Merrist Wood Agricultural College in Surrey. He still pursues this career today, branching out into giving gardening advice on television and giving lectures at Crystal Palace for a national magazine.

It was not long after their first meeting that Princess Margaret began to include her new friend in private dinner parties at Kensington Palace – not candlelit dinners for two, but always with close friends. Part of the initial attraction at this time was the fun of showing him off to her friends, those who knew that Tony was now hardly ever at home. It was as if Princess Margaret was proud that a forty-three-year-old woman could attract a twenty-seven-year-old man. After the oppression of her marriage, Roddy and his circle made the Princess feel young again, and it was with a rejuvenated spirit that when she next holidayed in Mustique, she invited Roddy along too. On the island Princess Margaret is queen. At this time Mustique became like one large party, with herself as hostess. She must have known that being seen publicly with a younger, unattached man was asking for trouble, but she preferred to enjoy his company, and to hell with the consequences. It was obvious to her friends that Roddy was becoming emotionally attached to the Princess while she merely enjoyed having him as a friend. This time she was determined not to be hurt, neither did she intend to be taken for granted. Once she went to Mustique with friends but did not include Roddy on her guest list. He gatecrashed the party and met with royal disapproval, apparently flying on to the island only to see the Princess flying out. Once this lesson was learned, he was quickly restored to favour.

In 1975 Roddy, with a group of friends, took over a derelict farm in Wiltshire and formed a self-sufficient commune, growing vegetables and living off the land. Princess Margaret eventually visited, once staying for a whole weekend, and immediately fitted into this world of 'drop outs'. Perhaps she identified with them. Like Mustique and Rotherhithe, Surrendell Farm offered a retreat from royal life. When photographs of her in Wiltshire (for which she had innocently posed) were published worldwide, the expected barrage of criticism began. By now, Princess Margaret was weary of public censure and appeared at her most rebellious. She openly ate in restaurants with Roddy Llewellyn, flew to the Caribbean with him on an ordinary charter flight (booked under the pseudonymns of Mr and Mrs Brown), as if flaunting her sexuality in the face of convention. Gossip columnist Nigel Dempster became one of the first to reveal her friendship with Roddy, and soon pictures of them were circulating around the world. One was captioned 'The photograph a husband could not take'. By this time Princess Margaret's husband no longer cared.

Rumour finally became public scandal when the *News of the World* printed an exclusive photograph of Princess Margaret with her paramour, apparently alone together on Mustique. Only much later was it revealed that other friends had been present but had been carefully obliterated from the printed picture, giving the impression of greater intimacy. When, just weeks later, the official announcement of her separation came, Roddy Llewellyn immediately found himself branded the cause of the marriage breakdown. This, as we know, was not the case. After a semi-official statement in which Roddy apologised for any embarrassment caused to the Royal Family, he maintained a very low profile. He retained his friendship with the Princess and tended her Kensington Palace Garden, but encountered hostility from Viscount Linley and Lady Sarah Armstrong-Jones. By 1978, when the Snowdon's divorce became absolute, Roddy seemed to disappear from Princess Margaret's circle completely.

In recent years Princess Margaret has denied that she was in love with Roddy Llewellyn, but that it was instead a close friendship, which once again had been severely damaged by external intervention. There was never any question that Princess Margaret might actually marry this man just fourteen years older than Viscount Linley. He provided light relief from a soured marriage, and it flattered the Princess's ego to have an attractive male escort. When their friendship was temporarily terminated, Roddy made a brief but unsuccessful venture into the world of showbusiness by launching a career as a singer. On his one album called simply *Roddy* (a name with high public profile at that time), released on the Philips label, is a song called *Who's Got The Last Laugh Now?* Its lyrics tell of a starry-eyed young man who meets a rich lady and falls in love. Finding that there was a price to pay in this world with no room to breathe, that the streets he believed to be paved with gold were really made of stone, he flies back to his garden and people of his own kind. Is there a meaning behind this choice of song, or was it purely coincidental? Within a short time,

Roddy fell in love with dress designer, Tania Soskin and married her in 1981. They now have two children, Natasha and Alexandra. Although Princess Margaret agreed to attend the Llewellyns' wedding, the chosen date coincided with an official visit to Canada. She must have felt relieved to have a legitimate excuse for not attending, knowing that the world media would have a field day photographing her at this particular ceremony. Roddy Llewellyn turned down £200,000 offers from tabloid newspapers to reveal the full story of their 'friendship', and has continued to work for his income. Probably his silence has only served to give the relationship far more sordid connotations than the stark truth, but the Princess has appreciated the loyalty. Roddy and Tania are on very friendly terms with the Princess as are Tony and his new wife Lucy. Some ex-husbands and wives cannot bear even to speak to each other, let alone maintain a true friendship, but once the fighting had ceased Margaret and Tony saw through the smoke those qualities which had initially attracted them.

Public affirmation of this came in 1984 when Princess Margaret asked Lord Snowdon to take the official photographs for her forthcoming tour of Bermuda. Her visit was to commemorate the 375th anniversary of the wreck of the ship *Sea Venture* which brought about the settlement of the island. Some fifteen years had passed since he had taken portraits of her, the last being in 1969 before they jointly visited Japan. The resulting photographs in 1984 demonstrated more than any words to the public how relaxed Princess Margaret appeared. The once vitriolic press described her skin as 'flawless', her eyes 'sparkling blue'. The 1969 photograph has a look of grim determination, the eyes petrol blue, the mouth grimly set, disguised dark shadows are apparent under her eyes yet fifteen years on, the eyes are sapphire blue, the smile natural, there is no sign of tension. With typical Snowdon flair, after the formal photographs of the Princess swathed in kingfisher blue taffeta, he took her out into the garden of his Kensington home, put her in a dramatic black cloak with just a red scarf at the neck for colour and photographed her in gothically dramatic splendour. In 1980 the Royal Family's favourite photographer, the late Norman Parkinson, had also photographed the Princess in a cape. Parkinson decided that if he dressed the Queen, Queen Mother and Princess Margaret in identical blue satin capes, the result would not only be unusual, but timeless. Photographing the three royal ladies at the same time, however, was not without its problems. 'Chin up a little, Ma'am. Could you just turn to the right, Ma'am,' the photographer instructed.

'It's absolutely no use you Ma'aming us like this,' said Princess Margaret eventually. 'We haven't the slightest idea who you are referring to. We are all Ma'am.'

The serious photo session at Royal Lodge (in front of the same fireplace that appeared in James Gunn's 1950 painting) disintegrated into uncontrollable fits of hysterical laughter.

The success of Princess Margaret's relationships with friends, ex-lovers, working colleagues and family stems from her ability to see humour in every situation. If the chemistry works with someone, it is usually because they share a sense of fun. Princess Margaret has come through many rough patches by not taking herself too seriously. When she has, it has resulted in depression. When her marriage was at its lowest ebb, she suffered a minor nervous breakdown and there were rumours that she had attempted suicide, but her method of coping with the mental and physical stress was to seek the comfort and security of her bed and sleep. On the occasion in question, prescribed sleeping pills put her into a deeper sleep, but as someone who enjoys life, she would never have any intention of deliberately terminating it.

Princess Margaret's home life today is more relaxed than it has ever been. There is no set routine because of the nature of her public life, but she seldom wakes early, and starts the day with a tray of Lapsong Souchong tea, brought to her by her housekeeper, Elizabeth Greenfield. Always the day begins by reading personal mail, followed by breakfast which consists of little more than her favourite Brazilian coffee, taken black without sugar, some fruit and sometimes toast. Aware of public criticism when she puts on weight, the Princess has eaten sparingly over the last ten years and her weight has remained consistent. The absence of high-caloried alcohol has helped, and she always eats small portions at lunch and dinner, enjoys chicken and fish and describes mixed salads as her favourite meal.

Mornings at Kensington Palace are usually spent dealing with personal and business correspondence. Lord Napier will present her with any important letters, and she will discuss with the Lady-in-Waiting on duty the outline of the day's events. All are personal friends, Elizabeth Blair, Lady Glenconner, Jane Stevens,

Lady Elizabeth Cavendish, and another Margaret, the Countess Alexander of Tunis, so after the first curtsey of the day on meeting there are very few formalities. Usually the Princess will speak to her mother on the telephone, and invariably she will have guests to lunch. Occasionally she will do some personal shopping or may perhaps have a dress fitting, or be visited by her milliner, Simone Mirman. Royal duties are usually carried out in the afternoon, but even a two-hour engagement can require a morning's preparation if there are long distances to travel. If there are no official engagements, there is never a shortage of invitations from friends to attend parties, the theatre, cinema or dinners. In fact the Margaret 'set', although it has evolved and matured, still exists to an extent. It may no longer make headlines, but Princess Margaret does not lead a lonely, secluded life when not on public show.

Foreign travel will never cease to excite Princess Margaret because of the adventure. Each year she visits Mustique at least once, and she always holidays in Italy in late summer. Despite the fact that the venues are the same and often her companions will be the old familiar crowd, it seems characteristic of the Princess that not one of her trips is without incident. Setting out for Mustique in February 1989, Princess Margaret was less than happy to be delayed at Heathrow Airport for more than three and a half hours. Her irritation subsided once it was pointed out to her that there is a clause on the Concorde ticket which enables passengers unavoidably delayed to claim a £250 payment for the inconvenience. The Princess quickly made her way to the Duty Free shop to buy gifts for her hosts.

Later in the year, on her thirty-eighth visit to Italy, she was taken to a small trattoria called Locanda del Falco at Costello di Rivalta where she was staying. She was told by the owner and chef, Carlo Piazza (obviously a man with an eye for business), that it was the local custom to sample every dish. In holiday mood, the Princess did exactly that, tasting everything from steamed sturgeon to ravioli filled with buttermilk-curd, despite being a modest eater usually.

Les Jolies Eaux, on Mustique, the only home that Princess Margaret actually owns, was designed by Oliver Messel. It took more than a decade to come to fruition, partly because Tony did not share in Princess Margaret's dream, which may account for why the house was not actually built until after the marriage began to go awry. The house is an impressive villa, built in a U-shape

around a courtyard, and can sleep ten people. The sitting-room
is on two levels, with magnificent views across Gelliceaux Bay. It
has numerous doors which can be opened wide so that the entire
room becomes like a large veranda. The floor is uncarpeted and is
made up of octagonal slabs of local stone. The sitting-room at Les
Jolies Eaux lacks the grandeur and elegance of Kensington Palace.
Although all the furniture was shipped over from England, it has
a colonial feel. There are many armchairs and small glass-topped
coffee tables constructed from bamboo. There are numerous seat-
ing areas to accommodate a large number of people, with chairs
ranging from very English-looking plain three-seater sofas, to
chrome-based tubular-framed armchairs in which it would be
virtually impossible to sit up straight. As with her London home,
there are table lamps everywhere, and numerous glass lights lit
by candles. Arrangements of local flowers and palms are dotted
throughout the apartment, books and ashtrays are scattered on
every table, and, looking totally out of place in this Caribbean
sitting-room, there is a white model of an English church. Because
of the climate, on average 78°F in February, the dining-room is a
completely open terrace, so that eating turns into a permanent
picnic. Part of the sitting-room was demolished in 1989 when
Princess Margaret's chef on the island, Dalton Williams, lost
control of his jeep and ploughed straight through the French
windows. The Princess was in England at the time and the
damage was repaired in time for her next visit.

Despite the close proximity to the sea, steps lead out of
double doors, beneath an ornately arched window, into the
tropical garden designed by Roddy Llewellyn, to a swimming
pool. Whenever Princess Margaret visits, her garden seems to
have an almost permanent display of strongly scented lilies, pink
and white hibiscus, perfumed oleanders, and for shade there are
citrus trees if the Princess does not wish to sit on her balcony
with its roof of thatched palm leaves. Princess Margaret's arrival
is always in time for the St Valentine's Fancy Dress Party on 14
February, after which night life centres around Basil's Bar. Here
you might see Mick Jagger and Jerry Hall, Barbra Streisand, or
Government Minister Paul Channon, who also has a house on
the island. Amid the scent of bougainvillaea and the sound of
the surf, Princess Margaret entertains her friends. A houseparty
might include the Glenconners, Lord Napier and his wife Delia,

Lord and Lady Tollemache, Lord and Lady Tryon, Roddy and Tania Llewellyn, Lord Lichfield, Ned Ryan, Norman Lonsdale, Reinaldo and Carolina Herrera, and of course, Viscount Linley and Lady Sarah Armstrong-Jones and their respective guests. Lord Snowdon still has not fallen for the island's charms, and does not visit, nor do the Queen and the Royal Family. Only the Duke and Duchess of Kent have sampled the delights.

On Mustique, Princess Margaret can really let her hair down at parties, wearing cool flowing kaftans. Her rendition of the song 'Buttons and Bows' has become a part of Mustique history even though it was fifteen years ago that she gave the memorable performance. It is easy to see the attraction of Mustique. Whatever worries Princess Margaret may have at home, they are left behind, and are meaningless the very moment she steps off the plane 8000 miles away. Of Scottish birth and from a thrifty family, Princess Margaret makes sure that Les Jolies Eaux more than pays for itself whenever she is away. Providing you pass the strict vetting process, the villa can be rented at 8000 dollars a week, which includes the services of a cook, two maids and a gardener, but you still have to buy your own food and pay the air fare. This ensures that Princess Margaret's paradise island remains exclusive, and her property well cared for.

From Mustique, Princess Margaret can fly home with her batteries recharged, equipped once more to face whatever brickbats may be thrown at her. Without this annual retreat she just might not have survived the course.

CHAPTER TEN

Misreported, Misrepresented

It was no coincidence that Princess Margaret chose the Ninth Beatitude to be read aloud in ringing tones at her marriage ceremony: 'Blessed are ye, when men shall revile you, and persecute you, and shall say all manner of evil against you falsely, for my sake.' She, more than any other member of the Royal Family, understands what it is like to be persecuted by the press, and has suffered greatly from false accusations for most of her life.

In January 1955 the *Observer* newspaper accurately stated:

> Most of what is written about her is awry, some of it scurrilous, as if the dry shade of Wilkes had returned to focus his vile, distorting mirror on royalty. There is a peering and a prying . . . and a pantomime-simple idea that while the Queen must be portrayed as an icon of seriousness, opposite qualities must be found in her sister.

Thus, in a few lines, the paper had struck at the very crux of Princess Margaret's relationship with the press, whom she had admonished for making Lilibet 'the dull one' and herself 'the gay one'. The Princess was only twenty-four and yet already most of what was written about her was 'awry' and 'scurrilous'. Even she could not have imagined how much worse it would get as she passed through thirty-four, forty-four, fifty-four . . . the stories becoming more outrageous as the years progressed because she was a sitting target, just ripe for firing at. As the Civil List income is rarely understood by the public, who wrongly assume that the

British tax-payer provides the Royal Family's money, it is felt that journalists have a right to attack the recipients. Princess Margaret became fair game very early on because her social life entered the gossip columns, and she was seen in public to be quick witted and intelligent and therefore capable of fielding off the attacks.

Everyone is aware that the British press build people up only to knock them down again. The Princess of Wales suffered greatly because she truly was the 'fairytale', the girl who married a Prince. For the first few years she could do no wrong. Then the strain became too much and the Queen had to intervene personally when the press hounded the Princess to such an extent that she could not even visit a local shop to buy a packet of wine gums without its becoming headline news. When the press finally toppled the pedestal, Diana could not cope. When one newspaper accused her of drinking too much, she publicly announced in a speech that she was 'not about to become an alcoholic'. She desperately needed to put her side of the story, and it proved that media criticism had hurt. Princess Margaret, however, never has provided that satisfaction. Born in an era when royalty did not give interviews to the press and retained an air of remoteness, she has never let it show when press stories have hurt. 'She's a tough cookie,' said one journalist who had frequently written inaccurately about her, perhaps confusing her stiff upper lip with hardness. 'She can take it, she's used to it,' reporters have said, but there is nobody who can really tolerate a constant barrage of criticism. Princess Margaret has learned to grin and bear it, but will never accept it. Looking back, some of the more outrageous stories must amuse her, no matter how angry they made her at the time, but today she simply refuses to read them.

While many early press reports were at least based on a modicum of truth, later stories became more and more ludicrous. People who began collecting fabricated stories had to weigh the cuttings rather than count them. Many now can only be treated with amusement rather than contempt. Did a gossip columnist really write that Princess Margaret had been seen dressed as a nun, riding a motorbike? Yes, a journalist actually sat at his typewriter and compiled the fanciful story. Could there possibly be any truth in it? No. The vision of Princess Margaret in nun's habit entered someone's vivid imagination when she visited Pope John XXIII at the Vatican dressed from head to toe in the requisite black dress and veil. Put this together with the fact that Antony Armstrong-Jones owned a motorbike, on which the Princess occasionally rode pillion, and, with a stretch of the imagination . . .

What journalists did not see was the seventeen-year-old Princess Margaret after she had just passed her driving test. Not having a car of her own, when being driven away one weekend in the King's Daimler, she had scarcely got outside the Castle precincts when she asked the chauffeur to stop. She made him get into the back of the car with her maid while she drove the vehicle herself. Imagine the footman's expression on their arrival when he opened the car door expecting Princess Margaret to step out gracefully only to see a chauffeur and a maid sitting sheepishly in the back.

The young Princesses Margaret Rose and Lilibet did not know of the earliest press fabrications that claimed Princess Margaret had been born deaf and dumb, nor later false accounts that they were known by Palace staff as P1 and P2. More disconcerting were later reports that claimed Lilibet would definitely receive the title Princess of Wales when she reached the age of eighteen. So forceful were the rumours that Buckingham Palace had to take one of their rare steps and issue a formal denial. In her seventh year Princess Margaret attended her parents' Coronation in Westminster Abbey, and although photographs of the occasion clearly show the Princess carefully resting her head on the side of the Royal box, she is still quite obviously concentrating on the proceedings. She was, therefore, angered by American press reports that she had disruptively rustled the pages of her hymn book.

Frightening was the story that Princess Margaret had inherited the disease haemophilia. Other rumours suggested that Princess Margaret had inherited porphyria, a disease which can lead to madness and is now believed to have been the medical problem of King George III. Princess Margaret does not have porphyria, but the idea and misunderstanding came from a conversation about porphyrogenitism, the technical term for a younger son inheriting the throne in preference to an older son.

Little wonder that when the Princess appeared on *Desert Island Discs* she bemoaned the fact that she had been 'misreported and misrepresented since the age of seventeen', although she should perhaps have said seven rather than seventeen. Once she had blossomed into an attractive young woman, photographers, too, began to dog her every footstep. When she visited Italy and the

Island of Capri in 1949 there were rumours that the Princess would be sunbathing and swimming in the sea. What followed is reminiscent of the furore in 1982 when photographers waited in undergrowth on the cliffs with zoom-lenses to photograph the pregnant Princess of Wales in a bikini. Fortunately for Princess Margaret, the press had greater concern for public decency, and she was aware that photographers were bound to be hiding somewhere. Was it mere coincidence or a deliberate antagonistic act on her part that the one-piece swimsuit she wore in Capri was flesh-coloured? When the press crew looked through their lenses from afar, she appeared to be completely naked. These were not the kind of photographs that the *Daily Express* could publish. So desperate were they to publish pictures, that eventually it was decided to use the 'apparently naked' shots and a swimsuit was painted on to them. The result fooled very few people and only added to Princess Margaret's daring reputation. What had she really been wearing? people wondered. Had she actually sunbathed nude?

The demand for photographs of the Princess sunbathing has apparently never diminished. As recently as September 1988 the *People* had a centre-page spread with the headline 'MARGARET'S HOT SUMMER NIGHTS IN THE TEMPLE OF LOVE', with four photographs of the Princess in Italy, picnicking in the apparent seclusion of the Countess of Warwick's holiday home, the Villa Sola. The photographs are taken on two different occasions, once when she was with Norman Lonsdale, and later, in a different swimsuit, sitting alone eating grapes. The patio is completely surrounded by shrubbery and the Princess and her escort are obviously blissfully unaware that they are being photographed. 'Margaret smoked through a familiar long holder,' wrote the journalist, 'the scar marks from the surgery clearly visible above her sun top.' The accompanying photographs, however, show the Princess from both left and right angles; her swimsuits are low cut and completely strapless and there are no signs of surgery scars whatsoever. Had there been, it is unlikely that the Princess would wear such a revealing sun suit, even in the presence of very close friends. 'For ten long, hot summer days and nights the princess and her perfect gentleman kissed and caressed as they strolled near the remains of an ancient temple of love – and shared intimate meals under the Italian skies . . . ' the article continued. Lucky that Princess Margaret 'gave up long ago' reading about herself.

The interest in Princess Margaret's love life never seems to wane. If she had married at the age of twenty and was now celebrating her Ruby Wedding Anniversary, perhaps press coverage would have been very different. Instead she has become the good-time girl, and if she dares to sunbathe with a man then she must face the consequences. After the Peter Townsend episode, royal authority Audrey Whiting informed her readers that she had exclusive information that revealed Princess Margaret would never marry. If she could not have Peter Townsend, then she would not have anyone, Miss Whiting declared. She continued with this reliable information even when the Princess was falling in love with Tony. 'She is deeply in love with Townsend,' wrote Audrey Whiting in the *Sunday Pictorial* and Princess Margaret was grateful. It allowed her relationship with Tony to develop relatively unhindered.

When she did marry Tony, there were press reports that she was pregnant and therefore had to get married. As their first child was not born until eighteen months after the wedding, the rumour died. Even the most fertile imagination could not believe that Princess Margaret could have such a lengthy pregnancy.

Throughout the marriage, Tony's public profile was built up to match Princess Margaret's – rumours of other women or even other men. In 1972, when Tony was involved in a car accident, the story arose that he was not alone, but there was a 'mystery blonde' in the passenger seat. Indeed, Tony was not alone, but his travel companion was Prudence Penn, the wife of Lieutenant-Colonel Sir Eric Penn, Comptroller of the Lord Chamberlain's Office and Extra Equerry to the Queen. She was a friend and utterly respectable. So the story died. Maybe it was with some satisfaction that Tony also accidentally crashed his car into one belonging to Raymond Belisario, notorious for taking intimate royal photographs. It was worth the £20 fine he received. Reports of imminent divorce began in 1967 and were to hound Margaret and Tony until they finally separated. In 1976 those who had written of the marriage in the past could smugly say, 'I told you so'.

One area which has severely angered Princess Margaret is that frivolous stories have taken precedence over her work, which has been boringly successful and unnewsworthy. In 1965 she and Tony undertook a twenty-two-day tour of America and Bermuda, fulfilling more than sixty official engagements. Every day they left their hotel to begin engagements between 9.30a.m. and 10.30a.m.

and on some days of the schedule they did not return to their hotel until after midnight, after a full day of duties, and an official dinner most evenings. The *New Statesman* described their programme as making the 'odd working visit here and there'; the British press commented on her wardrobe and highlighted one dance which the Princess did not leave until 3.30a.m. Readers in England had no idea of the schedule; only Lord Snowdon knew that his wife was suffering from a heavy cold and a high temperature through part of the tour. Nevertheless Princess Margaret's work won over the Americans, and she fell in love with the cities that never sleep. She declined a visit to Disneyland, knowing that photographs of her in this centre of fun would give the impression that she had only gone to America to enjoy herself, but did revel in visiting the Universal Studios in Hollywood, lunching with representatives of all the major film studios and watching filming. The magic world of cinema had held a fascination since childhood, and she remembered peering from the windows of Buckingham Palace to watch Anna Neagle in an open landau, dressed as Queen Victoria, arriving and departing from the Grand Entrance for the film *Sixty Glorious Years*; it was in the private Peter Sellers film that Princess Margaret played Queen Victoria herself.

Visits to America have not been without their problems regarding the press, most notably in 1979 when Princess Margaret visited Chicago shortly after the assassination of Lord Mountbatten. At an official reception given by the Mayor of Chicago it was reported by an American gossip columnist that Princess Margaret had called the Irish 'pigs' for murdering Mountbatten. As she had already encountered pro-IRA demonstrations on her arrival, the report was guaranteed to whip them into a frenzy, and it was not long before the Princess's life was threatened. Pouring oil on the passionate flames, the Mayor made a statement saying that Princess Margaret had actually been discussing Irish 'jigs'. This fooled no one and Kensington Palace had to release a further statement pointing out that the Princess had not mentioned 'pigs' or 'jigs', but the damage was done. Although Princess Margaret is quite capable of calling the IRA 'pigs', and has probably called them even worse in private, she has more sense than to make defamatory remarks in public about such an emotive subject. Nevertheless, she was justifiably angry and deeply upset by Lord Mountbatten's death, and equally shocked when a gun was aimed at the Queen during the 1981 Trooping the Colour ceremony. The gun fired blanks, but had the bullets been real, her sister would have been dead. Living with the ever-present threat that she or a member of her own family might be murdered or maimed purely for political reasons is a fact of life that Princess Margaret must resign herself to.

In 1983 there was press anger in Britain that the thirty-year rule, which allows Cabinet papers to be made public, did not reveal any information about Princess Margaret's relationship with Peter Townsend, which had become common knowledge in 1953. The American press however, concentrated on a private visit made by the Princess to Virginia in October, where she stayed with attorney, Neil Phillips. A story circulated that the reason for Princess Margaret's visit was that she was going to be secretly married to Norman Lonsdale. Knowing that re-marriage in Britain because of 'the church's teaching' would cause an ecclesiastical outcry, it was decided that the Princess had crossed the Atlantic for a clandestine ceremony. As Norman Lonsdale was actually on a business trip to Rome at the time it would have been a very strange wedding indeed. Lord Napier issued an official statement eventually to say that there was no truth whatsoever in the story. Seven years on, Norman Lonsdale seems no nearer to leading the Princess down the aisle.

In London, the Princess's image was not helped by an encounter with the pop singer Boy George. The heavily made-up lead singer with the group Culture Club once described himself as 'a poof with muscles'. In 1982 the group's song 'Do You Really Want To Hurt Me?' became a number one hit record in 51 countries, and led to a meeting with Princess Margaret at an award ceremony. Boy George wanted the Princess to pose for a photograph with the group, but she reportedly said that she did not want 'to be photographed with that over-made-up tart. I'm too old for that sort of thing.' When he heard what the Princess had supposedly said, Boy George replied, 'I don't give a damn. I didn't want to talk to her anyway. She doesn't mean a thing to me . . . I bring more money into this country than she does.' In what became an excellent publicity campaign, the singer demanded an apology from the Princess. Naturally this was not forthcoming. It was pointed out that Princess Margaret had likened Boy George's make-up to a mask from the *Commedia dell'Arte*, and Lord Napier said that the Princess had not called Boy George an over-made-up tart. She would never 'dream of saying such a thing'. Eventually Viscount Linley resolved the situation when he met Boy George in a restaurant and told him how upset his mother had been over the incident. All was forgiven.

That same year Viscount Linley had himself remarked that dinner with Princess Michael of Kent was the gift he would give his worst enemy. Although he apologised to Prince Michael, he refused to speak to the subject of his attack. Another feud began. 'If there are any men among you who are responsible for the three sackloads of mail I received this morning,' said Princess Michael in a public speech, 'all assuring me that you are in fact the worst enemy of a cousin of mine, then when can you come to dinner?' In private she joked that to her worst enemy she would give a table made by Viscount Linley. Princess Margaret was amused. She did not want her son to receive bad publicity, but she knew that the general public saw the episode only as the joke that it had been intended to be. For once, the lighter side of the Royal Family had reared its head. From death threats and false marriage rumours, it made a change to find the media had a less serious 'scandal' to bandy about. 'Like mother, like son,' winked those in the know, conscious that Viscount Linley's humour could be as caustic as Princess Margaret's if the occasion presented itself.

Unlike the younger generation of the Royal Family, Princess Margaret has suffered because she has never deliberately co-operated with the press. The Princess of Wales struck up a rapport with the newsmen who surrounded her home in Coleherne Court, London, before the announcement of her engagement to Prince Charles; Prince Charles and his brothers are happy to give a quote to waiting journalists; the Duchess of York has even given exclusive interviews to the *Daily Express* who paid her an estimated £120,000 for a series including extracts from her children's books. They did, however, say: 'There will be more children but not just yet . . . The new slimline Duchess has worked hard to get herself into the great shape she's in now and she is definitely going to hang on to it for a little while longer.' The following day the Duchess announced that she was pregnant for the second time. Princess Margaret has never given a newspaper interview. On rare occasions she has spoken to authors, such as Andrew Duncan and Christopher Warwick, and television presenters, speaking about her wartime memories on a programme to commemorate the Queen Mother's eighty-fifth birthday, but when out on official duties her expression is often so formidable when she passes waiting journalists that not one dares throw a question at her. When Princess Anne was asked how she was enjoying her visit to New Mexico in 1982 she snapped, 'Keep your questions to yourself,' and when asked that same year how it felt to be an aunt when the news of Prince William's birth was on everyone's mind, she said, 'That's my business, thank you.' Media men clearly fear that Princess Margaret's approach might well be the same.

When Lilibet and Margaret Rose were out in public with the King and Queen, or their grandparents, King George V and the severe Queen Mary, royalty were unapproachable. Not only that, they were revered and above criticism. The change came in the mid-1930s, when the then Prince of Wales, Princess Margaret's uncle David, who frequently visited London nightclubs and led a boisterous social life. If he enjoyed listening to a band, he would sometimes go up to the drummer and ask to have a play on the drums. When his relationship with divorcee Mrs Simpson became common knowledge, he became the subject of public censure, and when he eventually abdicated from his position as King Edward VIII he received harsh criticism. This marked a turning point in royalty's relationship with the press. When the Prince visited those without work in Wales, Durham and Glasgow and said that 'Something must be done' about their hardship, he was idolised; when the public felt let down by his abdication, then he was knocked from his pedestal. Princess Margaret has often been likened to her Uncle David in character, even though she scarcely knew him, and it was in this new climate that she grew up. It still remained sacrilege to criticise the King and Queen or Princess Elizabeth, which left Princess Margaret. When she grew up and seemed to ape her uncle's social lifestyle, even becoming involved with a divorcé herself, then history seemed to repeat itself. Royalwatcher James Whitaker has likened himself to a hunter, with the Royal Family as the prey. He and his newshounds must wheedle them out of cover at every available opportunity. It is Princess Margaret's misfortune that she has found herself in their sights just a little too often.

CHAPTER ELEVEN

A Happy Ending?

The year 1989 ended with Princess Margaret recuperating from the 'flu virus which had caused the worst epidemic in Britain for more than eighteen years. First the Queen Mother was confined to bed with a 'feverish cold', according to Clarence House, and within days the Queen succumbed and was forced to cancel her engagements. Although already suffering from 'the sniffles', Princess Margaret gamely gave a large dinner party as planned at Kensington Palace to mark the birthdays of her cousin, the Earl of Lichfield, Earl Alexander of Tunis (husband of her Lady-in-Waiting) and the Swiss banker, Nicholas Villiers, all celebrating their half-century that year. The three men had been friends for more than thirty years since sharing an apartment whilst in the Brigade of Guards. Later that night Princess Margaret joined some 400 guests at Claridges for the official birthday party organised by Patrick Lichfield's sister, Lady Elizabeth Anson.

Princess Margaret, wearing a cerise skirt and black silk top, was described by the press the next day as 'stunning . . . slim as a whippet and looking a decade younger than her 59 years'. One of her friends later described her as 'looking prettier, happier and sexier' than he had ever seen her. Within a few days the Princess developed full-blown influenza, forcing her to reluctantly cancel all her engagements. It was a bad end to one of the most peaceful decades of her life.

As she began to recover from the debilitating virus, the year 1990 dawned. The year that would be one of many significant birthday parties: the thirtieth birthday of her nephew, Prince Andrew, the Duke of York, born in the year she had married

Antony Armstrong-Jones; the fortieth birthday of Princess Anne, now the Princess Royal; more remarkably, the ninetieth birthday celebrations of the Queen Mother, and on 21 August, her own sixtieth birthday. While somehow we accept the passing of the years with other members of the Royal Family, as I looked back myself over the last six decades, time and time again people would say to me, 'It's so hard to believe that Princess Margaret is sixty'. No doubt the Princess herself feels the same.

Princess Margaret is a survivor, yet there is a certain irony that someone born to such privilege, into the most noble of families, with the option, one would think, to live a carefree life, has actually met with such misfortune. Although she was not granted the personality to live a quiet, uneventful existence, not all the troubles laid at her door have been through her own invitation. She never planned to fall in love; as her aunt, the late Duchess of Windsor, entitled her memoirs, 'the heart has its reasons'. Margaret would never have made a success of a marriage to Billy Wallace, and the collapse of her union with Lord Snowdon was not entirely her fault. Many felt that she should have made the relationship work, just as her niece the Princess Royal received severe criticism for ending her marriage to Captain Mark Phillips, but being royal is no guarantee of being happy. Regardless of public opinion, both Princesses lived out the role of wife long after the marriage was dead. In the end separation and divorce became the only option.

The attacks on Princess Margaret by the world press have been fast and furious for half a century. She was the sitting target, with no effective means of retaliation other than developing a metaphorically thick skin to prevent permanent damage. Only her health has suffered over the years, through the use of alcohol and cigarettes; smoking now causes her bronchial problems when she has a cold and undoubtedly exacerbated the 'flu symptoms of 1989. Perhaps both stimulants were used initially to give her confidence in her duties as Princess, and to cope with the stress that the constant heat of the limelight inevitably put upon her. Whatever the reason, it is only recently that the Princess has had to come to terms with the cost to her health.

The first major scare came in April 1978 when she developed what appeared to be influenza. In a determined effort to shake off the virus, she resumed her official engagements at the end of the month, but returned from a strenuous day in Manchester aware that something more serious seemed to be developing. She was admitted to the King Edward VII Hospital for Officers for tests, and hepatitis was diagnosed. Just as she had appeared to be blooming at the Claridges birthday party in 1989, while in the early stages of severe 'flu, so on that day in Manchester the Princess outwardly looked extremely healthy. Although hepatitis is made worse by alcohol, drink was not the cause of her illness as many newspapers suggested. Infective hepatitis is caused by a virus, and because the incubation period can be very long, it is frequently impossible to calculate where and when it was contracted. Severe sickness and prolonged debilitation result from the virus and, as the liver is affected, alcohol is strictly forbidden. It is probably no coincidence that the Princess caught the virus when her spirits were particularly low due to the final collapse of her marriage. Less than two weeks after she left hospital a decree nisi was granted in the divorce courts.

In the summer of 1978 Princess Margaret undertook an official visit to the Ellice Islands in the South Pacific to represent the Queen at Tuvalu's celebrations of independence. Recovery from hepatitis is slow; her defences were still down, and she contracted viral pneumonia. The combination of the two illnesses nearly killed her. With a dangerously high temperature of 105° and chronic chest pains, she had to endure a nine-hour flight to the nearest hospital. Originally the idea of the visit was that warmer climes might be beneficial to the Princess's health, but a 6000-mile flight can exhaust even the healthiest person. Because of the strain, and the complete abstention from alcohol, she was smoking noticeably more cigarettes. The onset of pneumonia did not surprise many doctors. The severity of her illness was not appreciated by people back in England.

Princess Margaret still smokes to this day. Many condemn her. Many look upon it as an act of defiance, boldly flaunting her mortality in the knowledge that cigarettes killed both her father, King George VI, and his brother, the Duke of Windsor. The implication is that she has not tried to give them up, but this is untrue. Unfortunately her addiction began forty years ago, at a time when smoking was seen as being vaguely daring but never injurious to health. At home people smoked, and when she married, Lord Snowdon smoked heavily too. The addiction is stress related. At official dinners it was noticed that she lit up between each course, yet when she is relaxing with friends on the island of Mustique she is scarcely seen with a cigarette. Certainly she is seen far less with a cigarette in public in the 1990s than she has ever been.

If ever the Princess was going to kick the habit, it would most surely have been in 1985 when, on 5 January, she was driven unexpectedly from Kensington Palace to the nearby Brompton Hospital, at a time when everyone believed her to be enjoying the New Year at Sandringham with the family. The Brompton Hospital specialises in heart and chest problems, and it was later revealed that she had been suffering from chest pains for several weeks and had developed an abnormal cough. Fortunately the Princess was not able to watch the television news that evening, which even gave details of her childhood illnesses – completely unrelated to the condition for which she had been admitted. A biopsy on the Princess's lung revealed that the tissue sample taken was non-malignant. To her great relief the Princess did not have lung cancer as she had feared, but spent nine days in hospital being treated for a lung infection. Determined to retain her dignity, the Princess would not allow any visitors while she was on a saline drip, and still feeling weak and unfit for conversation, the only visitors she eventually allowed were her children. The extra fuss and protocol that would have been involved for even the most private of visits by the Queen or the Queen Mother seemed unnecessary. The Princess was able to speak to her family on the telephone, and she must have been aware that press photographers were camped outside the hospital twenty-four hours a day. Had the Queen broken her Sandringham holiday and travelled from Norfolk to London there would have been increased speculation as to the severity of Princess Margaret's illness. As with all such occurrences, the Royal Family naturally tried to play the situation down. For the Princess herself there were to be stern words from the anti-smoking lobby and inevitable comparisons with her father, who had lost his left lung because of a malignant growth, almost certainly brought about by cigarettes. The episode weakened the Princess considerably and when she left the £165-a-day private room, she looked extremely delicate and unsteady. It is a reflection on the progression of royalty into the late twentieth century that she actually went into hospital for the operation. King George VI's condition had been far more serious, yet he refused to be admitted. 'I've never heard of a King going to hospital,' he grumbled and a room in the Belgian Suite at Buckingham Palace served as an operating theatre.

Scarcely had Princess Margaret returned to Kensington Palace on 13 January 1985 than London experienced its coldest day since 1963, with temperatures barely rising above -4°C, and much of Britain being covered in snow. It was hardly beneficial to someone with a lung complaint. As soon as she felt stronger the Princess was determined to visit the one place where she knew that she would be able to recover in warmth and peace – Mustique. Looking pale and drawn, she left Heathrow Airport in February for the $8^1/_2$-hour flight to her beloved haven, but without the usual excitement and jollity. By the time her plane landed at Barbados, before the final stage of the journey Princess Margaret was suffering from total exhaustion, and her staff immediately called a physician. Much to her dismay the Princess had to spend thirty-six hours in Barbados, temporarily lodged at the British Embassy, before she could continue on the short flight to Mustique. Although it was summer in the Caribbean, Princess Margaret was in no mood for the usual holiday activities. Instead of beach parties and sunbathing, the Princess slept solidly for the first forty-eight hours, just as her father had once slept for two days when he felt unable to cope. She is renowned for keeping late hours, and it was a sign of malady that even when she did feel strong enough to get up, she was rarely seen in the evenings. Equally, it was a sign of recovery when she became bored and house guests began to arrive – Viscount Linley and his reported girlfriend at the time, Susannah Constantine, the daughter of a haulage millionaire, the Glenconners and Lord Buckhurst (now the Earl De La Warr) and his wife Anne. The sun and the sea worked their usual wonders and soon the Princess was looking her former self. She returned to England early in March and stepped off Concorde at Heathrow Airport looking immaculate, her hair fashionably layered, her pale skin now glowing healthily.

Her first public appearance was in fact a private visit to see her nephew Prince Edward, on the eve of his twenty-first birthday, take part in a review as a member of the Cambridge University Light Entertainment Society. Wrapped warmly in a full-length fur coat (a garment she is now unable to wear, five years on, without causing offence to animal rights campaigners) Princess Margaret accompanied the Queen to watch the Prince

dance, sing and act his way through the show that he had helped
to write, called *Catch Me Foot*. It must have brought back memories
of wartime pantomimes at Windsor, especially with the inevitable
references to the royal family. 'It's HM here from BP,' said the
Prince in one sketch, playing the role of a Master Spy. During the
interval, Princess Margaret opened her evening bag, fished out the
familiar tortoiseshell cigarette holder and lit her first cigarette in
public since her cancer scare. The boredom of recuperation had
again only led to an increase in the number smoked. Her only concession appeared to be a change to a brand that were filter tipped.
This one personal conflict seems to have beaten the Princess. She
knows the risks only too well and is obviously prepared to accept
the consequences.

Within a short time Princess Margaret made a remarkable
recovery. In late March, at a centenary dinner at the Guildhall
in London for delegates attending the International Orchid Conference, arranged by the Royal Horticultural Society, she looked
extremely frail. She managed to visit Newcastle-upon-Tyne for an
NSPCC function on 28 March, but was forced to cancel an engagement in Glasgow the following day. Two weeks later, on 10 April,
the Princess arrived at the Hippodrome Theatre in Birmingham
for a Gala performance by the Royal Ballet. Resplendent in a
full-length orange evening dress, she looked in excellent shape and
well enough to embark on a four-day official trip to Hungary. One
of the highlights, which she had been determined not to miss, was
the opening night of *Manon* at the State Opera House in Budapest.
It did not seem to matter that this was the same ballet she had seen
in Birmingham two weeks earlier. As always, she enjoyed the sense
of occasion and sat on the very edge of her seat. 'It's been forty
years since there has been blue blood in the Royal Box,' revealed
a member of the audience emotionally, and as she entered the box,
wearing pale blue silk and looking at her most regal, she received
what seemed like four decades of pent-up applause that had finally
been unleashed.

Throughout the four days the Princess looked at her most
relaxed, chatting animatedly throughout, even during a fifteen-
minute talk with the Hungarian president who was unable to
speak English. She stayed at the official residence of the British
Ambassador, on the banks of the River Danube, and he and his
wife escorted the Princess throughout her visit. Although the ballet

was the main event, the remaining time was fully organised. They took the Princess on a tour of the Bukk mountains and visited the historic town of Eger. She rode in an open carriage in Szilvasvarad, had a two-hour tour of the Herend porcelain factory, visited the Mátra State Forestry Farm, watched horsemen, or 'chikos' as they are called, at work with the famous Lippizaner horses, and attended receptions and informal dinners eating traditional Hungarian fare. She was taken to the National Museum in Budapest to see the crown worn by King Stephen I nearly 1000 years ago. He is now the Patron Saint of Hungary as their first Christian king, and the ancient crown is a prized relic with supposedly mystical powers. Although Hungary is still a monarchy, there has been no king since the end of the First World War, and there has not been a regent since the end of the Second World War in 1945, which is why Princess Margaret's visit, forty years later, was an emotional occasion for many.

By June, Princess Margaret was back to a full schedule of engagements and when on the 4th she attended the Victoria League's Four Hundred Ball at the Hyde Park Hotel, more than a few heads were turned. The Princess arrived in a pure white evening dress, with slashed sleeves to reveal very tanned arms, and at her ears and throat were the largest diamonds that she owns. What was apparent to all was not only that the recovery was complete, but that a new Princess Margaret had emerged. The general consensus was that she was now looking better than she had for years and the public's perception of her suddenly began to turn. Critics became kinder; those who had once attacked her for not working hard enough looked more closely at her engagement diary and saw not only that it was full, but that the Princess had striven on often at the risk of her own health. That summer she undertook official duties throughout Britain, from Glasgow to Gwynedd, from Stoke-on-Trent to Dorset, as well as the usual family events, such as Royal Ascot and a private visit to the Chelsea Flower Show, plus an official visit to Scandanavia. It was almost as if the Princess was proving to herself that life was back to normal.

It is said that in 1985 Princess Margaret's staff became much closer to her and more understanding of their employer. Not until you face the risk of losing something do you become fully appreciative of its value. The majority of the population today cannot remember a time without Princess Margaret. The older generation remember being charmed by little Margaret Rose and her personal life has been of public interest for some forty years; she has become a piece of Britain itself. In her autumn years it is with sympathy and affection that the majority view her. Now that she has reached the age of sixty, a time when many women retire, few would condemn her if she withdrew totally from official life, but this is unlikely. The Queen Mother remained sprightly and extremely active in her ninetieth year and there is no reason to believe that her daughter, thirty years younger, will be any different.

In her private life, Princess Margaret now has something that she appreciates and treasures – her independence. She is more in control of her life than ever before. Viscount Linley and Lady Sarah Armstrong-Jones are self-sufficient and are carving out their own niches. There is no shortage of escorts to keep the Princess company at social functions and she enjoys having the companionship without the commitment. She is a free spirit and much of the frustration she has felt in past years has been caused by her sense of being trapped: trapped in the gilded royal cage with little privacy; trapped in a stale marriage that had lost its sparkle, once so exciting; trapped with an image that was way off the mark from her true nature. The 1980s were a time of renewal, of casting off that which held her back. At sixty the pressures have subsided. In what has undoubtedly been a somewhat stormy passage through the years Princess Margaret is now enjoying the tranquillity that has followed. Because of her volatile nature, her life will never completely be free from conflict. Unlike the Queen, whose life has been very much on an even keel, Princess Margaret has encountered very distinct episodes in hers – the restrictions of wartime childhood, years dominated by Peter Townsend, Antony Armstrong-Jones and Roddy Llewellyn, in a quest for emotional fulfilment, and then a period dogged by ill health – almost as if her time has been clearly mapped out in a series of cycles over which she has had no control. When one looks back, for example, over the forty years of Queen Elizabeth II's reign almost every year has followed a basic pattern, so that in retrospect any year becomes almost indistinguishable from the next. How different Princess Margaret's years have been. Elizabeth seems almost to revel in the routine of her role whereas Princess Margaret has a much lower boredom threshold and requires new experiences to keep her going.

When she once said that there was 'nothing more marvellous than being a Princess', she meant it, because the title is the key to opportunity. A passport to adventure.

Unexpectedly to those who do not know her, Princes Margaret is deeply religious and it is her faith that has pulled her through each personal crisis. This is not new, but a lifetime's spiritual experience. At the age of fourteen she wanted to be confirmed, but was forced to wait until she had reached the age of sixteen. In 1953, after the Townsend 'scandal' had broken, she attended a very High Church service incognito; there were even false rumours that she was studying Roman Catholicism. Certainly she had found her meeting with the Pope, a short time earlier, a deeply moving experience, and her crucifixes are still in a prominent place on her desk. In 1953 she also attended a course of eleven lectures on 'The School of Religion' at St Paul's, Knightsbridge, and went to post-confirmation classes at the vicarage. Often she was spotted going to church at dawn, and many felt that perhaps she was seeking the answers to certain questions, looking for a meaning to her life, even searching for the Church's views on divorce. She had a strong friendship at this time with the curate, the Reverend Simon Phipps, who later went on to become the Bishop of Lincoln. They would spend many hours together discussing theological issues, and he was himself surprised at the depth of her knowledge and the conviction of her beliefs.

Attending an official engagement at a church in Harlesden, London, in 1979, Princess Margaret was expected to stay for only ten minutes after a service. During the service she took Holy Communion for the first time since her divorce, and remained afterwards for an hour and a half. She admired a statue of the Virgin Mary, chatted to a group of West Indian children, tucked into sausage rolls, and revealed how much she enjoyed playing hymns on the piano. When she departed it was as if spiritually renewed. Through her Christian beliefs she has an inner peace, which her friends have described as a 'regal calm', and certainly during times of stress she has been known to play hymns seemingly interminably on the piano. Her leaning towards High Church services is in keeping with her love of the theatrical and sense of drama, but there has never been any question of a conversion to Roman Catholicism. Such a move would prove extremely embarrassing with her sister as Head of the Church of England.

At the end of 1989, the *Daily Mail's* 'Woman Writer of the Year', Lynda Lee-Potter, printed a list of selected mottoes for the 'Rich and Famous'. Some were tongue-in-cheek, most were intended seriously. For Princess Margaret she selected words from Thomas Fuller, a seventeenth-century clergyman: 'If it were not for hope the heart would break.' It is the Princess's religious beliefs and zest for life that have indeed kept her going. Where there's life there's hope, and when rumours spread that the Princess had made a suicide attempt those who knew her were adamant that her love of life was so great that she would never deliberately end it. 'Mindful also of the Church's teachings . . . '

Life has changed dramatically for Princess Margaret throughout her sixty years. It has been a journey across a minefield and it is as if today she has reached the side of safety. The little Princess who once said, 'Now that Papa is King, I am nothing,' has striven to become *something*. Some say she wields her royal position like a sledgehammer, demanding special privileges such as a bevy of police outriders to escort her on even the shortest of journeys, but that is part and parcel of her position. It happens automatically for Lilibet, why should she not receive the same treatment? While it is easy to see and criticise her impressive motorcade, it is not so easy to see the sensitive work and achievements behind the scenes. Much has been made, for example, of the Princess of Wales's work with AIDS patients, and she received universal praise for shaking hands with victims of the deadly virus without her customary white gloves. Yet almost three years ago, when Princess Margaret attended a charity performance of 'Ian McKellen Acting Shakespeare', and shook hands with AIDS sufferers, minus gloves, to allay public fears, it went almost unnoticed. In October 1988 the Princess officially opened the London Lighthouse, the residential and support centre for people affected by AIDS, and she continues to support their work. On 5 January 1990, she attended, for example, a late-night charity performance of the Austen Brothers Circus in Battersea Park to raise money for the London Lighthouse. As members of the Royal Household have now died of AIDS, it is not an issue that anyone in the Royal Family has wanted to ignore. When visiting the London Lighthouse, Princess Margaret received admiration for the compassion shown and her relaxed manner. Some might have felt uncomfortable in such a situation, but the Princess knows the facts and was aware that she was not at any risk. She had afternoon tea and although she carefully dissected a sandwich before eating it, this was to discover the contents rather than for reasons of hygiene.

Of his younger daughter, King George VI once said, 'Margaret is the kind of child who could persuade a pearl to come out of an oyster,' and she has never lost that early ability to charm those with whom she comes into contact. Princess Margaret's staff are long serving and intensely loyal. It is because she can charm that they stay, because they feel needed. Some say that the Princess fusses around them like a mother hen, but she demands high standards. Some feel that she has a love-hate relationship with the staff; on one occasion, during a heated discussion, one member of staff threw cold coffee over her, and on another a young under-butler accidentally set fire to her dress while serving *Crêpes Suzette*. Neither lost their job, nor was there any feeling of animosity. Each member of staff is a cog in the machinery that keeps her Household running smoothly; most of what they do is unappreciated by the public. When Princess Margaret arrives at a function in a long full-skirted evening gown, the public have not seen her staff frantically holding down a red carpet in the gusty wind so that she can walk to her car without getting the hem soiled or her shoes dirty. No one knows why it has to be a *red* carpet, but may be it gives the Princess a feeling of importance.

Despite constant statements to the contrary from some writers, Princess Margaret has never wanted to be Queen. Yes, she was at times jealous because Lilibet was treated as being more important than her, but it was a sisterly rivalry, never one of power. The restrictions and pressures of monarchy would have been too great a burden for Margaret. Her freedom would have been strictly curtailed. Lilibet is Queen with every fibre of her being and places this before her duties as wife and mother. Princess Margaret is prepared to undertake her share of duty, but her personal life is as high on her list of priorities. She enjoys her femininity. Elizabeth wears her jewels as symbols of monarchy, but when Margaret adorns herself with diamonds it is because she enjoys wearing them. She wears her brooches, not on her left-shoulder in the time-honoured tradition like her mother or sister, but nearly always in the centre of her collar or at her cleavage, as a fashion accessory. It is as a woman that she likes to sparkle, not just as a Princess. Above all Princess Margaret is an extremely sensual person, glorying in her sexuality. She went with Tony to see X-rated films which would have shocked Elizabeth, but Margaret enjoyed the sense of daring. It is this enjoyment of human pleasures that have made her at times seem less than royal, but have given her the charisma and panache that draw people to her.

In June 1949 during Ascot week, the social commentator Henry 'Chips' Channon, wrote that at Windsor Castle the Princess had nearly fifty young friends staying as guests. 'Princess Margaret was simply dressed,' he wrote, 'but already she is a public character, and I wonder what will happen to her? There is already a Marie Antoinette aroma about her . . . ' Princess Margaret has not lost her head like the ill-fated Queen of France, but did the shrewdly observant Channon notice something portentous about her? A flawed facet in her dazzling character that might lead to unhappiness? Was she born under an unlucky star? Many feel that the circumstances of her birth, on a wild and treacherous night in the haunted Castle of Glamis, home of the ill-fated Macbeth, have left their mark. The curse of Glamis is too fanciful a notion to consider seriously, but a shadow has been cast over much of the Princess's life.

Not all Princess Margaret's troubles have been unbidden, however. Sometimes she has deliberately flaunted convention, and walked into situations with eyes wide open, prepared to chance the consequences. For much of her life she has been mistress of her own fate. She has not always gone out of her way to make things easy for herself, but has the satisfaction of knowing that she has lived a full and rewarding life. Her search for personal happiness may have seemed thwarted, but although her relationships with Peter Townsend, Antony Armstrong-Jones and Roddy Llewellyn ultimately ended, they were happy and fulfilling for much of the time. She has remained close friends with Tony and Roddy and would adhere strongly to the adage that it is better to have loved and lost than never to have loved at all. The double-edged sword throughout her life has been her noble birth, offering great privilege but with it a golden ball and chain. The question as to whether or not the Princess will marry again is frequently the subject for conjecture, but having enjoyed fourteen years of independence she would now find total commitment to someone difficult.

At the age of sixty Princess Margaret has at last found peace. Her public duties are now beyond criticism, her social life is full of rewards, but it is not in her nature to lay down the weapons completely and her defences will always remain up in case of attack. Once her own worst enemy, Princess Margaret has finally come to terms with her lot in life and she now has the upper hand. The combat over, in her own power lies the ability to make this an enduring truce – in harmony with both herself and the world, at last.

APPENDIX I

Princess Margaret Factfile

BORN
  Thursday, 21 August 1930 at Glamis Castle, Tayside, Scotland

CHRISTENED
  October 1930, at Buckingham Palace by the Archbishop of Canterbury,
  Dr Cosmo Lang
  Names: Margaret Rose
  Godparents: Prince of Wales (later Duke of Windsor)
                Princess Victoria
                Princess Ingrid of Sweden
                Lady Rose Leveson-Gower
                David Bowes-Lyon

EDUCATION

1935	Taught at 145 Piccadilly by Marion Crawford
1936	Began singing lessons with the Countess of Cavan, music lessons with Mabel Lander, and was taught to swim by Amy Daly
1937	Buckingham Palace schoolroom
1939-1945	Windsor Castle schoolroom
1946	Took madrigal lessons
1947	Passed driving test at Ballater, Scotland
1953	Attended a course of 11 lectures on 'The School of Religion', at St Paul's, Knightsbridge

ENGAGEMENT
  26 February 1960, announced in the Court Circular

MARRIAGE
  Married Antony Charles Robert Armstrong-Jones, 6 May 1960, at
  Westminster Abbey
  Officially separated 19 March 1976

182

Granted a decree nisi on 24 May 1978 in Court 44, London Divorce
Court
Granted a decree absolute on 11 July 1978

CHILDREN
David Albert Charles Armstrong-Jones, Viscount Linley, born 3
November 1961 at Clarence House, London. Christened in the Music
Room, Buckingham Palace, on 19 December 1961
Lady Sarah Frances Elizabeth Armstrong-Jones, born 1 May 1964 at
Kensington Palace, London. Christened 13 July 1964 at Buckingham
Palace

RESIDENCES
1A Clock Court, Kensington Palace, London
'Les Jolies Eaux', Gelliceaux Bay, Mustique, Windward Islands

INTERESTS
Music, composing and playing
Theatre
Ballet
Opera
Art
Designing clothes, dinner services, collages and floral pictures, collect-
ing sea shells

APPENDIX II

Princess Margaret's Honours, Patronages and Appointments etc

DECORATIONS
Imperial Order of the Crown of India (1947)
Grand Cross of the Royal Victorian Order (1953)
Dame Grand Cross of the Order of St John of Jerusalem (1948)
Grand Cross of the Order of the Lion of The Netherlands (1948)
Order of the Brilliant Star of Zanzibar, 1st class (1956)
Grand Cross of the Order of the Crown of Belgium (1960)
Order of the Crown, Lion and Spears of Toro Kingdom, Uganda (1965)
Order of the Precious Crown, 1st class, Japan (1971)
Grand Cross (1st class) of the Order of Merit of the Federal Republic
of Germany (1972)

COLONEL-IN-CHIEF
Highland Fusiliers of Canada (Militia)
15th/19th The King's Royal Hussars
Queen Alexandra's Royal Army Nursing Corps
Royal Highland Fusiliers (Princess Margaret's Own Glasgow and
Ayrshire Regiment)
Princess Louise Fusiliers (Royal Canadian Infantry Corps, Militia)
The Bermuda Regiment

DEPUTY COLONEL-IN-CHIEF
Royal Anglian Regiment

FREEMAN
Worshipful Company of Haberdashers (1966)
City of London (1966)
Royal Burgh of Queensferry (1972)

HONORARY DEGREES
    Hon. D. Music, University of London (1957)
    Hon. Doctor of Law, University of Cambridge (1958)
    Hon. Doctor of Laws, University of British Columbia (1958)
    Hon. Doctor of Letters, University of Keele (1962)

HONORARY AIR COMMODORE
    Royal Air Force, Coningsby (1977)

HONORARY FELLOW
    Royal Institute of British Architects (1953)
    Royal Society of Medicine (1957)
    Royal College of Surgeons of England (1963)
    Royal College of Obstetricians and Gynaecologists (1966)
    Royal Photographic Society (1983)

HONORARY LIFE FELLOW
    Zoological Society of London

HONORARY MEMBER
    Automobile Association
    Order of the Road
    Royal Automobile Club
    Sealyham Terrier Breeders' Association

HONORARY LIFE MEMBER
    Century House Association (British Columbia)

HONORARY MEMBER AND PATRON
    Grand Antiquity Society of Glasgow

HONORARY PATRON
    The Winnipeg Art Gallery

LIFE MEMBER
    British Legion Women's Section

MASTER OF THE BENCH
    The Honourable Society of Lincoln's Inn

PATRON
    Architects' Benevolent Society
    Association of Anaesthetists of Great Britain and Ireland
    Barnardo's
    Barristers' Benevolent Association

Bristol Royal Society for the Blind
British Sailors' Society Ladies' Guild
Cambridge Festival Association
Combined Theatrical Charities Appeals Council
Friends of Kenwood
Friends of Southwark Cathedral
Friends of St. John's (Smith Square)
Hallé Concerts Society
Heart Disease and Diabetes Research Trust
Japan Society of London
Light Infantry Club
Linked Cities Congress (Great Britain and North
  Rhine-Westphalia)
Mary Hare Grammar School for the Deaf
Mathilda and Terence Kennedy Institute of Rheumatology
Migraine Trust
Mustique Educational Trust
National Pony Society
Northern Ballet Theatre
Olave Baden-Powell Society
Pottery and Glass Trades' Benevolent Institution
Princess Margaret Hospital and Lodge (Canadian Cancer Society
  Auxiliary)
Princess Margaret Rose Orthopaedic Hospital, Edinburgh
Queen Alexandra's Royal Army Nursing Corps Association
Royal College of Nursing and National Council of Nurses of the
  United Kingdom
Royal National Hospital, Bournemouth
St Margaret's Chapel Guild, Edinburgh Castle
St Pancras Housing Association in Camden
Scottish Association of Youth Clubs
Scottish Ballet
Scottish Community Drama Association
Services Sound and Vision Corporation
Suffolk Regimental Association
Tenovus (Institute for Cancer Research)
Union of Schools for Social Service
University of London Choir
West Indies Olympic Association
Zebra Trust

PATRON-IN-CHIEF
English Harbour Repair Fund

VICE-PATRON
Royal Anglian Regimental Association

APPENDIX II

PATRON (TEMPORARY)
   Royal Caledonian Ball

PRESIDENT
   English Folk Dance and Song Society
   Friends of the Elderly and Gentlefolk's Help
   Girl Guides Association
   Horder Centre for Arthritics
   National Society for the Prevention of Cruelty to Children
   Royal Ballet
   Royal Scottish Society for Prevention of Cruelty to Children
   Sadler's Wells Foundation
   Scottish Children's League
   Sunshine Homes and Schools for Blind Children (Royal National
      Institute for the Blind)
   Victoria League for Commonwealth Friendship

GRAND PRESIDENT
   St John Ambulance Association and Brigade

JOINT PRESIDENT
   Lowland Brigade Club

PRESIDENT AND CHAIRMAN OF COUNCIL
   Invalid Children's Aid Nationwide

VISITOR
   King George VI and Queen Elizabeth Foundation of
      St Catharine's

APPENDIX III

Official Overseas Visits

1947	South Africa
1948	The Netherlands
1949	Italy, Switzerland, France
1950	Malta, Tripoli
1951	France
1953	Norway, Southern Rhodesia
1954	Federal Republic of Germany
1955	West Indies
1956	Sweden, East Africa, Indian Ocean Dependencies
1958	Federal Republic of Germany, West Indies, Canada, Belgium
1959	Portugal
1960	Belgium
1961	Norway
1962	Jamaica
1963	Federal Republic of Germany
1964	Denmark
1965	Uganda, Netherlands, United States of America
1966	Hong Kong, France
1967	Belgium
1968	United States of America
1969	Japan, Cambodia, Thailand, Iran
1970	Yugoslavia
1971	France, Canada
1972	British Virgin Islands, Italy, Federal Republic of Germany, Seychelles, Western Australia, Singapore
1973	Barbados, Federal Republic of Germany
1974	Cyprus, United States of America, Canada
1975	Federal Republic of Germany, Australia, Bermuda
1976	Morocco, Tunisia, Cyprus
1977	Italy, United States of America
1978	Tuvalu, Japan, Dominica
1979	United States of America
1980	Federal Republic of Germany, Philippines, Singapore, Malaysia, Canada

APPENDIX III

1981	Greece, Federal Republic of Germany, Canada, Swaziland, Antigua, St Vincent
1982	Federal Republic of Germany, Italy
1983	St Kitts, Nevis
1984	Bermuda, United States of America
1985	Hungary, Denmark, Sweden
1986	The Netherlands, Canada
1987	China, Hong Kong
1988	Canada, United States of America

APPENDIX IV

Engagement Diary for October/November 1989

OCTOBER

4   As Grand President of St John Ambulance Association and Brigade, attended a Reception and Dinner given by Garrard and Company in aid of the Order of St John.

5   As Patron of the Friends of St John's, Smith Square, attended the 20th Anniversary Concert given by Dame Joan Sutherland and Mr Richard Bonynge.

6   Attended a service at the Church of St Philip and St James, Up Hatherley, Cheltenham, during the Parish Preaching Mission.

8   As Patron of the Hallé Concerts Society, attended a performance by the Hallé Orchestra at Henbury Hall, Macclesfield.

9   Visited the Northern Ballet Theatre in Manchester.

11 As President of the National Society for the Prevention of Cruelty to Children, opened the Hertfordshire Child Protection Team's Unit, Hemel Hempstead.

16 Attended the Women of the Year Luncheon at the Savoy Hotel, London. In the afternoon, as Patron of the St Pancras Housing Association, visited Goldington Court, Camden, to open the refurbished development.

18 As Colonel-in-Chief attended the Annual Cocktail Party of Queen Alexandra's Royal Army Nursing Corps at the Royal Hospital, Chelsea.

20 Attended a Gala Evening at the Theatre Royal, Glasgow, organised by the Society of Friends of Glasgow Cathedral.

29 As Patron of the Combined Theatrical Charities Appeals Council, attended a performance of *Peace in Our Time* at the Theatre Royal, Windsor.

NOVEMBER

2   As President of Invalid Children's Aid Nationwide, visited Pilgrims School, Seaford, East Sussex.

190

7   Attended Evensong in Westminster Abbey to mark the Quincentenary of the death of Archbishop Thomas Cranmer.

10   Visited the University of Keele to attend the dedication of the restored fountain. Later opened the new factory extension of Steelite International PLC, Burslem, Staffordshire.

13   Visited the Potteries Shopping Centre, Hanley, Staffordshire. Later attended a luncheon at the City Hall, Stoke-on-Trent. As President of the National Society for the Prevention of Cruelty to Children, opened the Staffordshire Child Protection Team's Unit, Tunstall.

15   Visited the Bishop Grosseteste College, Lincoln. As President of the National Society for the Prevention of Cruelty to Children, opened the Lincolnshire Child Protection Team's Unit in Lincoln.

17   Opened the Eldon Garden Shopping Precinct, Newcastle-upon-Tyne. As Grand President of St John Ambulance Association and Brigade, accepted the Freedom of the City of Newcastle-upon-Tyne on behalf of the Order of St John for Northumbria.

20   Undertook engagements in Berwick-upon-Tweed.

24   As President of the National Society for the Prevention of Cruelty to Children, opened the Derbyshire Child Protection Team's Unit, Ripley.

27   Visited the Assembly Rooms, Derby, to meet workers and sponsors of the National Society for the Prevention of Cruelty to Children Appeal. Attended a luncheon for the NSPCC in the Royal Banqueting Suite, Derby, and reopened the suite. Visited the restored Market Hall, Derby.

APPENDIX V

On 21 July 1989, in her capacity as President of the Girl Guides Association, Princess Margaret made a three-hour visit, including a luncheon, to Foxlease in Hampshire, to open The Coach House and visit the British Guides in Foreign Countries Camp. Just three days before the visit the final programme was drawn up:

Programme

Opening of The Coach House and visit to the British Guides in Foreign Countries Camp, Foxlease, Lyndhurst, Hampshire, on Friday 21 July 1989.

12.45   Her Royal Highness arrives at the main entrance to Princess Mary House (Foxlease), and is greeted by The Lord Lieutenant, Lieutenant Colonel Sir James Scott.
Sir James Scott escorts Her Royal Highness into the Entrance Hall where he presents:
Mr Derek Burdle
Chairman of the New Forest District Council
Mr P.A.D. Hyde
General Manager
Mrs P.A.D. Hyde
Dr June Paterson-Brown
Chief Commissioner
Mrs R.A. Chermside
Chairman of the Foxlease Committee
Mrs H. Chittock
Guider in Charge, Foxlease
Retiring room (South Africa Room) has been set aside for use by Her Royal Highness.

12.50   Her Royal Highness is escorted to Scotland Room where approximately 60 guests will be gathered.

192

Drinks will be served

1.05   Some guests will move to the Dining Room.

1.15   Her Royal Highness, Sir James Scott, Dr June Paterson-Brown, and others will be escorted to their places in the Dining Room by Mrs Chittock.

Her Royal Highness will be seated at the top table with:

Sir James Scott

Dr June Paterson-Brown

Mrs R. Chermside

Mr James Morgan

(Mr Morgan works for John German, the Land Agents appointed to Foxlease as Consultants. He worked on the designs for The Coach House)

Mr R. Smith

(Mr Smith is Vice Chairman of the Foxlease Committee)

Mrs H. Chittock

Her Royal Highness and her guests will be served by Mrs Rosemarie Dodd (Cook at Foxlease) and two young members of staff.

2.00   Her Royal Highness and her guests are invited to take coffee in London Room with Foxlease staff.

Miss Christine Davies	–	Assistant Guider in Charge
Miss Alison Baillie	–	Housekeeper
Mrs Rosemarie Dodd	–	Cook
Miss Sarah Field	–	Administrator
Miss Susan Moloney	–	Secretary

2.25   Guests proceed to the area in front of The Coach House.

2.30   Her Royal Highness

Sir James Scott

Dr June Paterson-Brown

Mrs R. Chermside

Mrs H. Chittock

leave Princess Mary House and proceed to the rostrum in front of The Coach House.

Mrs Chermside will make a short speech and invite Her Royal Highness to unveil a plaque and declare The Coach House open.

The main door will be opened from inside by Ranger Guides.

Sarah Chittock (daughter of the Guider in Charge) will come from inside to present Her Royal Highness with a posy.

Her Royal Highness, escorted by Mrs Chittock and Mr James Morgan, will be shown around The Coach House.

Ground Floor

Guiders' Room	–	adopted by The Friends of Foxlease
Living Room	–	adopted by Canada

Kitchen	–	adopted by Sussex Central	
Dormitory	–	adopted by Sussex East	

First Floor

Bedrooms	–	adopted by:	
		Essex	Norfolk
		Birmingham	Worcestershire
		Gloucestershire	Leicestershire
		Rutland	Wadhurst

One or two people representing those who have adopted rooms will be in each of the rooms.

3.00 Her Royal Highness leaves The Coach House
Dr June Paterson-Brown will present:
Mrs Anne Dunford
Deputy Chief Commissioner and Commissioner for British Guides in Foreign Countries
Mrs Ann Mitchell
Adviser to the Commissioner for British Guides in Foreign Countries
The party, escorted by Mrs Chittock, will proceed to the camp site.
(A car will be available at this point should Her Royal Highness require it or in case of bad weather)
During the tour of the camp site Her Royal Highness will have the opportunity to meet and see girls involved in the following activities:
Cooking without utensils
Baking bread in camp
Maori stick game and/or putting on and wearing a sari
Blindfold tent pitching
Origami water bombs
Resussi-Annie or other visual First Aid
Mini orienteering
Basic life saving skills
Flower arranging
Mouth and foot painting
'Scouting for Boys' Hike fires
Plaster of Paris prints
Stalking games
(Retiring Room (South Africa Room) has been set aside for use by Her Royal Highness).

3.45 approx Dr June Paterson-Brown, Mr D. Burdle and Sir James Scott take their leave of Her Royal Highness at the main entrance to Princess Mary House.

Bibliography

Aronson, Theo, *Royal Ambassadors: British Royalties in South Africa 1860-1947*, David Philip, 1975

Aronson, Theo, *Royal Family – Years of Transition*, John Murray, 1983

Barry, Stephen P., *Royal Service*, Macmillan, 1983

Barry, Stephen P., *Royal Secrets*, Villard, 1985

Batchelor, Vivien, *HRH The Princess Margaret Gift Book*, Pitkin, 1952

Beaton, Cecil, *Self Portrait with Friends*, Weidenfeld & Nicolson, 1979

Beaulieu, Lord Montagu of, *Royalty on the Road*, Collins, 1980

Bloom, Ursula, *Princesses in Love*, Robert Hale, 1973

Bolitho, Hector, *Their Majesties*, Max Parrish, 1952

Cathcart, Helen, *Princess Margaret*, W.H. Allen, 1974

Colville, John, *Footprints in Time*, Collins, 1976

Coolican, Don, *The Story of the Royal Family*, Colour Library, 1982

Crawford, Marion, *The Little Princesses*, Cassell, 1950

Cunliffe, Lesley, *Great Royal Disasters*, Arthur Barker, 1986

Davies, Phyllis, *HRH The Princess Margaret Comes of Age*, Pitkin, 1951

Dempster, Nigel, *HRH The Princess Margaret: A Life Unfulfilled*, Quartet, 1981

Duncan, Andrew, *The Reality of Monarchy*, Heinemann, 1970

Edgar, Donald, *Happy and Glorious*, Arthur Barker, 1977

Edgar, Donald, *Palace*, W.H. Allen, 1983

Ford, Colin, *Happy and Glorious*, National Portrait Gallery, 1977

Hall, Trevor, *The Royal Family Today*, Colour Library, 1983

Hamilton, Alan, *The Royal Handbook*, Mitchell Beazley, 1985

Huth, Angela, *The Englishwoman's Wardrobe*, Century, 1986

James, Paul, *The Royal Almanac*, Ravette London, 1986

James, Paul, *Anne: The Working Princess*, Pan, 1988

James, Paul, *Diana: One of the Family?*, Sidgwick & Jackson, 1988

James, Paul, and Russell, Peter, *At Her Majesty's Service*, Collins, 1986

Keay, Douglas, *Royal Pursuit*, Severn House, 1983

Lacey, Robert, *Majesty: Elizabeth II and The House of Windsor*, Hutchinson, 1977

Laird, Dorothy, *How The Queen Reigns*, Hodder & Stoughton, 1959

Lindsay, Loelia, *Cocktails and Laughter*, Hamish Hamilton, 1983

Longford, Elizabeth, *Elizabeth R*, Weidenfeld & Nicolson, 1985

Longford, Elizabeth, *The Oxford Book of Royal Anecdotes*, O.U.P., 1989

Masters, Brian, *Great Hostesses*, Constable, 1982

Menkes, Suzy, *The Royal Jewels*, Grafton, 1985

Mortimer, Penelope, *Queen Elizabeth: A Life of the Queen Mother*, Penguin, 1987

Nash, Roy, *Buckingham Palace: The Place and The People*, Macdonald, 1980

Nicholson, J. Haig, *HRH The Princess Margaret in The British West Indies and The Bahamas*, Pitkin, 1955

Packard, Anne, *HRH The Princess Margaret 20th Birthday Book*, Pitkin, 1950

Saville, Margaret, *Royal Sisters*, Pitkin Pictorials, 1953

Thornton, Michael, *Royal Feud*, Michael Joseph, 1985

Warwick, Christopher, *Princess Margaret*, Weidenfeld & Nicolson, 1983

Winn, Godfrey, *The Younger Sister: An Intimate Portrait Study of HRH The Princess Margaret*, Hutchinson, 1951

Ziegler, Philip, *Crown and People*, Collins, 1978

INDEX